(SCTS) SYMANTEC CERTIFIED TECHNICAL SPECIALIST

(SCTS) SYMANTEC CERTIFIED TECHNICAL SPECIALIST

SMALL BUSINESS SECURITY STUDY GUIDE

NIK ALSTON, MIKE CHAPPLE, AND KIRK HAUSMAN

♦ Addison-Wesley

Upper Saddle River, NJ • Boston • Indianapolis • San Francisco
New York • Toronto • Montreal • London • Munich • Paris • Madrid
Capetown • Sydney • Tokyo • Singapore • Mexico City

Many of the designations used by manufacturers and sellers to distinguish their products are claimed as trademarks. Where those designations appear in this book, and the publisher was aware of a trademark claim, the designations have been printed with initial capital letters or in all capitals.

The authors and publisher have taken care in the preparation of this book, but make no expressed or implied warranty of any kind and assume no responsibility for errors or omissions. No liability is assumed for incidental or consequential damages in connection with or arising out of the use of the information or programs contained herein.

Publisher Symantec Press: Linda McCarthy
Editor in Chief: Karen Gettman
Acquisitions Editor: Jessica Goldstein
Cover Designer: Alan Clements
Managing Editor: Gina Kanouse
Senior Project Editor: Kristy Hart
Copy Editor: Krista Hansing
Indexer: Lisa Stumpf
Proofreader: Debbie Williams
Compositor: Interactive Composition Corporation
Manufacturing Buyer: Dan Uhrig

The publisher offers excellent discounts on this book when ordered in quantity for bulk purchases or special sales, which may include electronic versions and/or custom covers and content particular to your business, training goals, marketing focus, and branding interests. For more information, please contact:

> U.S. Corporate and Government Sales
> (800) 382-3419
> corpsales@pearsontechgroup.com

For sales outside the U.S., please contact:

> International Sales
> international@pearsoned.com

Visit us on the Web: www.awprofessional.com

Library of Congress Cataloging-in-Publication Data

Alston, Nik.
   (SCTS) Symantec Certified Technical Specialist : small business security study guide /
Nik Alston, Mike Chapple, and Kalani Kirk Hausman.
        p. cm.
   ISBN 0-321-34994-6
   1. Electronic data processing personnel—Certification. 2. Computer security—
Examinations—Study guides. 3. Internet—Security measures—Examinations—Study guides.
I. Chapple, Mike. II. Hausman, Kalani Kirk. III. Title.

   QA76.3.A5245 2005
   005.8—dc22

                                              2005019935

   ISBN 0-321-34994-6

Text printed in the United States on recycled paper at Courier in Stoughton, Massachusetts.
First printing, September 2005

Table of Contents

Acknowledgments

Like most projects, this book, and the SCTS program in general, could not have been produced without the help and assistance of a great many people.

First and foremost, I'd like to thank Kathleen Bissonnette, our SCTS program manager and official whip cracker. She played such an enormous role in managing the creation of this book that her name should have been on the cover, but unfortunately the printer didn't have enough Ss, Ns, or Ts. Without her calming influence and nefarious attention to detail, you would not be reading this book. Kathleen broke barriers (often quite literally in the office) to get this book produced, and still kept up her day-to-day routine and work responsibilities. Her energy never ceases to amaze me. Kathleen, "thank you" is simply not adequate.

I'd also like to acknowledge those that took part in the technical review for the certification exam and others who helped review the book and CD for accuracy. Thanks go to Brian Antolin, David Bain, Linda Baxter, Christophe Bouscaut, Sean Conrad, Esper Chawah, Larry Cox, Deirdre Crossan, Blaise Fallon, Julia Green, Justin Harshbarger, Melonia Musser-Braune, Brandon Noble, Michael Plavin, Brian Powell, Joezen Punongbayan, Brian Rosenbery, John Stone, Karen Torimaru, Joseph Rodgers, and Moira Waddell.

A special note of thanks goes to Peter Quicken for his meticulous final review of the all the materials against the exam objectives and questions.

Linda Scrivano and Deb Calhoun were the driving force behind the exam development including the sample tests on the CD. One day they will achieve their goal of making me understand Psychometrics.

Thanks also go to Linda McCarthy of Symantec Press and Jessica Goldstein of Addison-Wesley for their guidance and support. Who would have thought that writing a book involved more than just turning in a handful of manuscripts.

Lastly, but by no means least, I'd like to thank Graeme Johnston, Jill Guardia, and Carrie Cuhaci—their initial vision which was the driving force behind the creation of the SCTS program, including the certification exam and this study guide.

About the Authors

Nik Alston has been involved in computers and networking for longer than he cares to admit, working mainly for systems software vendors selling into large corporate environments. He has experience covering most of the major platforms, including IBM mainframes, Novell, UNIX, OS/2, and all Microsoft Windows versions. For the last 10 years he has worked for computer-security companies in various technical roles, including support, pre- and post-sales, consulting, and management. Nik has been with Symantec Corporation since 1999. He is a Certified Information Systems Security Professional, a Symantec Certified Security Practitioner, and a Symantec Certified Technical Specialist, Small Business Security. Originally from the UK, he now lives in Franklin, Massachusetts with his wife Alyson and their 3 children.

Mike Chapple has a number of writing credits, including the *CISSP: Certified Information Systems Security Professional Study Guide, 2nd Edition* (Sybex, 2004, 0782143350), *The GSEC Prep Guide: Mastering SANS GIAC Security Essentials* (Wiley, 2003, 0764539329), the *TICSA Training Guide* (Que, 2002, 0789727838), and *Information Security Illuminated* (Jones and Bartlett, 2005, 076372677X). He is a technical editor for *Information Security Magazine* and a frequent contributor to the About.com Database site and SearchSecurity.com.

Kirk Hausman's studies include security, computer science, electronics technology, electrical engineering, mechanical engineering, and philosophy. His hobbies include designs in high-speed transportation, submersible propulsion, cosmology, interactive telepresence, technology in education, and virtual reality for use by those with disabling conditions.

CHAPTER 1

Introduction

Issues Facing Small Businesses

In today's digital age, businesses face unprecedented information security challenges that can be distilled into the four following statements:

- To effectively use information, you must trust it.
- To trust it, you must secure it.
- To secure it, you must manage it.
- To manage it, you must think ahead.

In the early days of computing and the Internet, many small businesses simply didn't see the need to be online. However, those that did, saw the Internet as a valuable tool and not as a threat to their business.

Today two factors have combined to cause small businesses to focus on the importance of information security. First, those businesses have become dependent upon the Internet for their daily business activities. For many businesses, access is more than a convenience; it's a business necessity. Second, the number and magnitude of threats and security risks in the modern computing environment have multiplied. Spyware, adware, viruses, worms, Trojan horses, and other risks are prevalent on the Internet today. Insightful small business owners and managers understand these risks and are willing to make investments in information security now to prevent large business headaches down the road.

The risks facing businesses of all sizes are similar. Symantec™ has a four-dimensional model of business risk (illustrated in Figure 1-1) that outlines the following four types of risk:

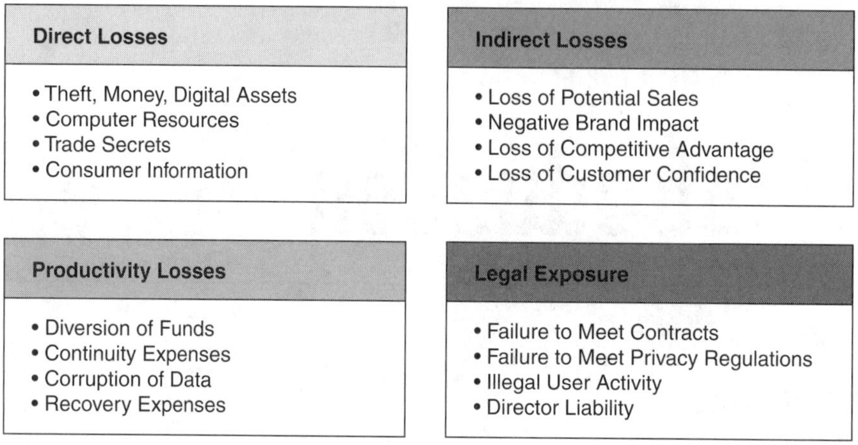

Direct Losses	Indirect Losses
• Theft, Money, Digital Assets • Computer Resources • Trade Secrets • Consumer Information	• Loss of Potential Sales • Negative Brand Impact • Loss of Competitive Advantage • Loss of Customer Confidence
Productivity Losses	**Legal Exposure**
• Diversion of Funds • Continuity Expenses • Corruption of Data • Recovery Expenses	• Failure to Meet Contracts • Failure to Meet Privacy Regulations • Illegal User Activity • Director Liability

Figure 1-1 Four dimensions of business risk.

- **Direct losses** might be short-term in nature, such as the theft of money and equipment. However, they are often the precursor to long-term losses from the other three dimensions.

- **Indirect losses** can be extremely damaging to a business but are also very difficult to quantify. For example, if a bank suffers a computer intrusion, there might be an insignificant monetary loss that's covered by the bank's insurance policy. However, if the story is reported by the media, it could result in widespread loss of consumer confidence in the bank's capability to safeguard their money. This indirect loss could be far more damaging to the bank's overall business than the simple theft it initially suffered.

- **Productivity losses** occur tangentially to other risks. For example, if a company's computer systems are infected by a virus, it might cause some direct and indirect losses. However, it's also going to have a productivity cost. If company employees aren't able to access the network, they might be unable to do their jobs for a period of time, resulting in lost revenue to the business.

- **Legal exposure** is one of the most damaging types of risk in today's regulated society. Information-based businesses are subject to numerous regulatory requirements. Laws such as the Health Insurance Portability and Accountability Act (HIPAA), the Gramm-Leach-Bliley Act (GLBA) and the Sarbanes Oxley Act (SOX) require businesses to protect the confidentiality, integrity, and availability of information assets under their stewardship. Failure to meet those requirements could place the organization in civil or even criminal jeopardy.

In this chapter, we take a brief look at the security risks and threats facing small businesses and some of the products offered by Symantec to help deal with them. We also discuss the Symantec Certified Technical Specialist, Small Business Security program, including certification requirements and an overview of the examination process.

The remainder of this book is dedicated to providing you with the practical, hands-on knowledge that you'll need both to be successful on the SCTS, Small Business Security exam and to provide you with the knowledge to assist small businesses in need of information security.

We begin with a look at the risks on the Internet.

Security Risks and Threats

Often, when people think of information security, the phrase "malicious code" pops into their heads. They might not use that terminology, but the words *virus*, *worm*, *Trojan horse*, *spyware*, and *adware* are all specific examples of a more general menace. How prevalent are these items? The *Symantec Internet Security Threat Report VIII*, published in March 2005 as an update to the Internet community, estimated that *every* organization connected to the Internet experiences an *average* of 13.6 attacks directed against its network *each day*.

The risks facing modern organizations are serious and significant. In this book, you'll learn how you can counter them by developing robust security infrastructures for the organizations with which you work.

Before we can study malicious code prevention, we must have a general understanding of the threat. Simply put, malicious code is any computer program that carries out an unwanted activity without the consent of the system operator. The activities performed may range from annoying (such as displaying a message on the screen every few minutes or popping up ad content) to downright destructive (such as erasing all data stored on the system's hard drive).

Viruses

Viruses, the most commonly known type of threats, are similar to biological viruses. Just as biological viruses spread in a number of ways— you might have direct contact with an infected person, drink out of a cup that person used, or merely be present in the same room and become infected—computer viruses spread from computer to computer carrying their malicious activity.

Worms

Worms are viruses' more insidious cousins. Like viruses, worms spread from system to system carrying a malicious payload. They range in severity from minor nuisances to catastrophically damaging.

What makes worms different from and more dangerous than viruses is that they spread without any user intervention. Worms exploit vulnerabilities in operating systems to infect weak systems. After they establish themselves on an infected host, their mission changes to one of rampant propagation. They attempt to spread as far and wide as they can, searching for other vulnerable systems on the local network or across the Internet.

Worms can take advantage of vulnerabilities in common operating systems and applications The SQL Slammer worm of early 2003 infected Windows® systems running the popular SQL Server 2000 database system and brought financial networks to their knees for a number of hours, leaving ATM users stranded without cash.

Trojan Horses

In ancient history, the Greeks laid siege against the city of Troy for almost 10 years during the Trojan war. Weary of battle, the Greeks resorted to trickery and built a giant wooden horse that they presented to the Trojans as a gift. The Trojans graciously accepted the gift and wheeled it within the walls of their city. When night fell, the horse opened up and Greek warriors rushed out, quickly conquering the city.

Malicious code also uses this type of trickery. Electronic Trojan horses present themselves as a beneficial "gift" to computer users. They might appear to be a computer game, utility, or screen saver downloaded by an unsuspecting user, when, in reality, they contain dangerous malicious code. To top it all off, the Trojan program usually works in the manner you'd expect it to but, while you're happily playing a downloaded game, it delivers its payload behind the scenes.

Spyware/Adware

Spyware and adware are two of the newer security risks to face organizations. If you've been following the media, you've probably heard these two buzzwords tossed around quite a bit recently. They're part of a new class of code designed to sit quietly on computer systems and remain unnoticed while they perform their mission. Depending upon the purpose of the code, this mission might be simply to cause pop-up ads to appear on the infected computer, or it might be more mischievous.

Spyware programs have the capability to scan systems or monitor activity and relay information to other computers or locations in cyber-space. Among the information that may be actively or passively gathered and disseminated by spyware: passwords, log-in details, account numbers, personal information, individual files, or other personal documents. Spyware may also gather and distribute information related to the user's computer, applications running on the computer, Internet browser usage, or other computing habits.

Adware facilitates delivery of advertising content to the user through his own window, or by utilizing another program's interface. In some cases, these programs may gather information from the user's computer, including information related to Internet browser usage or other computing habits, and relay this information back to a remote computer or other location in cyber-space.

Spam/Phishing

Spam, or unsolicited commercial email (UCE), is an ever-increasing problem for business users, who are forced to wade through a myriad of advertisements for prescription drugs, get-rich-quick schemes, and free timeshare vacations in order to get to their real email. Email has become a mission critical application and spam has a negative impact on the productivity of employees. Spam also causes potentially more serious threats due to some spam emails carrying viruses and phishing attacks.

One form of spam you might be familiar with is the phishing attack. In this type of spam, the goal is to trick users into revealing private information that the spammer can use to his or her advantage.

One of the more common phishing attacks is to fake an email from eBay® or PayPal® telling the user that there's a security problem with his or her account. When unsuspecting users receive this official-looking email, they might be tempted to click the link, which then presents a page that looks very much like the eBay or PayPal home page. The page then asks them to enter their account information for security-verification purposes.

The problem is, the Web page the email links to isn't actually run by eBay or PayPal. It's a phishing site that dutifully records account information and tells users that the problem has been resolved. The users then happily go their way, thinking that the problem has been fixed. Unfortunately, the problem has just begun. The account information now goes off into the hands of unscrupulous individuals who attempt to clean out bank balances or use it for other dubious purposes.

Symantec Solutions

The earliest threats were simple viruses and worms. The threats have increased as the propagation methods have become more sophisticated to include mass mailing worms and blended threats. In addition to the traditional threats of viruses, worms, and Trojan horses, new types of risks have emerged in the recent years. Organizations are now faced with protecting their infrastructure from a wider threat landscape.

There's no reason to avoid contact with the Internet at large. It's important to ensure that small businesses practice safe computing. Symantec provides solutions to help safeguard networks, including software, hardware, and services. In this section, we look at security offerings designed to protect small business networks from the modern threats and security risks found on the Internet.

- Symantec AntiVirus™ 10.0
- Symantec™ Client Security 3.0
- Norton AntiSpam™ 2005

We explore them briefly here, but the remainder of this book is dedicated to exploring them in further detail. Part 1, "Symantec AntiVirus," explains the proper use of Symantec AntiVirus to protect your organization from malicious code. Part 2, "Symantec Client Security," provides you with a detailed look at using Symantec Client Security, including the firewall and intrusion prevention capabilities. This book concludes with Part 3, "Norton AntiSpam," which explores the use of Norton AntiSpam to protect your organization from unsolicited email.

Symantec AntiVirus

A component of Symantec's strategy to protect the small business is Symantec AntiVirus. Symantec AntiVirus (shown in Figure 1-2) provides small-business users with a desktop solution for real-time virus and spyware

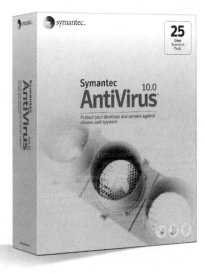

Figure 1-2 Symantec AntiVirus.

protection for workstations and network servers. The solution automatically detects and repairs the effects of spyware, adware, viruses, and other threats and security risks.

Symantec Antivirus provides centralized configuration, policy management, alerting, and logging, enabling administrators to determine which nodes are vulnerable to virus attacks. It uses LiveUpdate technology to keep definitions and program components up to date.

Symantec Client Security

Another component of Symantec's strategy to protect the small business is Symantec Client Security (see Figure 1-3). This package provides all the functionality of Symantec AntiVirus, with the addition of intrusion-prevention and firewall capabilities designed to keep out unwanted traffic. It monitors the system's network connection to block unwanted incoming traffic and also watches for signs of viruses, worms, Trojan horses, spyware, and other programs that attempt to spread from your system to others via the network.

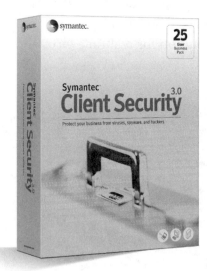

Figure 1-3 Symantec Client Security.

Symantec Client Security automatically removes detected malicious code and provides a comprehensive approach to protecting systems against threats that exploit multiple vulnerabilities.

Norton AntiSpam

The last component of Symantec's strategy to protect the small business is Norton AntiSpam, a desktop solution for spam prevention (see Figure 1-4). Norton AntiSpam uses automatically updated filters in combination with logic that determines what you consider spam and what you consider legitimate for filtering email. Norton AntiSpam provides the capability of blocking unwanted Web advertisements and pop-ups. In addition it provides easy integration with programs such as Microsoft® Outlook®, Outlook Express, and Eudora®, and is also capable of filtering Yahoo!® Mail accounts.

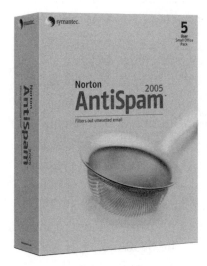

Figure 1-4 Norton AntiSpam.

Small Business Protection

These three products covered in the SCTS, Small Business Security certification, will provide small businesses with a proactive security stance against the myriad of today's online threats and security risks. In addition, Symantec has many other offerings to provide a defense in depth for all sizes of organizations from small business to large enterprise.

Additional Solutions

Symantec offers a variety of products and solutions designed to work at different layers of the network, that are complementary to those spoken about in this book. These include Symantec™ Mail Security for Domino®, Symantec™ Mail Security for Microsoft® Exchange, and the Symantec™ Gateway Security Appliance family. This section discusses a partial list of the products.

The Symantec Gateway Security family of products provides protection at the gateway. The Symantec™ Gateway Security 300 Series (see Figure 1-5) is an easy-to-use firewall/VPN appliance with integrated security for the small business and remote office with simple network requirements. It combines high performance for the entry-level with firewall, VPN, IDS/IPS, antivirus policy enforcement, content filtering, and optional VPN secured wireless. These products sit on the network between the protected LAN and the Internet.

The Symantec™ Gateway Security 5400 Series (see Figure 1-6) is a Firewall/VPN appliance that integrates full inspection firewall technology, IPsec-compliant virtual private networking, intrusion prevention, intrusion detection, antivirus protection, URL-based content filtering and antispam technology. There are a range of models that provide scalability from small enterprise and corporate branch offices, up to large enterprise, data centers, and service providers.

The Symantec™ Mail Security 8200 Series appliances (see Figure 1-7) offer a hardware-based approach to protecting the enterprise by combining antispam and antivirus protection in an appliance. The 8240 model provides protection from 100 up to 1,000 users. The 8260 provides protection for

Figure 1-5 Symantec Gateway Security 300 Series.

Figure 1-6 Symantec Gateway Security 5400 Series.

Figure 1-7 Symantec Mail Security 8200 Series.

1,000 plus. Software solutions exist specifically for Lotus Domino® and Microsoft® Exchange.

More information on these enterprise products is available at http://enterprisesecurity.symantec.com.

SCTS Certification Program

Symantec created the Symantec Certified Technical Specialist, Small Business Security program to provide Symantec partners and customers with an opportunity to validate their knowledge of Symantec security solutions suitable for implementation in a small business environment. SCTS, Small Business Security is a desktop security solution, certifying that an information technology professional has the skills and knowledge necessary to build a solid defensive posture for workstations. It's designed for security consultants, sales engineers, system engineers, and system administrators who work with Symantec products in the small business market.

Overview

Earning the SCTS, Small Business Security credential requires candidates to pass a single computer-based test that covers the material presented in this book. You'll need to demonstrate your understanding of the planning, installation, configuration, and management of the following:

- Symantec AntiVirus 10.0
- Symantec Client Security 3.0
- Norton AntiSpam 2005

When you've successfully completed the exam and have accepted the Symantec Certification Agreement you earn the right to use the SCTS logo, shown in Figure 1-8, on your business cards.

symantec.
SCTS

Figure 1-8 SCTS logo.

> **Note**
> Your Symantec Certified Technical Specialist credential is valid for two years from the time you complete certification requirements (passing the exam and accepting the certification agreement).

After you pass the exam, you need to log in to the Symantec certification program tracking site, CertTracker, and accept the terms of the Symantec Certification Agreement. Symantec utilizes CertTracker, a secure database hosted by Integral 7, to track and manage candidates' certification activities. Through CertTracker you can access your exam records, track fulfillment status, and monitor your progress toward achieving a targeted level of Symantec certification.

This is found at www.symantec.com/certtracker. This interactive tool helps you confirm your contact information and track the shipment of your certification kit.

> **Tip**
> CertTracker is preloaded with the contact information you used to register for the exam, so be certain to provide accurate address information when you sign up. This will ensure that you receive your certification materials in a timely fashion.

The Exam

The SCTS, Small Business Security exam is offered via Computer-Based Testing (CBT) at Prometric locations throughout the world. You have

90 minutes to complete 75 questions, with the exception of additional time for the list below.

An automatic 15 minutes is added for English language exams for the following countries:

- France
- Germany
- Italy
- Spain
- Austria
- Switzerland
- Belgium
- Luxemburg

- Monaco
- San Marino
- Liechtenstein
- Cameroon
- Comoros (Madagascar)
- Mauritius
- Reunion
- Senegal

An automatic 30 minutes is added for the English language exams for Japan.

Registering for the Exam
Prometric offers thousands of testing locations throughout the world. To register for the exam, visit www.2test.com and select the testing center near you. You'll need to provide payment details for the $100 fee at the time of registration.

Exam Outline

The exam is divided into three content areas, corresponding to the three products covered in the SCTS, Small Business Security certification. The 75 exam questions are distributed among the three content areas according to the following proportions:

- Symantec AntiVirus: 50.7%
- Symantec Client Security: 32%
- Norton AntiSpam: 17.3%

> **Tip**
> Take these proportions to heart: If you're new to all three solutions, you should spend approximately half of your time working with Symantec AntiVirus and the remainder of your time divided between Symantec Client Security and Norton AntiSpam.

Following is a list of the specific exam objectives that we cover in this book:

- Symantec AntiVirus Overview
  - Describe the business problem that Symantec AntiVirus addresses
  - Describe types of viruses
  - Describe the architecture of Symantec AntiVirus technology
  - Describe the components of the Symantec AntiVirus solution

- Symantec AntiVirus Planning
  - Conduct deployment planning activities, taking into consideration varying technologies, platforms, and business environments
  - Describe the top three deployment scenarios for a small business environment

- Symantec AntiVirus Installation and Configuration
  - Describe all required preinstallation tasks
  - Perform an installation
  - Configure the product for use

- Symantec AntiVirus Management
  - Describe the management components
  - Perform management tasks
  - Perform an AntiVirus upgrade/renewal

- Symantec Client Security Overview
  - Describe the business problem that Symantec Client Security addresses
  - Describe types of attacks

- Describe the architecture of the client-based Symantec Client Security technology
- Describe the components of the client-based Symantec Client Security solution

- Symantec Client Security Planning
  - Conduct deployment-planning activities, taking into consideration varying technologies, platforms, and business environments
  - Describe the top three deployment scenarios for a small business environment

- Symantec Client Security Installation and Configuration
  - Describe all required preinstallation tasks
  - Perform an installation
  - Configure the product for use

- Symantec Client Security Management
  - Describe the management components
  - Perform management tasks
  - Perform Symantec Client Security upgrade/renewal

- Norton AntiSpam Overview
  - Describe the business problem that the Norton AntiSpam technology addresses
  - Describe the types of spam
  - Describe the architecture of the client-based AntiSpam technology
  - Describe the components of the client-based AntiSpam solution

- Norton AntiSpam Planning
  - Conduct deployment-planning activities, taking into consideration varying technologies, platforms, and business environments
  - Describe the top three deployment scenarios for a small business environment

- Norton AntiSpam Installation and Configuration
  - Describe all required preinstallation tasks
  - Perform an installation
  - Configure the product for use

- Norton AntiSpam Management
  - Describe the management components
  - Perform management tasks
  - Perform a Norton Antispam upgrade/renewal

Use this list of objectives to help guide your studying efforts. When you're finished reading this book and working with the software, you should be able to review this list and clearly articulate the meaning of each step and the process used to complete it.

Question Types

You'll find four types of questions on the SCTS, Small Business Security exam. Let's take a brief look at each type of question:

- **Single-response questions** are straightforward multiple-choice questions with one correct answer. You'll be able to select only a single answer. These options are in the radio button format.

- **Multiple-response questions** have more than one correct answer, and you'll need to select all of the correct answers. These options are in the check box format. You will be told the number of answers to select.

> **Tip**
> Always read the question text carefully; it will tell you the number of correct answers that you need to select. You'll never be forced to guess the correct number of answers on the SCTS, Small Business Security exam.

- **Matching questions** ask you to match items in one column with items in another column. Typical exercises might ask you to match words with their definitions or products with their capabilities.

- **Ordering questions** ask you to place a series of items in the appropriate sequence. For example, you might be asked to sort a series of installation steps in the order they should be performed.

Exam Preparation

A recent survey revealed that taking an exam is one of the most stressful activities in the lives of adults. After all, school is behind us and many years might have elapsed since the last time we picked up a no. 2 pencil. Fortunately, it's possible to alleviate the majority of the fear created by a test with one tool: preparation.

We've created an eight-step process designed to provide you with a solid foundation to prepare for the exam. It revolves around the use of this book, the accompanying CD-ROM, and Symantec's security products. Here are the eight steps in our recommended preparation plan:

1. **Register for the exam.** That's right. The first step of our process is registering for the exam! When you finish reading this introductory chapter, quickly skim through the rest of this book to get a feel for how much time it will take you to master this material and be fully prepared for the exam. This will prevent you from the most common failing of certification candidates: never taking the exam. If you're new to the field of information security, give yourself plenty of time. You might want to choose an exam date that's about two months from now. If you have some experience under your belt, you might be ready to take the exam sooner. It's your decision. Just make the commitment to this program by signing up for a date now.

> **Note**
> To register for the exam, visit the Prometric Web site at
> www.2test.com.

2. **Read this book.** All of the topics you need to master to pass the SCTS, Small Business Security exam are contained within the covers of this

book. Read this book cover to cover. You might want to combine this with step 3, but it's essential that you read every word contained in this book. If you find yourself reading quickly and skipping sentences without really comprehending them, it's time to take a break, go get a glass of water, and come back when you're ready to devote your full attention to learning.

3. **Use the CD-ROM that accompanies this book.** The CD-ROM contains simulations and activities to reinforce the topics covered in this book. When there is an associated simulation or activity, it will be identified by the following icons:

   Indicates an activity

   Indicates a simulation

Insert the CD-ROM and work though the related simulations and activities.

4. **Install and configure the products.** The SCTS, Small Business Security exam covers three products: Symantec AntiVirus 10.0, Symantec Client Security 3.0, and Norton AntiSpam 2005. To succeed on the exam you need to have hands-on experience with the software, especially during the installation phase. If you're able to obtain this experience on the job working with live systems, great. If not, you'll need to obtain a couple of practice systems and use them to install and configure these products. If you'd like, it's perfectly acceptable to complete this step as you're completing step 2 so that you can follow along with the book.

5. **Work with the products on a regular basis.** Gaining a full understanding of any security product requires that you use it on a regular basis and understand how it helps you deal with security risks and threats as they arise in real time. As with the last step, more power to you if you're able to get this experience at work. If you're not, leave your test environment up and running for a few weeks, and use it to practice the administration skills you learn in this book.

> **Tip**
> Successful completion of the SCTS, Small Business Security exam depends upon hands-on experience with Symantec products. Don't attempt the exam without working with the software products, even if you need to do so in a lab environment.

6. **Review this book.** After you've gained experience with the products, turn back to the book again. You'll probably want to use it as a reference while you're experimenting. This will help you firm up your knowledge from an experiential point of view.

7. **Take a practice test.** Now it's time to see how prepared you are! Use the CD included with this book to take a practice exam. Do it all in one sitting without referencing the book, to best simulate the real testing environment. Pass or fail, this process will provide you with valuable information to help your study process. Most important, the exams on the CD closely resemble the actual test environment and will help you feel comfortable with the test before sitting for the exam.

8. **Repeat, Repeat, Repeat.** Repeat steps 6 and 7 until you're confident that you're well prepared for the real exam.

Following this process strictly will ensure that you'll have the confidence you need when exam time rolls around. Confidence breeds success.

Program Guidelines and Policies

Symantec has laid out the following SCTS, Small Business Security program guidelines and policies for SCTS, Small Business Security candidates and credential holders:

- Candidates must meet all published requirements to achieve Symantec certification designations.
- All Symantec exams related to security products are delivered through Prometric Worldwide Testing Centers.

- Before taking the exam, candidates must agree to keep exam content confidential.
- Candidates must electronically accept the Symantec Certification Agreement via www.symantec.com/certtracker.
- Candidates must adhere to Certification Logo Usage Guidelines.
- Candidates pay all required fees for exams to Prometric.
- Symantec strongly recommends building appropriate hands-on experience before taking exams.
- Candidates maintain their profile information via CertTracker, Symantec's Certification Tracking Tool, and on the Prometric Web site.
- Before retaking a failed exam, Symantec recommends that candidates evaluate area(s) for further development and experience.

Finding More Information

Further information on the SCTS, Small Business Security certification, as well as other Symantec certification programs, can be found on the Web at www.symantec.com/education/certification. You can also contact Symantec's certification experts directly via e-mail at certification@symantec.com.

Conclusion

Symantec provides small businesses with a robust set of tools designed to increase their security posture: Symantec AntiVirus, Symantec Client Security, and Norton AntiSpam. The SCTS, Small Business Security certification is designed to demonstrate a candidate's ability to plan, install, configure, and manage these three Symantec products in a small business setting. As you explore the rest of this book, you'll develop the knowledge base necessary to work with these products in a production environment.

Chapter Review Questions

Question 1-1

Which two Symantec security solutions help protect desktop systems against spyware? Select the two correct answers.

- ❑ A. Symantec AntiVirus
- ❑ B. Norton AntiSpam
- ❑ C. Symantec Client Security

Question 1-2

Which three types of program are generally considered to be threats? Select three correct answers.

- ❑ A. Viruses
- ❑ B. Worms
- ❑ C. Phishing
- ❑ D. Spyware
- ❑ E. Spam
- ❑ F. Adware
- ❑ G. Trojan horses

Question 1-3

What type of malicious code spreads from system to system with some user intervention? Select the correct answer.

- ◯ A. Viruses
- ◯ B. Worms
- ◯ C. Phishing
- ◯ D. Spam

Question 1-4

What type of malicious code spreads from system to system without user intervention? Select the correct answer.

- ◯ A. Viruses
- ◯ B. Worms
- ◯ C. Phishing
- ◯ D. Spam

Question 1-5

What type of malicious code spreads by deceiving computer users into thinking it is a beneficial program? Select the correct answer.

◯ A. Viruses

◯ B. Trojan horses

◯ C. Worms

◯ D. Spam

Question 1-6

After you pass the Symantec Certified Technical Specialist exam, for how long does your certification remain valid? Select the correct answer.

◯ A. Six months

◯ B. One year

◯ C. Two years

◯ D. Three years

◯ E. Five years

Question 1-7

A brokerage's computers were hacked into, causing a network failure. No customer accounts were affected, and the brokerage didn't suffer any monetary loss. However, the brokerage was forced to stop business operations for several hours, causing employees to sit idly waiting for the repair. The brokerage also suspects that some customers might have switched to another brokerage as a result of the incident. What type of losses has the brokerage incurred? Select the two correct answers.

❑ A. Direct loss

❑ B. Indirect loss

❑ C. Productivity loss

❑ D. Legal exposure

Chapter Review Answers

Answer 1-1

Answers **A** and **C** are correct. Both Symantec AntiVirus and Symantec Client Security provide automatic detection and removal of spyware, adware, viruses, worms, and Trojan horses on desktops, laptops, and file servers. Symantec Client Security adds firewall intrusion prevention capabilities to defend against blended threats such as Nimda and Blaster.

Answer 1-2

Answers **A, B,** and **G** are correct. Viruses, worms, and Trojan horses are all threats. Phishing is a variant of spam, neither of which is considered a threat. Spyware and adware are classified as security risks.

Answer 1-3

Answer **A** is correct. Viruses are malicious code that spread from system to system with some user intervention. Worms are similar to viruses but spread without requiring user intervention. Phishing and spam are not types of malicious code.

Answer 1-4

Answer **B** is correct. Worms are malicious code objects that spread from system to system without user intervention. Viruses are similar to worms but require user intervention. Phishing and spam are not types of malicious code.

Answer 1-5

Answer **B** is correct. Trojan horses present themselves to the computer user as a beneficial program, such as a game or utility. While they're running the advertised function, they deliver their malicious payload in the background.

Answer 1-6

Answer **C** is correct. Symantec Certified Technical specialist credentials are valid for two years from the date you pass the SCTS, Small Business Security examination and accept the Symantec Certification Agreement.

Answer 1-7

Answers **B** and **C** are correct. The brokerage suffered a productivity loss when employees were forced to sit idly waiting for the network to be repaired. They also suffered an indirect loss when customers switched to another brokerage firm as a result of the incident. There was no direct loss or legal exposure described in the scenario.

PART I

SYMANTEC ANTIVIRUS

CHAPTER 2

Security Risks and Threats

Terms and Techniques to Remember

- Threats
- Security risks
- Blended threats
- Social engineering
- Denial of Service
- Impact caused by security risks and threats

Security Risks

When computers were large monolithic devices standing alone and loaded from verified software packs provided directly by commercial vendors, applications were validated before installation and only an administrator with proper permissions could add new programs. Today, always-on high-speed broadband connectivity is common, and even dial-up users are able to maintain a high degree of constant connectivity to the Internet. Users are beset by a constant stream of toolbar helpers, cursor animations, browser plug-ins, and other types of software they are prompted to install.

The term *malware* (short for "malicious software") has been commonly used to refer to the traditional threats posed by viruses, Trojan horses, and worms. Over the last few years, the risks introduced by a number of other types of programs, including spyware and adware, have been steadily increasing. Spyware programs can spontaneously pop up advertisements, hijack browser sessions, redirect browsers to select target sites, or compile tracking information on user browsing habits. They can make use of a user's computer resources without his or her informed consent, or even log a user's keystrokes and form data—including sensitive data such as credit card and personal information that might then be used for identity theft or other illegal actions.

Makers of these programs often package their wares in a bundle with other packages the user wants, such as in the case of Kazaa, a peer-to-peer file-sharing application. Packaged within Kazaa, users unknowingly agreed to allow Brilliant Digital Entertainment to make use of "unused" computer capacity when they selected to accept the very lengthy terms of service required to download and install Kazaa. Without realizing what they had done, these users had given an unknown company the right and ability to make use of their computer's storage, CPU, memory, and network connectivity as this clandestine agency saw fit.

Although Symantec and other security providers have identified thousands of different security risks, most fall into a few general categories of operation. These can impact the performance or security of an infected host, posing an ever-expanding threat that must be addressed if a user is to maintain an acceptable level of operational capacity.

Symantec recognizes a number of different types of security risks present in the modern network environment. Although some of these risks are present only when a computer is actively connected to a network, it is important to remember that other vectors can be used to transfer security risks of many types. Technologies such as flash drives, floppy disks, portable hard drives, CD-ROM and DVD optical media, and wireless connectivity provide avenues for the introduction of undesirable software onto unprotected computers.

Spyware

Spyware is software that has the capability to scan computers or monitor activity and relay information to other computers or locations in cyberspace. Among the information that can be actively or passively gathered and disseminated by spyware are passwords, log-in details, account numbers, personal information, and individual files or other personal documents. Spyware can also gather and distribute information related to the user's computer, applications running on the computer, and Internet browser usage or other computing habits.

Spyware frequently attempts to remain unnoticed, either by actively hiding or by simply not making its presence on a computer known to the user. Spyware can be downloaded from Web sites (typically in shareware or freeware), email messages, and instant messengers. Additionally, a user might unknowingly receive and/or trigger spyware by accepting an End User License Agreement from a software program linked to the spyware or from visiting a Web site that downloads the spyware with or without an End User License Agreement.

A survey in late 2004 examined the prevalence of spyware on consumer PCs. This survey found that more than two-thirds of all computers surveyed had some form of spyware present, commonly with multiple forms or variants present on a single computer. The burgeoning growth of these risks has reached such proportions that the Electronic Privacy Information Center (EPIC) has listed the need for antispyware, antivirus, and firewall software as the no. 3 item on their "Top Ten Consumer Privacy Resolutions."

Adware

Adware is designed to deliver advertising content to a user, often mining the user's browsing habits to provide directed advertising of products or services the user is most likely to want. As a result of this practice, many users see this type of software as somewhat innocuous, without realizing that this information is being gathered and may be sent to other parties elsewhere without their consent. Spammers often buy lists compiled by such programs to target a flood of unsolicited email to the user's address.

Browser-hijacking adware programs can redirect a user's home page to a different site, intercept search engine, or browsing URLs, and redirect the user to alternate locations or otherwise attempt to control the user's Web browser client. Programs such as Xupiter and CoolWebSearch are examples of this type of adware.

Hack Tools

These are tools that a hacker or unauthorized user can use to attack, gain unauthorized access to, or perform identification or fingerprinting of your computer. Hack tools generally do the following:

- Attempt to gain information on or access hosts surreptitiously, utilizing methods that circumvent or bypass obvious security mechanisms inherent to the system they are installed on.

- Facilitate an attempt at disabling a target computer, preventing its normal use.

- Facilitate attacks on third-party computers as part of a direct or distributed Denial-of-Service attempt.

One example of a hack tool is a keystroke logger, a program that tracks and records individual keystrokes, and can send this information back to the hacker.

Joke Programs

Mostly harmless, these programs generally create distractions by causing animated characters to wander around a user's screen randomly or by interrupting normal operations to display a fake computer crash message. Such programs are typically benign but can cost a business a great deal of lost time trying to eliminate programs from infected hosts.

Dialers

Dialers are a form of risk that intercept connectivity requests to a user's normal ISP and instead dial on their own to connect a user to an alternate phone service. Often these numbers are long-distance calls, sometimes dialing numbers with exorbitant per-minute toll fees. Although decreasing in number due to the expansion of cable modem and DSL broadband connectivity, these programs can cost users money and effort, and can also endanger user information.

Remote Access

Remote access programs allow an unauthorized user or remote terminal to interact with a user's desktop or other devices connected to a running computer. Some of these programs relay the desktop to a remote viewing client so that the originator can observe exactly what the user sees. Others actually allow the originator to take over a user's console by entering keystrokes or moving the mouse as if the hacker were sitting at the compromised computer's console.

A few of these programs can be used to surreptitiously access a computer's attached devices, such as webcams and microphones, to better spy on users without alerting them to this behavior. Although there are a number of valid uses for remote access clients in the modern business environment, most of these programs hide their existence from the user and can present an extreme risk to users working with sensitive or protected information, trade secrets, or other similarly valued data.

Summary

Table 2-1 details some of the typical impacts caused by security risks.

Table 2-1

Typical Impacts Caused by Digital Infections	
Impact	**Risks**
Performance	Computer slowdown. Computer instability.
	Active conduit for download and installation of additional security risks.
Privacy	Release of confidential, protected, or sensitive information.
	Release of browser-tracking information, logged keystrokes, or other forms of data.
	Violations of privacy policies or legal requirements.
Operation	Infections can allow programs to spread to other computers, mobile devices, or network file shares.
	Infections can lead to data loss, corruption, or other forms of operational impairment to infected hosts.
Liability	In additional to legal issues surrounding violations of privacy laws, owners of infected hosts might find themselves liable for harm or loss caused by their infected computer's actions.

Removal of infections can also cost time, personnel, and possible loss of critical data within an enterprise. Viruses, worms, and Trojan horses can add significantly to the total cost of ownership (TCO) of a company's network.

Threats

Unlike security risks, threats can be much more malicious and widely distributed. Based on the manner in which a threat spreads and how it acts after infecting a new host, it is referred to as a virus, worm, Trojan horse, or blended threat.

Viruses

A virus is a program or code that replicates itself onto other files with which it comes in contact; that is, a virus can infect another program, a boot sector, a partition sector, or a document that supports macros by inserting itself or attaching itself to that medium. Most viruses only replicate, although many can do damage to a computer or to the user's data as well. Unlike worms, which are discussed later in this chapter, viruses generally require human action to propagate.

Risks from Viruses

Symantec has identified more than 10,000 variations of viruses, with multiple new viruses added to this list every day. Some of these simply seek to spread copies; others can be used to weaken a computer's defenses against later attacks in a process referred to as softening the target. Other viruses have deleted files of a particular type on local and network-shared file stores, while some are programmed to lie in wait until a particular date or time and then enact a preprogrammed process, such as attacking antivirus Web sites in an effort to create a distributed Denial-of-Service of a Web site.

Viral Propagation

Just as a biological virus can find its way to a new host by air, contact, or water, digital viruses can be transmitted between hosts via a number of different avenues, including removable storage, downloads, network file shares, wireless connectivity, and email.

Removable Storage

Early virus propagation occurred when a medium, such as a floppy disk, was loaded into an infected computer. The virus copied itself to this medium so that when the floppy was inserted into another host, the viral code executed and spread to this new computer. Common removable media exploited by viral code included floppy disks, Bernoulli cartridges, removable drive platters, and any other form of medium that could carry the infection between computers. Today removable optical media and the ubiquitous USB flash drives provide a convenient transport mechanism between unprotected computers.

Downloaded Information

With the advent of networked operating systems and the development of the global Internet, users can transfer data without requiring a physical medium of transport. Data downloaded from Web sites, electronic mail, and peer to peer file-sharing services such as BitTorrent or Kazaa all provide a conduit for potential viral transmission. Users who download cracked applications or illegally downloaded audio and video files commonly encounter viral programs masquerading as the desired file. Legitimate users might find themselves attacked by a newly released virus if they visit an infected Web site or otherwise download virus-laden data.

Network File Shares

In modern network scenarios, multiple users often share common file storage on a centralized file server. This allows mobile users to access their data from the central repository without requiring that they always log on from a particular client computer, while also allowing centralized management of backup/recovery and file-storage policies. Some viruses can replicate themselves to an available file, potentially corrupting key data or providing a vector for transmission to other users who might access infected files from a shared directory that has been compromised in this manner.

Wireless Connectivity

Viral programs are evolving into forms capable of being transmitted via wireless connectivity, including Bluetooth and WiFi wireless data connections. As mobile devices employ greater data-sharing capabilities and expanding computer resources, many devices and embedded control computers might become capable of being infected by viruses.

Windows and the World

Because of the dominance of the Microsoft Windows® operating systems, on computers around the world, virus writers have focused on this platform and its common applications. However, other operating systems are not without risk; for example, viruses are now being seen infecting mobile devices such as cell phones, personal digital assistants (PDAs), and other mobile devices. Like their server and desktop-computing counterparts, these devices can also be vulnerable to viruses and other forms of threats.

BRAIN

One of the earliest documented computer viruses to strike systems "in the wild" was the BRAIN virus, which originated in Pakistan in 1986. The BRAIN virus is a boot-sector infector that spreads through infected magnetic media. When the computer starts, it reads the infected boot sector and loads itself into memory.

A nasty twist implemented by BRAIN is its stealth capabilities. BRAIN watches for attempts by user programs (such as antivirus systems) to read the boot sector and intercepts them. It feeds back a copy of an uninfected boot sector, making detection difficult.

PCs Are Not Alone

In July 2004, proof-of-concept threats were identified that were targeted at the Symbian operating system used by many mobile devices, including personal digital assistants (PDAs), cell phones, vending machines, environmental controls, and many other forms of wirelessly connected electronics. Some of these threats were capable of taking advantage of the Bluetooth connectivity built into mobile devices to spread to nearby devices configured for Bluetooth access. Symantec lists 31 variations of SymbOS-based threats at the time of this text's writing.

As with biological viral infections, a digitally infected mobile device can potentially spread to other susceptible devices that passed close by—much like having a co-worker with the flu come to the office and share his or her biological virus with those who come too close. This is not limited to cell phones, laptops, and PDAs alone. *SC Magazine* recently detailed the potential for viral infection of the onboard computers on some late-model automobiles.

With the capability to infect other devices without direct contact, the potential for rapid viral propagation between automobiles and other devices becomes a very complex issue. Users passing through a crowd, walking past parked cars, or walking near other wireless devices in their office or home could find their personal devices infected simply by their proximity.

Executable Files

By attaching itself to an executable file, viral code can be executed by the operating system when the executable file is run. Some viruses are capable of renaming common executable files and duplicating themselves in place of the replaced application so that when a user attempts to open a common application such as notepad.exe, the virus executes in its place. A few of these viruses can attempt to hide their existence by also executing the renamed program the user sought after they have completed their own operation.

Kernel Attacks
In addition to normal executable files, the core executable component of the operating system, termed the *kernel*, can also be targeted by a virus.

File Attachments

With the growing use of email for personal and professional uses, file attachments have become a common means of viral transmission. Many viruses arrive in a user's inbox pretending to be from a known source, offering some type of information of interest to the target. Little does the user know, when he or she launches the attached file, a virus and is activated.

Macro Viruses

Within some applications, such as the Microsoft Office Suite of products, users can record macros, allowing a set of common tasks to be executed. Macro viruses append themselves to common file types, such as document (.doc) or spreadsheet (.xls) files, and execute their payload when an infected document is opened by the application or some other program capable of executing embedded macro code.

Direct Infection

Some viruses directly damage files by replacing the original file with a copy of the virus named the same as the deleted file, or by embedding their code within an existing file by discarding the original file contents beyond the file's header segment. Other viruses can attach their code to the beginning or end of existing files, to conceal the infection more effectively. Many viruses hide copies of their code within the System Restore on Windows XP computers, requiring that a user disable this feature to be able to remove the infection. Others write keys into the Registry that must be removed to clean out the viral code.

Boot-Sector Viruses

Boot-sector viruses directly infect the first sector of a computer's hard drive. When a computer is first powered on, its built-in programming is capable of performing only simple Power-On Self-Test (POST) operations and then accessing the first sector on the configured boot device (typically a hard drive). Code loaded from this boot sector directs the computer through additional steps necessary to load software drivers and the operating system itself.

Worms

A worm is a program that makes and facilitates the distribution of copies of itself—for example, from one disk drive to another, or by copying itself using email or another transport mechanism. The worm can do damage and compromise the security of the computer. It can arrive via exploitation of computer vulnerability or when a user clicks on an infected email.

The World's First Worm

The very first worm to terrorize the Internet occurred long before the word *Internet* became a household term. On November 2, 1988, a strange affliction struck the young Internet. Systems around the network suddenly began acting strangely, and network traffic grew at an exponential pace.

Internet experts quickly discovered that a new type of malicious code was spreading. This "worm" was infecting entire networks and quickly winding its way throughout the fledgling Internet.

Security officials responded quickly (at least, by 1988 standards) to dissect the worm and determine the methods by which it was spreading. Experts throughout government and academia (the two major players on the Internet in those days) convened a conference at the National Computer Security Center in Baltimore and developed a response plan.

Six days later, on November 8, the worm was declared eradicated. Authorities tracked down the worm's author, Robert Tappan Morris, a graduate student in computer science at Cornell University who claimed that the worm was an academic experiment gone wild. The courts didn't believe his claim and, after he was found guilty, sentenced him to a fine and community service under a felony violation of the Computer Fraud and Abuse Act.

Vulnerabilities

Worms have been developed to attack vulnerabilities in operating systems, services and daemons. Worms such as the Morris Worm (one of the first in-the-wild worm programs that impacted overall network performance, released in the late 1980s) spread through UNIX® and VAX™ computers that shared a common vulnerability, allowing execution of code through improperly secured debugging routines and other vulnerabilities.

Rate of Propagation

Unlike viruses, the automatic replication of worms can allow even seemingly benign worms to congest networks and impair recovery procedures. Although the Nachi worm downloaded an update from Microsoft to patch the very vulnerability it exploited, the worm generated considerable traffic and impacted network performance even for users who had already installed the patch on their own computers.

In March 2004, the Witty worm set a new record for the speed at which a discovered vulnerability has been used to generate a live worm program, a record that stands at the time of this text's writing. Less than two days after the initial advisory announcing a newly discovered vulnerability, the Witty worm was released to take advantage of the vulnerability before the operating computer vendor could develop and distribute a patch for this newly discovered security weakness.

Zero-Day

Many analysts predict that some type of "zero-day" threat will soon be developed, taking advantage of a totally unknown vulnerability to gain almost universal distribution across all unprotected computers on the Internet before developers have an opportunity to begin fashioning a countering patch or hot fix. Without antivirus protection, users would be faced with the decision to shut down their infected computer until a patch could be developed or to risk whatever threat the worm produced. Symantec AntiVirus™ and Symantec™ Client Security can aid in defending against many of the potential avenues that might be exploited if such a zero-day threat were ever to emerge by providing proactive defenses for vulnerable computers.

The popularity of the Microsoft Windows operating system has been suggested as one factor contributing to the incredible rate of propagation experienced by recent worm releases. However, the implementation of complex worms capable of spreading through many different vectors provides a strong indication that even if there were two or three equally dominant platforms sharing the market, worm authors would simply target vulnerabilities present in multiple platforms and so gain near the same distribution levels.

Trojan Horses

A Trojan horse portrays itself as something other than what it is at the point of execution. Although it might advertise its activity after launching, this information is not apparent to the user beforehand. A Trojan horse neither replicates nor copies itself, but causes damage or compromises the security of the computer. A Trojan horse must be sent by someone or carried by another program, and can arrive in the form of a joke program or software of some sort. The malicious functionality of a Trojan horse is anything undesirable for a computer user, including data destruction or the compromise of a computer by providing a means for another attacker to gain access, bypassing normal access controls. Like spyware discussed earlier in this chapter, Trojan horses might offer interesting new games, desktop themes, or all manner of other enticements to a user, to get the user to install the Trojan package.

Once installed, a Trojan horse typically provides some type of apparent functionality to the user, while performing many other tasks behind the scenes, leaving the user unaware. Trojan horse programs often communicate with their creator through Internet Relay Chat (IRC) communications, allowing the creator to modify these programs once installed and even to publish updates that can be applied automatically by the program itself. Table 2-2 lists a few of the more common security risks posed by Trojan horse infections.

A subtype of the Trojan horse is the "back door," which refers to a programmatically created mechanism for bypassing normal security measures in accessing resources on the vulnerable computer. Occasionally, programmers put into place various hidden shortcuts in their code, designed to ease the

Table 2-2

Common Risks Carried by Trojan Horses	
Risk	Examples
Remote access	Services can be enabled or ports can be opened.
	Remote-control utilities can be installed, allowing control of the computer's console.
Monitoring	Console duplication can allow shoulder-surfing by remote operators.
	Keystrokes, URL history, and other data can be collected and relayed to the creator.
Data relay	Unauthorized file-sharing services can be implemented, allowing the creator to distribute contraband data through the compromised host.
	Spam relay programs can be implemented, allowing the creator to hide the origin of spam messages.
Softening	Trojan horse programs can replace common applications on the host computer, creating vulnerabilities and softening the host's defenses.
	Trojan horse programs can also be used to coordinate mass network-scanning or network attack efforts, making it harder to detect the profiling scan or attack coming from tens of thousands of separate computers controlled by the creator of the program.

process of development or testing. Attackers might utilize one or more security risks to plant their own back-door program somewhere within the network.

Back doors are implanted by the attacker to allow later access to a computer. Remote-access tools can provide an attacker with a back door or allow the attacker to obtain sufficient information to bypass normal authentication measures using key-logged information. Back doors are particularly troublesome for network administrators responsible for tracking down the party responsible for network misuse.

Blended Threats

Blended threats combine the characteristics of viruses, worms, and Trojan horses with server and Internet vulnerabilities to initiate, transmit, and spread an attack. By using multiple methods and techniques, blended threats can rapidly spread and cause widespread damage. Characteristics of blended threats include the following:

- **Causes harm**—Launches a Denial-of-Service (DoS) attack at a target IP address, defaces Web servers, or plants Trojan horse programs for later execution.

- **Propagates by multiple methods**—Scans for vulnerabilities to compromise a computer, such as embedding code in HTML files on a server, infecting visitors to a compromised Web site, or sending unauthorized email from compromised servers with a worm attachment.

- **Attacks from multiple points**—Injects malicious code into the .exe files on a computer, raises the privilege level of the guest account, creates world-read and writeable network shares, makes numerous Registry changes, and adds script code into HTML files.

- **Spreads without human intervention**—Continuously scans the Internet for vulnerable servers to attack.

- **Exploits vulnerabilities**—Takes advantage of known vulnerabilities, such as buffer overflows, HTTP input-validation vulnerabilities, and known default passwords to gain unauthorized administrative access.

Effective protection from blended threats requires a comprehensive security solution that contains multiple layers of defense and response mechanisms.

Blended threats such as Code Red spread by exploiting services running on vulnerable computers, which in Code Red's case was the Miscrosoft IIS service's HTTP implementation. Code Red took advantage of a flaw in the initial coding that allowed the arbitrary execution of code on the server hosting the IIS service. Others spread by taking advantage of vulnerabilities discovered in various services, such as the Windows DCOM Remote Procedure Call (RPC) vulnerability exploited by Blaster, or through code injection and buffer overflows, such as those generated by malformed UDP datagrams exploited by the SQL Slammer worm. Nimda and its variations made use of multiple vectors for transmission in a single package by spreading through vulnerable file shares and buffer overflows, or by sending itself as an email attachment.

> **Note**
> As an item of interest, Nimda is believed to be named because it spells *Admin* backward. Code Red gained its name from the caffeinated soda product popular at the time.

Blended threats are becoming increasingly sophisticated, allowing viruses, worms, and Trojan horses to spread through any of a number of different mechanisms, in case a vulnerable computer's defenses are only partially in place. This multifaceted attack strategy requires administrators to plan their network defense carefully, to contain multiple layers of defense and response mechanisms implemented at the client, server, and the gateway.

Proliferation of Viruses, Worms, and Trojan Horses

With dozens of new variations of viruses being released daily, one might ask who is developing so many sophisticated programs. Although the first exploits to take advantage of a newly discovered vulnerability are generally released by highly skilled programmers, the creation of viruses and worms requires no more skill than any other point-and-click GUI to create a seemingly infinite stream of new customized viral programs. Hundreds of ready-made GUI and command-line virus generators can be downloaded from the Internet, with names such as Acid Flowing Trojan Generator or the Batch-O-Matic.

By selecting options on a GUI, such as shown in Figure 2-1, a hacker might elect for his or her new creation to spread by one or many different means, using customized file names, polymorphic restructuring capabilities, and many other details that can make the newly generated program unique in its methods of attack and distribution. Because researchers also use these tools, they remain legal in most countries and are easily accessible through a simple Web search. The danger inherent in these tools is that, through their use, relatively unskilled hackers could generate continuous streams of new threats.

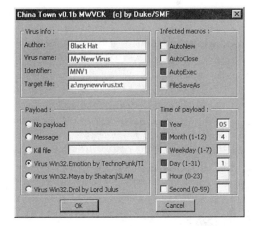

Figure 2-1 An example virus-generating GUI tool, configuring a virus called My New Virus to deliver a payload that will act on April Fools' Day 2005.

Polymorphism

Polymorphism is the capability of a program to generate offspring copies that differ from the parent because of a mutated ordering of operations or functionality within the code. Viruses, worms, and Trojan horses that implement polymorphism are more difficult to identify because of the continual mutation in each generation.

Common Attack Strategies

Attackers targeting a network can leverage combinations of the various security risks and threats to enact their nefarious plans for vulnerable computers. The least sophisticated attacks might corrupt or delete data, potentially requiring a complete reformatting and reload for infected computers. More sophisticated attacks can produce even less desirable results, including placing illegal content on targeted computers, exposing protected data, or even utilizing the compromised computers to levy attacks against secondary targets.

Social Engineering

Many hackers make use of the practice of social engineering, which is a psychological scam intended to get users to reveal information or to provide details useful for a successful network attack. Email-borne viruses employ this technique by presenting an innocuously named viral attachment with a From email address matching that of a known associate. Spyware and other security risks can provide attackers with information that can be used to improve social-engineering efforts, such as by allowing a phishing attack to mimic a site the user is known to frequent.

Bots and Botnets

Botnet is a term used by the FBI to describe a group of compromised hosts controlled by a remote attacker, as illustrated in Figure 2-2. Communicating with their creator through Internet Relay Chat (IRC) or other anonymous methods of communication, compromised computers can reside quietly for a lengthy time until given a command to attack a chosen target. These networks can also be used to crack encryption keys and other CPU-demanding tasks, distributing a huge task among tens of thousands of personal computers located around the globe.

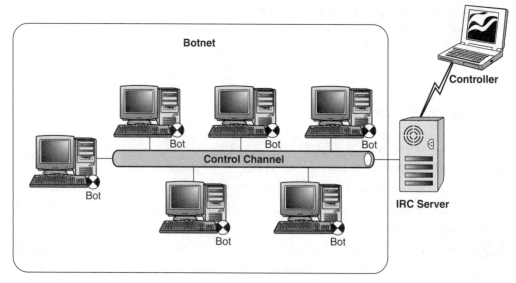

Figure 2-2 An idealized example of an IRC-controlled botnet.

Sometimes referred to as zombies compromised computers (bots) are often traded as coin of the realm among hackers seeking access within a particular network. Large botnets are status symbols among some groups, where their originators might fight silent wars against one another using corporate, educational, personal, and even governmental hosts as their playing pieces. Compromised bots in secure networks, such as .gov and .mil sites, can often be traded for thousands of compromised .edu and .com hosts, all traded by the controlling hacker to purchase status, bragging rights, or access to target networks. These transactions occur while the true owners remain unaware that the compromised computers are being bought, sold, and used as a weapon against other networks.

Beyond their value as currency among the various hacker communities, botnets are commonly used in various malicious ways:

- **Distributed–Denial-of-Service attacks**—The most common use of botnets is the massed coordinated attack against a target site or address to saturate the target's bandwidth or capability to respond to legitimate connections. These attacks have been levied against high-profile sites through the use of thousands of compromised bots scattered around the world. The distributed nature of these attacks makes it more difficult for the target to filter out only the undesirable traffic.

- **Remote control**—Bots provide their controller some measure of control over the compromised computer, allowing the introduction of malicious programs, back doors, spyware, or any of the other security risks previously discussed.

- **File sharing**—Botnets are sometimes used to host contraband files, cracked software titles, audio files, and even entire DVDs that have been ripped and stored on compromised computers with high-bandwidth broadband connections. By replacing valid services on compromised hosts, these bot programs can be configured to serve as HTTP or FTP servers that might appear valid to a cursory audit of the network.

Compromised computers in highly secure or limited-access areas are highly valued by controllers of these botnets, along with computers with high levels of connectivity and large storage capacity. Because of this, commercial targets are commonly identified for attack to compromise servers and other well-connected computers. Educational sites are also commonly targeted because they are generally comprised of large numbers of relatively new computers installed in default configurations, connected to wide-bandwidth Internet backbones, and supported by limited numbers of staff that take publicly posted holidays.

Root Kits

Extending the qualities of a Trojan horse or a back door, root kits replace or modify elements of the operating system to provide an attacker greater control over compromised hosts. These programs can replace or modify the system kernel, system binaries, or other elements of the host's operating system, often allowing an attacker's later efforts to pass unnoticed, provided with stealth and cover by the modified system binaries.

Implementations of root kits can replace common user interface functions, allowing an attacker to conceal their implanted services from the Task Manager or to hide files from the explorer interface when a user attempts to check for unexpected files that might reveal the compromise. Root kits can be used to implant a known master password or other mechanism for bypassing the normal protections of the host computer.

Root kits provide the greatest level of control over a compromised host because they target directly the basis for all other applications running on a computer. Attackers who can successfully deploy a root kit can be considered to "own" the compromised computer at a functional level to such an extent that only a full reformat-and-reload can be certain to remove the damage done. Protection strategies are vital to protect against this level of compromise, where backup and recovery strategies might provide the only path back to a functional network environment.

Impact of Security Risks and Threats

Viruses, worms, and Trojan horses can corrupt data on a user's computer, infect other computers, weaken computer security, or provide back doors into protected networked computers. Although seemingly less dangerous than viruses that can corrupt digital content on a user's computer, spyware, adware, and other forms of security risk also represent a significant problem to small businesses, their users, and the company networks. All types of threat and security risk can seriously impair business operations, network use, and computer performance while performing many tasks unknown to the user of an infected computer. Some of the areas of impact are discussed here.

Capacity

All software operating on a computer consumes a portion of the host computer's resources, whether its hard drive storage, CPU processing power, computer memory, or network bandwidth. Any threat or security risk resident on a computer can seriously impair the performance. They add to the load placed by normal use by consuming additional memory, processor or network resources as they perform their task, monitoring keystrokes, searching for private information, and possibly sending that data to a central location. In addition to this, the threat could be a virus or worm attempting to propagate or launch an attack against another computer or network

Your Computer Held Captive

It is easy to see how each small package can combine with others to quickly overwhelm a computer, much like Gulliver found himself bound by the many tiny strands woven by the miniscule Lilliputians in the classic tale *The Travels of Gulliver*. Each individual software package might consume only a tiny fraction of a computer's capacity, but when taken together in large numbers, these packages can rapidly overwhelm normal operations.

Time

In addition to time lost because of operational slowdown caused by the weight of a computer's parasitic population, computer users could lose time clicking to close the endless stream of advertisements that suddenly appear, or while attempting to navigate back through a redirected session to find meaningful Web content. Administrative staff are also overburdened responding to user issues stemming from the security risks and threats prevalent on computers.

Undesirable Content

A myriad of pop-up advertisements and browser redirection by various security risks often expose users to undesirable content, notably graphic images inappropriate in the workplaces. Distracting materials or contraband images can, at best, be an impediment to a user's focus on work and can, at worst, present legal liabilities for the organization.

Unexpected Hazards

In one instance, an investigation of a user's computer brought about by complaints filed by a co-worker who claimed a hostile workplace environment was being created by the user's pornographic screen saver. Unknown to the user, acceptance of a bundled desktop themes package had also included installation of a spyware program that presented advertising images as a changing screen saver—often advertising materials of a decidedly mature theme.

Data Harvesting

Data-harvesting is particularly troubling within the modern corporate setting because many different legal requirements exist to mandate protection of client information in a number of different industry settings. As mentioned earlier, legislative requirements in the U.S. include the Children's Online Privacy Protection Acts (COPPA), the Health Insurance Portability and Accountability Act (HIPAA), the Federal Educational Rights Protection Act (FERPA), the Gramm-Leach-Bliley Act (GLBA), and a wide assortment of other privacy and information-control laws. Violations of these provisions, even when inadvertently caused by spyware data harvesting, can carry heavy penalties for both individual users and their companies' owners and board members.

Users must also be concerned about data-harvesting programs when their own private information is being distributed without their knowledge;

such data can be used in a number of different scams to drain users' bank accounts, make use of their credit, or enact identity-theft crimes. These are merely some of the threats posed by data-harvesting programs that might have meaning to the user and their employer. Businesses conducting research, operating under protected network mandates, or involved in protecting trade secrets or other valuable information might find that unexpected spyware programs are busily transferring sensitive data elsewhere beyond their control.

Computer Security

Security risks such as spyware can perform any number of actions without the user's knowledge once installed, with or without the knowledge of the user. Because of this, these programs can cause almost any type of security breach. Coupled with viral threats, automated computer-profiling utilities, and many other tools employed by hackers, a seemingly innocuous game, screen saver, animated cursor, or toolbar could open the door wide to any type of mischief desired by the software's author.

Instability

Instability of computer systems infected by security risks and threats could be an intentional effect desired by the program's author, in the case of a malicious program, or a side effect of these unwanted applications competing for similar resources, along with the fact that they are often not well written or tested as with most commercial software. In addition to these difficulties, spyware can compromise computer operations through hijacking and browser redirection or when replacing normal components of the operating system.

Business Issues

IT staff are faced with increasing pressures to comply with regulations, increase the mobility of their workforce, provide access to the extended workforce, and increase the breadth of their value and supply chains, as well as prevent the latest Internet attacks from wreaking havoc on the infrastructure.

At the same time, they must maintain service-level agreements, keep executives out of jail, and keep hackers from preying on end users utilizing the network.

Many companies today live with a false sense of security. They believe that perimeter security alone is sufficient to keep unwanted intruders from the spread of security risks and threats. To the contrary, it is too easy for these to enter a company network and never touch perimeter security. For example, imagine that a mobile user takes a laptop to work at home. While at home, the user connects to a local ISP and accesses infected Web sites or downloads personal email with infected attachments. The user then reconnects to the corporate network the next day and launches an infected attachment from a local email download. Another example is the remote user who uses a VPN to access corporate resources. The remote user accesses a local ISP before initiating the VPN client. It is very easy for the user to access an infected Web site or download infected personal email. When a VPN tunnel is established, the client is essentially behind the corporate perimeter. The threat infestation can be sitting in memory and immediately take advantage of open file shares and Web server vulnerabilities to spread its payload.

To stay protected from the increasing number of methods and techniques that security risks and threats are utilizing, it is apparent that a "defense-in-depth" approach is required, creating multiple layers of protection around your computers and valuable data. Such an exhaustive approach is required because there are new and innovative types of security risks and threats, some of them using multiple methods and techniques to propagate themselves. It is now necessary to protect all endpoints with comprehensive security that prevents intrusions from either entering or spreading from client machines. Providing this level of protection on the client requires three crucial technologies:

- Antivirus software, to protect against known security risks and threats

- A client firewall, to block suspicious incoming and outgoing network traffic

- Intrusion detection and prevention, to identify and block known and unknown Internet intrusions such as those that are used in Denial-of-Service attacks (DoS)

Symantec documented more than 1,400 new vulnerabilities between July and December 2004. In addition to all the new vulnerabilities appearing, significant risks are still posed by old attacks. In the same 6 month period, the most common attack is one that emerged in January 2003, the Microsoft SQL Server Overflow Attack. This was used by 22% of all attackers. This highlights the need for an integrated approach to blended threats: inspect traffic before it gets on the computer.

Symantec Client Security plays a critical role in allowing customers to adopt this holistic and proactive security paradigm. Symantec has long tracked the evolution of security threats and has prominently exposed the rise in sheer number of threats. What is also evolving is the nature and type of threats. Today we see network-based threats that are designed to take advantage of widespread vulnerabilities, to compromise as many computers as possible in the least amount of time.

Targeted attacks, phishing, and spyware have become the spam of 2004. These attacks use multiple attack vectors that exploit unannounced vulnerabilities, phishing attacks, and insider threats. These attacks are motivated by extortions, information theft, and organized crime. Payloads are for the purpose of theft, data export, and destruction. Social engineering will continue to illustrate the ongoing need for end-user education.

What's To Be Done?

At first glance, it might seem that the only way to avoid the security risks and threats prevalent in today's interconnected world is to avoid using the Internet, to never download any content, and to never read active-content email messages. However, this is not practical in the business world. A number of steps should be taken to reduce the risks to an organization:

- **Install detection and protection software**—With the number of security risks and threats constantly expanding, all computers should have software installed to provide real-time detection and protection against identified security risks and threats.

Symantec Client Security
Symantec Client Security helps keep client systems safe by providing comprehensive and proactive protection against blended threats, spyware, unauthorized network access, and mass-mailer attacks, with vulnerability-based detection.

- **Perform regular software maintenance**—Regularly review and apply new updates, service packs, and hot fixes to the applications and operating system on computers to provide the best possible protection.

- **Secure browser settings**—Ensure that Web browser security settings are set to the highest level that still allows proper operation.

Tip
Corporate administrators who oversecure browsers, blocking highly desired functionality, might find that users work to actively circumvent these protections and so weaken security overall.

- **Educate Users**—Ensure end users are aware of the dangers of downloading content from unknown sources and opening attachments from unknown Senders. Inform staff to carefully read all "terms of service" agreements, and never select buttons on pop-up.

Note
Users should also be wary of anything offered for free, whether it is a game, a funny desktop theme, a file-sharing application, or a toolbar promising faster downloading. As a very old cautionary saying goes, "Anything that seems too good to be true will be."

Detection

Because of the huge number of threat and security risk variations that exist, detection of new infections must be performed in many different ways. Table 2-3 lists a few of the most common methods of identification used by Symantec AntiVirus and Symantec Client Security.

Table 2-3

Detecting Security Risks and Threats	
Method of Detection	**Detects This Type of Threat**
Auto-Protect	Auto-Protect is your best defense against security risks and threats. Whenever you access, copy, save, move, or open a file, Auto-Protect scans the file to ensure that a virus has not attached itself. Auto-Protect includes SmartScan, which scans a group of file extensions that contain executable code and all .exe and .doc files. SmartScan can determine a file's type even when a virus changes the file's extension. For example, it scans .doc files even when a virus changes the file extension to one that is different from the file extensions that SmartScan has been configured to scan.
Memory scan	Viruses, worms, and Trojan horses copy themselves into a computer's random-access memory (RAM), where they can reside and copy themselves onto other forms of storage media or across network file shares to other vulnerable computers.
Boot sector scan	Boot-sector viruses hide on a medium's master boot record or within its partition tables.
Floppy drive scan	Removable media, such as floppy disks, CD-ROMs, and flash drives, can harbor viruses, worms, or Trojan horse programs. Before the computer is allowed to access files on removable media, the media is scanned for software threats.
File scan	Infected files can be identified by comparing each file present on a computer against a definitions file that contains the signatures of all known threats and security risks.
Archive scan	Viruses, worms, and Trojan horse programs can hide within compressed file stores such as .zip, .arj, .lzh, .rar, and .exe self-extracting archives. By scanning each compressed file within these archives, infected files can be identified in the same manner as other forms of file scanning.
Heuristics	Symantec's Bloodhound engine provides a heuristic analysis to detect unknown threats by analyzing program structure, behavior, and other attributes. This allows newly emergent threats to be detected by observing their behavior where no signature exists. Heuristic analysis also protects against polymorphic threats, which can reconfigure the internal architecture between iterations.

Virus definitions files should be updated regularly to enable identification of newly emergent threats and security risks.

Responding to Detected Threats

Symantec AntiVirus and Symantec Client Security perform various types of scanning to detect known patterns identifying security risks and threats in much the same way that biological infections are detected within the human body. To follow the biological analogy, antivirus programs act to provide a computer with a form of digital immune system, one that rapidly adapts to protect against new threats.

The Definitions File

Signatures of known threats and security risks are maintained in a set of files known as the virus definitions files. These files contain signatures that are used to identify infections, although the definitions file does not contain live viral code and so does not pose a threat to the host computer's operation. Automatic updates to these definitions can be delivered to client computers from their parent server in the managed environment or directly from Symantec LiveUpdate.

Symantec AntiVirus and Symantec Client Security respond to files that are infected by threats or security risks with a first action and a second action. By default, when a virus is detected by Auto-Protect or during a scan, an attempt is made to clean the virus from the infected file. If the file cannot be cleaned, the second action is to log the failed cleaning attempt and move the infected file to quarantine so that the virus cannot spread, which denies you further access to the file. When a security risk is detected by Auto-Protect or during a scan, the infected file is quarantined and attempts are made to remove or repair the changes that the security risk has made on the computer. Quarantining the security risk ensures that it is no longer active on your computer and also ensures that Symantec AntiVirus or Symantec Client Security can reverse the changes, if necessary. If the first action cannot be done, the second action is to log the risk and leave it alone.

Outbreak Response

Handling threat and security risk outbreaks within the network requires planning and preparation beforehand to minimize the impact on network operations. The key to an effective response is the outbreak plan. Table 2-4 details an example outbreak plan.

Table 2-4

Example Outbreak Plan	
Task	**Description**
Maintain current definitions	Ensure that antivirus definitions are regularly updated.
Map network topology	Prepare a network map to ease isolation and cleaning of infected computers. This map might include:
	■ Subnet boundaries and gateways
	■ Server names and IP addresses
	■ Client names and IP addresses
	■ Network protocols
	■ Key service details (such as WINS, DNS, DHCP, and catalog servers)
	■ Shared resources and network file shares
Document security solutions	Prepare a map of firewall, gateway, antivirus, and other security applications within the enterprise. This map might include:
	■ Server-protection applications
	■ Workstation-protection applications
	■ Security appliances
	■ Update mechanisms and schedules
	■ Alternate update options if normal update methods are unavailable
	■ Document logs available for outbreak tracking
Perform backup and recovery	Develop a backup plan and test-recovery practices regularly to ensure that backup and recovery operations function as expected, that backup media remains viable, and that staff responsible for recovery are experienced in the steps required for recovery.
Isolate infected computers	To protect the network from further compromise, it is important to have in place a policy for isolating infected computers from the enterprise network.

continues

Table 2-4 continued

Example Outbreak Plan	
Task	Description
Identify the threat	Identification of the threat responsible for the infection is critical to removal and recovery procedures. Security and antivirus logs can provide details about the threats found.
Respond to the threat	Removal and recovery procedures vary among different viruses, worms and Trojan horses. Details on known and newly emergent threats and security risks can be found at http://securityresponse.symantec.com/.

Conclusion

Internet connectivity, email and the web, now vital for small business, pose many risks to computer systems and the privacy of the company's data. The onslaught of viruses, worms, and Trojan horses, compounded with the increasing problem of spyware, adware, and blended threats continue to attack an organization's network through multiple methods.

Without effective network-defense and disaster-recovery practices a business is constantly at risk. Defense requires continually updated products such as Symantec AntiVirus or Symantec Client Security, and a well-defined outbreak-response plan to identify and deal with this ever-expanding problem. Symantec AntiVirus and Symantec Client Security provide an effective barrier against security risks and threats, facilitating their identification and removal, and protect sensitive and private company data. Without this protection, companies might find themselves faced with an administrative nightmare, including time consuming and costly full system reloads to recover lost data.

Chapter Review Questions

Question 2-1

Which of the following are types of security risks? Select all that apply.

❑ A. Adware

❑ B. Dialers

❑ C. Hack tools

❑ D. Joke programs

❑ E. Spyware

Question 2-2

Spyware can impact computer performance and security in which of the following ways? Select all that apply.

- ❏ A. Overwhelming computer capacity
- ❏ B. Wasting time
- ❏ C. Displaying graphic content
- ❏ D. Harvesting sensitive data
- ❏ E. Weakening computer security
- ❏ F. Causing programs to fail

Question 2-3

What are some of the ways that computers can be protected from threats and security risks? Select all that apply.

- ❏ A. Update software regularly
- ❏ B. Run unknown applications received via email
- ❏ C. Make use of a firewall application
- ❏ D. Make use of an antispyware application

Question 2-4

Which of the following best describes a virus? Select the best answer from those provided.

- ◯ A. A malicious program capable of spreading itself automatically
- ◯ B. A malicious program that makes use of many different vectors of transmission
- ◯ C. A malicious program that usually requires user interaction to spread
- ◯ D. An application that provides some form of desirable functionality while also performing other undesirable tasks hidden from the user

Question 2-5

Which type of virus can execute before an operating system is loaded? Select the best answer from those provided.

- ○ A. Macro virus
- ○ B. File virus
- ○ C. Boot-sector virus
- ○ D. Blended threat

Question 2-6

A blended threat is what type of program? Select the best answer from those provided.

- ○ A. Both a virus and a worm
- ○ B. A program that can change itself during replication
- ○ C. A program that spreads using many different methods and techniques
- ○ D. A program capable of targeting only a single operating system
- ○ E. Both a virus and a Trojan horse

Question 2-7

Which of the following best describes a worm? Select the best answer from those provided.

- ○ A. A program capable of spreading itself automatically
- ○ B. A program that makes use of many different vectors of transmission
- ○ C. A program that usually requires user interaction to spread
- ○ D. A program that provides some form of desirable functionality while also performing other undesirable tasks hidden from the user

Question 2-8

Why do worms impact an organization much more than most viruses? Select the best answer from those provided.

- ○ A. Worms can spread by many different means.
- ○ B. Viruses automatically replicate themselves.
- ○ C. Worms can relay data without the user's knowledge.
- ○ D. Worms automatically replicate themselves.

Question 2-9

Which of the following best describes a Trojan horse? Select the best answer from those provided.

- ○ A. A malicious program capable of spreading itself automatically
- ○ B. A malicious program that makes use of many different vectors of transmission
- ○ C. A malicious program that usually requires user interaction to spread
- ○ D. An application that provides some form of desirable functionality while also performing other malicious tasks hidden from the user

Chapter Review Answers

Answer 2-1

Answers **A**, **B**, **C**, **D**, and **E**, are all correct. Common forms of security risks include adware, spyware, dialers, hack tools, and joke programs. In addition to these, browser cookies and applications pretending to be antispyware tools can pose risks to users.

Answer 2-2

Answers **A**, **B**, **C**, **D**, **E**, and **F** are all correct. Security risks can impact computer performance and security by consuming all available computer capacity or causing computer instability that requires frequent reboot or application restart actions. They can also waste user time through both distraction and removal requirements, or can display undesirable content such as graphic images. Security risks can threaten user privacy and security by harvesting sensitive data, profiling a user's computer for exploitable vulnerabilities, or directly impairing normal security procedures.

Answer 2-3

Answers **A**, **C**, and **D** are correct. Best practices recommended to reduce risks include regular software updates, secure browser settings, careful browsing, and the use of antivirus, antispyware, and client firewall applications such as those provided in Symantec Client Security. Running unknown applications received via email is never recommended, as this is a common way to be infected by security risks and threats.

Answer 2-4

Answer **C** is correct. A virus is a malicious program that requires user interaction or some other form of enacting process to infect a computer and spread.

Answer 2-5

Answer **C** is correct. A boot-sector virus can execute before an operating system is loaded, making later removal more troublesome than many other types of infection. Early detection before infection is highly desirable in all cases, but nowhere more so than with boot-sector infections.

Answer 2-6

Answer **C** is correct. Blended threats combine the characteristics of viruses, worms, Trojan horses with server and Internet vulnerabilities to initiate, transmit, and spread an attack. By using multiple methods and techniques, blended threats can rapidly spread and cause widespread damage.

Answer 2-7

Answer **A** is correct. A worm is a program that is capable of spreading without relying on user interaction. Because of this behavior, worms can spread to all network-connected vulnerable computers in a very short period of time.

Answer 2-8

Answer **D** is correct. Worms can impact an enterprise much more than most viruses because worms can self-propagate to all vulnerable computers. This allows a much wider distribution of newly released worms, which can also saturate a network's connectivity by attempting to spread to all available target addresses.

Answer 2-9

Answer **D** is correct. A Trojan horse is best described as an application that provides some type of desirable functionality while hiding other functions from the user.

CHAPTER 3

Symantec AntiVirus Installation

Terms and Techniques to Remember

- Managed client
- Unmanaged client
- Parent server
- LiveUpdate™
- Preinstallation requirements for Symantec AntiVirus™
- Local and remote deployments of Symantec AntiVirus
- Windows® Installer command-line options for installation
- Migration from previous releases

Introduction

The purpose of this chapter is to provide a detailed step-by-step approach to installing Symantec AntiVirus within the small business environment. Although not all components will be necessary in every computer network, you should be familiar with the use of each technology before deciding which components to deploy.

Before Beginning

Before installing Symantec AntiVirus, it is important to understand the various product components and the different types of installation that can be performed, in order to design and deploy a configuration that suits your customers' needs and environment.

Managed vs. Unmanaged

Symantec AntiVirus can be installed in a managed or unmanaged configuration. An unmanaged configuration protects an individual computer without centralized control over protection policy options. Unmanaged clients are not associated with a particular server for policy and definitions updates and are forced to retrieve updates on their own. Unmanaged clients can still be configured to receive regular updates to their antivirus definitions file directly through the LiveUpdate service, as long as the client's license is not expired. An unmanaged environment would typically be used where there are only a very small number of clients. In a small business environment a managed environment gives the benefits of centralized deployment and management of antivirus protection.

> **Note**
> Because unmanaged clients must individually download updates from the Symantec LiveUpdate server, large numbers of these clients configured to download updates should be scheduled in a staggered fashion, to avoid network bandwidth saturation. When moving beyond a small workgroup setting, managed clients provide a more effective solution.

Managed clients connect to a parent server to retrieve configuration and virus-definition updates. The parent server obtains a single copy of all updates and then pushes the new definitions directly to its clients. Figure 3-1 illustrates the basic differences between these options.

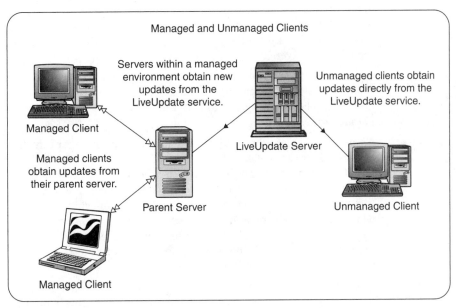

Figure 3-1 The update process for managed and unmanaged Symantec AntiVirus clients.

Symantec AntiVirus Servers

Within a managed environment, several types of Symantec AntiVirus server roles can be implemented. Antivirus servers are often grouped into different server groups. A server group is a logical grouping of servers in which a primary server and potentially one or more secondary servers can better manage the distribution of updates and antivirus policy settings within an environment. Table 3-1 details the different server roles that can be implemented within a managed Symantec AntiVirus scenario.

In very large network scenarios, additional servers can be configured as backup servers to ensure 100% up-time. Very few small business networks require these roles, but the terms should be familiar when taking the exam.

Table 3-1

Symantec AntiVirus Server Roles

Role	Purpose
Primary server	Server that is responsible for downloading new updates and then distributing them to secondary servers within the same server group, as well as to any clients that might be configured with this as their parent server.
Secondary server	An optional server type that obtains updates from the primary server within its server group. Secondary servers distribute their updates to clients configured to have the secondary server as their parent server.
Quarantine server	An optional server type that provides a secure data store for threats and security risks that are identified by clients but for which no specific remedy has yet been developed. Clients can forward newly emergent viruses, worms, or Trojan horses to a quarantine server so that later updates can be used to attempt to clean infected files, where possible. The quarantine server can also serve as part of the Digital Immune System™ by forwarding quarantined items to Symantec™ Security Response to aid in the identification of and response to emerging outbreaks.
Parent server	Any server to which a particular managed client has been assigned. A client's parent server provides updates and policy settings. Both primary and secondary servers can be configured as the parent server for one or more antivirus Symantec AntiVirus clients.

Symantec AntiVirus Components

Symantec AntiVirus includes a wide array of individual components that can be used to tailor the program to the customer's environment. These components are available within a Symantec AntiVirus installation:

- **Symantec AntiVirus client**—This component can be installed on either a workstation or server version of Windows to scan and monitor for threats and security risks.

- **Symantec AntiVirus server**—This component provides centralized configuration and virus-definitions file management within a managed environment. It provides antivirus protection for the server and centralized distribution of configuration and virus-definitions files to managed clients.

- **Symantec System Center™**—The Symantec System Center enables centralized management of clients, servers, client groups, and server groups within a managed environment. The Symantec System Center provides a single unified interface for management tasks and access to several configuration options that are not accessible through the Symantec AntiVirus client or server interfaces. If your organization is over several offices or you need to have multiple people administer the environment, you can install the Symantec System Center to as many computers as you need.

- **Alert Management System² (AMS²)**—This component allows the configuration of enhanced alert options. The Alert Management System supports notifications generated by Symantec AntiVirus servers and clients through the following:

  - Message Box
  - Broadcast
  - Send Internet Mail
  - Send Page
  - Run Program
  - Write to Windows Event Log
  - Send SNMP Trap
  - Load an NLM

- **Symantec AntiVirus snap-in**—This is a Symantec System Center snap-in used to centrally manage antivirus protection settings. This should be installed with the Symantec System Center and is required if you want to centrally manage antivirus protection.

- **AV Server Rollout tool**—This tool offers the capability to push the server installation to remote computers.

- **ClientRemote Install tool**—This tool adds the capability to push the Symantec AntiVirus client installation to remote computers that run supported Microsoft Windows operating systems.

- **Symantec Central Quarantine**—This works as part of the Digital Immune System to provide automated responses to heuristically detected new or unrecognized viruses. It does the following:
  - Receives unrepaired infected items from Symantec AntiVirus servers and clients
  - Forwards suspicious files to Symantec Security Response
  - Returns updated virus definitions to the submitting computer
- **LiveUpdate Administration Utility**—You can use the LiveUpdate Administration Utility to create a single download point for virus definitions and updates to Symantec products that use LiveUpdate. You can set up a LiveUpdate server on one or more Internet-ready computers to distribute updates across an internal local area network (LAN).

Windows® Server versus Symantec AntiVirus Server

A Symantec AntiVirus server is a computer that has been configured to host the Symantec AntiVirus Server service, and this should not be confused with a Windows Server operating system that has only the Symantec AntiVirus Client component installed for antivirus protection. Server operating systems such as Windows® Server 2000/2003 can be managed clients of a parent Symantec AntiVirus server, an important distinction for the exam.

Symantec AntiVirus Virus-Definitions Update

Antivirus definitions files can be updated through several means, depending on the type of operating system hosting the Symantec AntiVirus client. Table 3-2 details the available methods for updating virus files. Combinations of update methods are also possible, such as configuring a primary server to update its own files using the Intelligent Updater method in a scheduled batch file execution, and then allowing the updated definitions to be distributed to all secondary servers and managed clients through VDTM.

Table 3-2

AntiVirus Update Methods	
Update	Description
Virus Definition Transport Method (VDTM)	The method used by primary servers to push updates obtained from a LiveUpdate server to secondary servers, and for parent servers to push updates to managed clients. This is the preferred method for most environments, although it is not supported for 64-bit clients.
LiveUpdate	Provides the capability for computers to automatically pull updates of virus definitions files directly from the Symantec LiveUpdate server or an internal LiveUpdate server. This is the only method supported on 64-bit clients.
Central Quarantine polling	This method relies on a Central Quarantine Server to pull updates from the Symantec Digital Immune System Gateway. These updates are then pushed to managed clients using VDTM noted previously. As with VDTM, this method is not supported on 64-bit clients.
Intelligent Updater	This method relies on downloaded executable files that can update virus definitions. The executable file is downloaded from the Symantec™ Security Response Web site and can be distributed via network or removable media. This method is also easily scripted as a batch file but is not supported on 64-bit clients.

The Installation Environment

In the remainder of this chapter, we will examine the installation, configuration, and use of Symantec AntiVirus. In order to understand the installation of this protective technology, you may find it useful to review the environment in which these tasks will be performed. Here are details of the test network used in order to illustrate the various installation tasks.

Operating Systems

All workstations used in these examples are Windows XP with Service Pack 2 installed, while all servers use Windows Server 2003. For detailed listings of compatible operating system environments, please see each of the installation sections that follow.

The Testing Network

In the examples, we use the non-routable **.local** root in order to illustrate all concepts necessary for the installation and management of Symantec AntiVirus and Symantec Client Security. Most companies will make use of **.net**, **.com**, **.org**, or other such routable root domain designations, and the solutions provided herein will work just as well within such environments. Figure 3-2 illustrates the basic domain architecture used in this text.

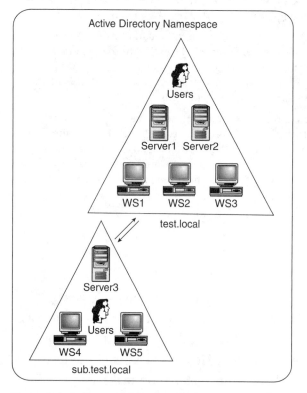

Figure 3-2 A diagram of the installation test network.

Root Domain

The root domain namespace for the test network utilizes a non-routable **.local** extension, which can be resolved locally because the test network includes a

DNS service that has been configured to resolve the **test.local** domain. Such a domain is not externally routable because it does not use one of the approved routable root domain designations like **.gov** or **.com**.

Within the **test.local** domain, there are two Windows 2003 Servers and three Windows XP workstations. **Server1.test.local** is the DC for this domain, while **Server2.test.local** is simply a Member Server uninvolved in Active Directory authentication. The three workstations in this domain are simply named **WS1.test.local**, **WS2.test.local**, and **WS3.test.local**.

Child Domain

The **test.local** domain has one child domain in the test installation environment: **sub.test.local**. Within this domain, **Server3.sub.test.local** has been configured as the DC supporting two workstations named **WS4.sub.test.local** and **WS5.sub.test.local**. Although these are registered within a separate sub-domain, they share a common schema that extends through the entire tree—which is a term that encompasses the entire namespace of **test.local** and all of its sub-domains.

Stand-Alone Systems

The test network also includes two stand-alone systems that are not members of the Active Directory environment. These systems are members of the workgroup **localtest**, but do not share a central authentication system. Logon accounts are maintained on each stand-alone system separately. **Server4** is a Windows 2003 Server configured for stand-alone operation, while the Windows XP stand-alone workstation is named **WS6**.

Nomenclature

Throughout the remainder of this book, all test network systems will be referred to simply by the computer name in order to simplify references to each. Table 3-3 presents a listing of the individual computers and their roles within the test network used in these scenarios.

Table 3-3

Test Network Computer Systems

Name	Domain/Workgroup	Role	Description
Server1	test.local	DC	Server1.test.local is the sole Domain Controller for the test.local domain
Server2	test.local	Member server	Server2.test.local is a member server within the test.local domain
Server3	sub.test.local	DC	Server3.sub.test.local is the sole Domain Controller for the sub.test.local child domain
Server4	Localtest	Stand-alone	Server4 is a stand-alone server that is a member of the localtest workgroup
WS1	test.local	Member	WS1.test.local is a workstation member of the test.local domain
WS2	test.local	Member	WS2.test.local is a workstation member of the test.local domain
WS3	test.local	Member	WS3.test.local is a workstation member of the test.local domain
WS4	sub.test.local	Member	WS4.sub.test.local is a workstation member of the sub.test.local domain
WS5	sub.test.local	Member	WS5.sub.test.local is a workstation member of the sub.test.local domain
WS6	Localtest	Stand-alone	WS6 is a stand-alone workstation that is a member of the localtest workgroup

The test network has been configured in order to illustrate the various different types of installation of the Symantec AntiVirus and Symantec Client Security products. Your own test network may be more or less complex, and may make use of very different domain and computer naming schemes.

Preinstallation

Before installing Symantec AntiVirus, it is important to perform a few simple preinstallation steps that are appropriate to most application installations:

1. Log in as a user with the appropriate privileges.

2. Close all open applications.

3. Ensure that mobile devices are plugged in, to prevent installation failure from exhausted batteries.

4. Ensure that scheduled processes such as full-system virus scans or system automatic updates will not occur during the installation.

System Requirements

Before installing the various components of Symantec AntiVirus, it is important to ensure that all target computers meet the minimum requirements for the installation. The amount of memory and storage required for installation varies by component, depending on options selected.

Time Synchronization

Because Symantec AntiVirus now makes use of SSL encryption when transmitting settings betweenclients and servers, it is important to ensure that all system clocks are synchronized to that of the primary server. The threshold for this synchronization is 24 hours plus or minus of the system clock time on the primary server.

Required Protocols

Symantec AntiVirus uses TCP and UDP for its communications. If client firewall software is already installed on target computers, it will be necessary to open ports 1024–4999 (TCP) and 2967 (TCP) for both console and support operations. For remote installation, TCP ports 137, 138, and 139 must also be opened. Server Discovery requires opening port 38293 (UDP).

Windows® XP with Service Pack 2 and later, as well as Microsoft Windows 2003 Server, include a basic firewall installed by default. To deploy Symantec AntiVirus to these hosts, you must manually configure all necessary ports or simply turn off the basic firewall during installation. This can performed by accessing the Windows Firewall MMC through Start, Control Panel, Security Center, Windows Firewall. Here, simply select the Off option and then close the console.

Windows XP systems with Service Pack 2 or later that are configured in a workgroup rather than as members of an Active Directory domain must also be configured to allow remote software installation. This can be accomplished by accessing the Local Security Policy console through **Start**, **Control Panel**, **Administrative Tools**, **Local Security Policy**. By navigating through Local Policies, Security Options, the Network Access: Sharing and Security Model for Local Accounts setting can be located. The setting here should be changed from **Guest Only** (the default) to **Classic.** Once applied, this console can be closed.

Symantec AntiVirus Client Requirements

Thirty-two-bit workstations and servers that host the Symantec AntiVirus client component must meet the following minimum requirements for installation:

- Windows 2000 Professional/Server/Advanced Server, Windows XP Home/Professional/Tablet PC, Windows Server 2003 Web/Standard/Enterprise/Datacenter
- 64 MB RAM and 55 MB of disk space available
- IE 5.5 with SP2 or later

Sixty-four-bit workstations and servers hosting the Symantec AntiVirus client require slightly reduced resources for Symantec AntiVirus client installation:

- Windows XP 64-bit Edition version 2003, Windows Server 2003 Enterprise/Datacenter 64-bit
- 80 MB RAM and 70 MB of disk space available
- IE 5.5 with SP2 or later

Symantec AntiVirus Server Requirements

Microsoft Windows systems that host the Symantec AntiVirus server component must meet the following minimum requirements for installation:

- Windows 2000 Professional/Server/Advanced Server, Windows Server 2003 Standard/Enterprise/Datacenter
- 64 MB RAM and 111 MB of disk space available (15 MB of additional drive space required if AMS[2] is installed)
- IE 5.5 with SP2 or later

Novell NetWare® systems that host the Symantec AntiVirus server component must meet the following minimum requirements for installation:

- NetWare 5.1 with SP 3 or higher, NetWare 6.0 with SP 1 or higher, NetWare 6.5

- 15 MB RAM available

- 116 MB of disk space available (70 MB for server files, 46 MB for client disk images and 20 MB of additional disk space required if AMS^2 is installed)

- 15 MB of additional drive space required if AMS^2 is installed

Central Quarantine Server Requirements

Microsoft Windows systems that host the Central Quarantine Server service must meet the following minimum requirements for installation:

- Windows 2000 Professional/Server/Advanced Server, Windows XP Professional, Windows Server 2003 Standard/Enterprise/Datacenter

- 128 MB RAM

- 40 MB of disk space available for the Quarantine Server service (500 MB or more disk space minimum recommended to store quarantined items)

- 250 MB minimum swap file

- IE 5.5 with SP2 or later

Tip
If running the Central Quarantine Server service on Windows XP systems, the System Restore option can increase disk space and throughput utilization.

Symantec System Center and Snap-In Requirements

The Symantec System Center and the Symantec MMC snap-ins require the following minimum requirements:

- Windows 2000 Professional/Server/Advanced Server, Windows XP Professional, Windows Server 2003 Web/Standard/Enterprise/Datacenter

- 64 MB RAM

- 36 MB of disk space available for the Symantec System Center (snap-ins can be individually selected and require additional space for each)

- 6 MB of disk space for the Symantec AntiVirus snap-in (if selected)

- 1 MB of disk space for the Symantec Client Firewall snap-in (if selected)

- 35 MB of disk space for the Quarantine Console snap-in (if selected)

- 24 MB of disk space for the AMS^2 snap-in (if selected)

- 130 MB of disk space for the Server Rollout tool

- 2 MB of disk space for the Client Remote Install tool

- Microsoft Management Console (MMC) version 1.2 or later (if not already installed, 10 MB of disk space is necessary to install MMC)

- IE 5.5 with SP2 or later

Installation Methods

Symantec AntiVirus uses Microsoft Windows Installer (.msi) technology for installation and deployment of its various components. Packages can be deployed in several different ways, including these:

- Local installation using the installation media

- Remote installation using the Rollout tools provided on the installation media

- Use of the Symantec System Center to deploy remote client and server installations

- Web-based installation

- Network-based logon scripts

- Third-party deployments (such as Microsoft Systems Management Server, Tivoli®, or ZenWorks®)

Administrative Rights

To install Symantec AntiVirus, the account used must have administrative rights to the computer. These rights can be directly assigned to the account, inherited through its group membership, or assigned using Windows Group Policy settings. For Novell NetWare installations, the account used must be an administrator or supervisor.

File sharing must also be enabled on computers that will host a Symantec AntiVirus Server installation. The installation package makes use of administrative shares (such as c$ and admin$) during installation, which might need to be enabled if the domain or local Group Policy settings have been configured to disable standard administrative shares. Administrators should also ensure that the IP protocol is enabled for network connectivity.

Installation

Symantec AntiVirus can be installed in a managed or unmanaged configuration, while the Symantec AntiVirus management components can be installed as needed on both Symantec server and Symantec client computers. Installation can be performed using the source media for local or remote installations, or across the network using the remote install tools provided, or using Web-based or network file-sharing deployment methods. The capability to centrally control the remote deployment of clients is of great benefit for companies with multiple offices or those that are geographically dispersed. We explore each of these alternatives throughout the rest of this chapter. Although you are provided with clear step-by-step walkthroughs of each installation procedure, you are encouraged to perform various types of installation on a test network, if at all possible.

Local Installation

The most basic form of installation relies on the source medium, which must be transported to the target system or shared on a LAN in a manner that allows direct access from the target computer. This scenario is typically not used beyond small workgroup settings, but it might still be used in remote locations or because of other considerations. Within our example network, detailed earlier in this chapter, we will configure a Windows XP workstation (WS6) as an unmanaged Symantec AntiVirus client and the

Windows 2003 Server (Server1) as a Symantec AntiVirus server using the local installation methods.

To install Symantec AntiVirus, the administrator should insert the installation media into the CD-ROM drive. If auto-play is enabled, the welcome screen (shown in Figure 3-3) appears; otherwise, you should navigate to the proper drive and select **SETUP** from the root folder.

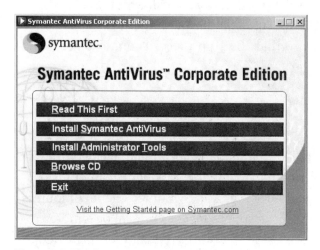

Figure 3-3 The Symantec AntiVirus welcome screen.

From this location, the user can choose to install Symantec AntiVirus, to install the Administrator Tools alone, to browse the installation media's contents, or to exit and abort the installation.

Local Client Installation

1. Selecting the option **Install Symantec AntiVirus** begins the installation process, displaying the installation options screen shown in Figure 3-4.

> **Note**
> The Deploy options are used later when performing remote rollouts to nonlocal installations.

2. Select the **Install Symantec AntiVirus** button to advance to the InstallShield Wizard screen, where the administrator must choose **Next** to continue or **Cancel** to terminate the installation (see Figure 3-5).

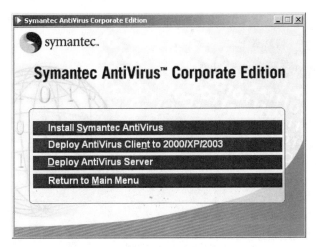

Figure 3-4 The Symantec AntiVirus installation options screen.

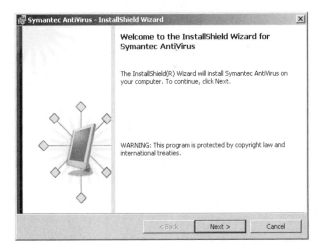

Figure 3-5 The Symantec AntiVirus InstallShield Wizard screen.

3. Selecting the **Next** button advances to the Licensing Agreement screen, where the administrator should read the licensing agreement and signify agreement to be allowed to continue (see Figure 3-6).

4. Selecting the **Next** button again allows the administrator to select the type of installation to be performed (client or server), as shown in Figure 3-7.

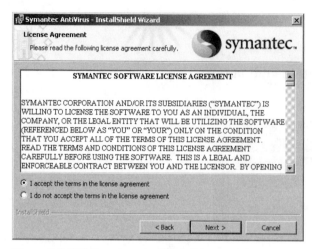

Figure 3-6 The Symantec AntiVirus License screen.

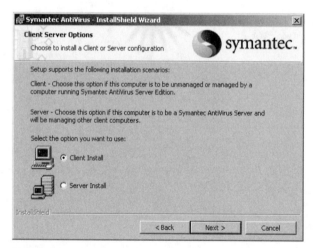

Figure 3-7 Selecting the type of installation to be performed.

5. Selecting **Client Install** and then the **Next** button allows the administrator to select whether a complete or custom installation is performed (see Figure 3-8).

The complete installation installs all normal components of the Symantec AntiVirus client; the custom installation option allows a more granular selection of individual components (see Figure 3-9).

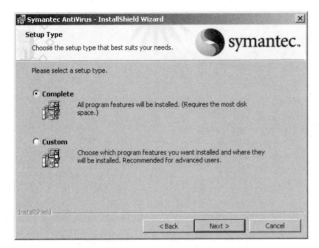

Figure 3-8 Selecting the setup type to be performed.

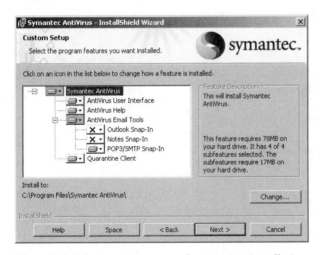

Figure 3-9 Selecting components for a custom installation.

6. After selecting a complete or custom installation and then pressing the **Next** button, the administrator is prompted to select a managed or unmanaged client installation, as shown in Figure 3-10. Here, we are installing an unmanaged (or stand-alone) client.

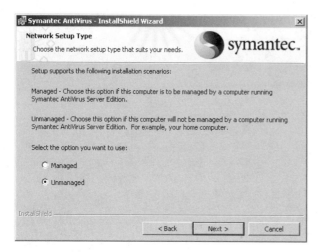

Figure 3-10 Selecting the client type for installation.

> 7. The administrator is prompted to select configuration options for the client, including whether to enable Auto-Protect or whether the client should immediately run LiveUpdate following installation (see Figure 3-11).

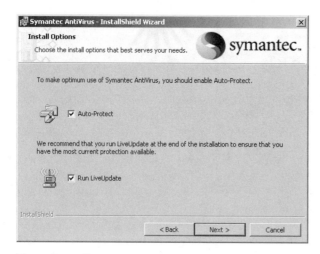

Figure 3-11 Client configuration options.

> 8. After selecting any desired options, selecting the **Next** button and then Install initiates the Symantec AntiVirus Client installation process. Depending on the available system resources and speed of the media drive, this process can take several minutes to complete.

9. When installation has completed, the administrator is prompted to finish the installation process. If the client computer is connected to the Internet and LiveUpdate was selected to execute following installation, the LiveUpdate screen is displayed (see Figure 3-12).

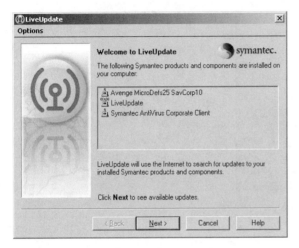

Figure 3-12 Initial LiveUpdate of the new unmanaged client.

10. After selecting **Next**, the client contacts the LiveUpdate service and begins to install any available updates, as shown in Figure 3-13.

Figure 3-13 LiveUpdate updates being installed.

11. When all updates have completed, the administrator will see a listing of all changes that have been applied (see Figure 3-14).

Figure 3-14 Updates applied by the LiveUpdate process.

12. Selecting Finish concludes the installation process. The Symantec AntiVirus client local interface (see Figure 3-15) can be accessed by

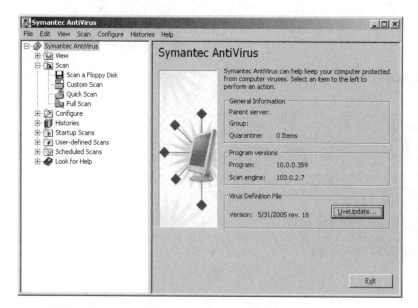

Figure 3-15 Administering the new unmanaged client.

Start, **All Programs**, **Symantec Client Security**, **Symantec AntiVirus**.
Here you can see that no parent server is present, identifying this as
an unmanaged client. The following chapters detail how to configure
the client to provide the best protection.

Local Server Installation

During a local Symantec AntiVirus Server installation, steps 1–5 are the same
as those taken during the local client installation process, except that a server
installation is selected in step 5.

1. If a custom installation is selected, the server installation process
   provides a slightly different set of options for installation (shown in
   Figure 3-16), but the process is not otherwise different.

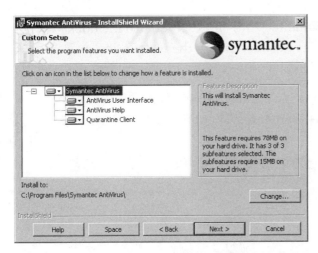

Figure 3-16 Symantec AntiVirus Server custom installation
options.

2. After selecting a complete or custom installation and then pressing
   the **Next** button, the administrator is prompted to provide a name and
   password for the new server group that will have the new server as its
   initial member (shown in Figure 3-17). Here, we name the group **Test
   Server Group A**.

3. After selecting **Next**, the administrator is prompted to verify the
   password once more. The installation process continues by asking for
   client configuration options, as in step 7 of the client installation

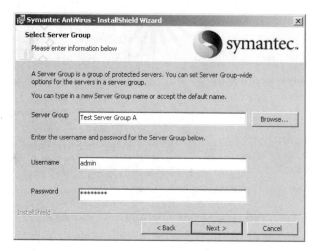

Figure 3-17 Creating the new server group.

process. Because the Symantec AntiVirus server also includes antivirus protection for its host computer, the installation process continues exactly as before.

After installation, the server's local interface (see Figure 3-18) can be accessed by **Start**, **All Programs**, **Symantec Client Security**, **Symantec**

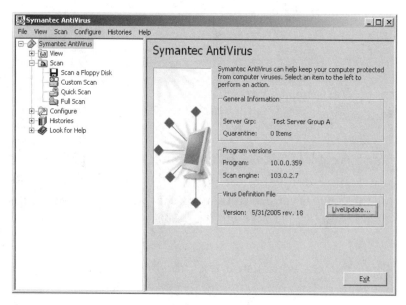

Figure 3-18 Managing the server's local protection settings.

AntiVirus. You will be prompted for the user name and password created during the installation. Here you can see that this server belongs to the **Test Server Group A** server group.

Local Administration Tools Installation

To effectively configure the new managed environment, you will now install the Symantec System Center. In this demonstration, the administrative console will be installed to a separate server (Server2) within the example network. This is done only to show that the console can be used to configure the managed environment on other servers as well; the Symantec System Center could be installed on Server1 just as easily.

1. Selecting the option **Install Administrator Tools** at the initial setup screen brings up the option **Install Symantec System Center**. Selecting this option begins the process of installation, as before navigating through an introductory InstallShield screen and license agreement before the component selection screen is presented (see Figure 3-19).

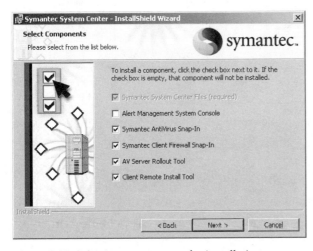

Figure 3-19 Selecting components for installation.

2. After selecting all components desired and selecting the **Next** button, the administrator is prompted for an installation location for several

processes (C:\Program Files\Symantec\Symantec System Center\, by default). After specifying a new location or accepting the default location for each, the administrator confirms the installation to begin installing all selected components. A reboot is required when this process has completed.

The Symantec System Center console can be accessed through **Start**, **All Programs**, **Symantec System Center Console**, **Symantec System Center Console**. When first opened, the console displays icons for the various components selected during installation, as shown in Figure 3-20. Had we unchecked some of the available snap-in components, those options would not be present here.

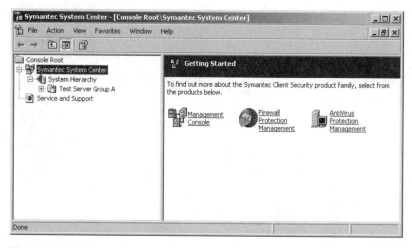

Figure 3-20 The Symantec System Center console showing available component snap-ins.

The server group is displayed with a small lock icon, which illustrates that the group remains locked. Selecting the server group causes a prompt to appear (see Figure 3-21) where the username and password provided during setup should be entered.

Before using the Symantec System Center to configure the managed environment, it is necessary to configure the first server as the primary server for the new server group. Right-clicking SERVER1 brings up a drop-down list

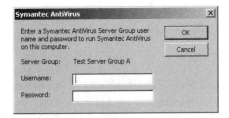

Figure 3-21 Supplying the username and password assigned to the server group.

with the option **Make Server a Primary Server**. Selecting this option configures SERVER1 as the primary server for the test server group. We will now use the initialized Symantec System Center to perform additional remote installation tasks in the next portion of this chapter.

Remote Installation

To support larger networks, Symantec AntiVirus includes a number of remote installation options. The installation media can be used to deploy (roll out) remote client and server installations of Symantec AntiVirus. This functionality is also included within the Symantec System Center, allowing easy deployment to multiple clients at one time. Client installation can also be performed using network file sharing and web-based distribution points. In addition, the .msi installation package can be distributed via Group Policy, or through SMS or another third-party tool used for package distribution. Command-line installations can also be used to specify options during scripted installation.

Deploying Symantec AntiVirus Clients to Windows 2000/XP/2003

Selecting the option to **Deploy AntiVirus Client to 2000/XP/2003** from the installation screen from the original medium's welcome screen makes it possible to begin a remote installation of the Symantec AntiVirus client.

Here, the client will be installed onto a remote Windows XP workstation (WS1), using the installation files found on Server1.

1. After initiating the remote installation process, the administrator is prompted for a source location where the client installation files can be found (see Figure 3-22). By default, this is the clt-inst directory within the VPHOME network share created during server installation, although an alternate location can be provided at this time, if desired. When we examine the installation of Symantec Client Security in Chapter 6, "Symantec Client Security Installation," the same folder will contain the Symantec Client Security client instead of the Symantec AntiVirus client.

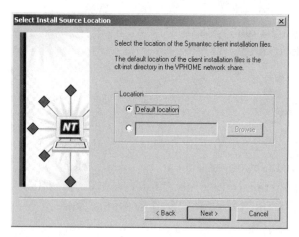

Figure 3-22 Selecting the source location for client installation files.

2. After specifying a source location and selecting **Next**, the administrator is prompted to select one or more clients to be targeted for client installation and to select the server that will be assigned as the parent server for the newly installed clients. In Figure 3-23, the Windows XP workstation (WS1) is selected for Symantec AntiVirus Client installation. Server1, the primary server for the first server group, has been selected as the parent server for the new client.

   When one or more clients and a parent server have been highlighted, selecting the **Add** button adds the target computers to the list for client installation. Adding computers in this manner requires the

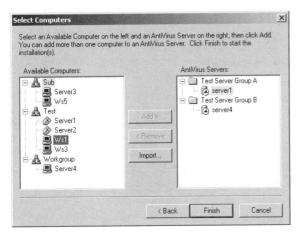

Figure 3-23 Selecting client installation targets and a parent server.

use of the Windows Internet Name Service (WINS). For computers that are located in a non-WINS environment (such as a native Windows 2000 network that uses the LDAP or DNS protocol), you must create a text file with IP addresses and then import it to be able to install to those computers.

If a listing of IP addresses for target installation has been created as a .txt file, the **Import** button can be used to select this file to mass-configure a large number of systems at once. Figure 3-24 illustrates the results of importing two IP addresses within the example network.

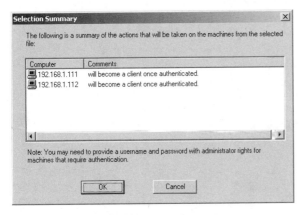

Figure 3-24 Two IP addresses imported for Symantec AntiVirus client installation.

3. After adding and importing all clients for installation, selecting **Next** begins the client installation process for each client. When installation is complete, the administrator can select the **Done** button to conclude the process.

Remote Client Installation

Remote client installation can also be initiated from within the Symantec System Center by selecting **Tools, ClientRemote Install** from the header. The process of remote client installation here is identical to that of deploying from the source media.

Deploying Symantec AntiVirus Servers

By selecting the option **Deploy AntiVirus Server** from the installation screen, it is possible to begin a remote installation of the Symantec AntiVirus server. Here, the server will be installed onto a remote Windows 2003 Server (Sever3), joining the server group currently managed by Server1 alone.

1. After initiating the remote installation process, the administrator is prompted to identify whether this will be a new server installation or an update of an existing installation. Upgrading from an earlier version is covered later in this chapter, so for now, the Install option is selected (see Figure 3-25).

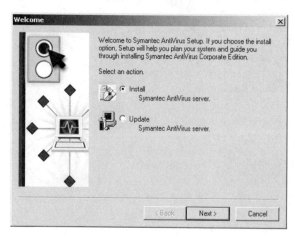

Figure 3-25 Electing to perform a new installation rather than an update installation.

2. After selecting **Next** and agreeing to the license agreement, the administrator is prompted to select the components to be installed to the remote computer, as shown in Figure 3-26. By default, the Alert Management System (AMS[2]) is not selected. If you plan to use AMS[2] to generate alerts based on antivirus events, you must install it to every primary server.

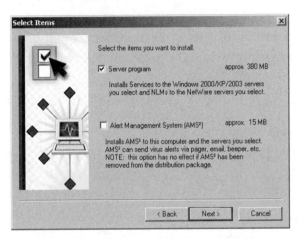

Figure 3-26 Components selected for remote antivirus server installation.

3. After selecting **Next**, the administrator is prompted to add the computer(s) that will be targeted for server installation (see Figure 3-27).

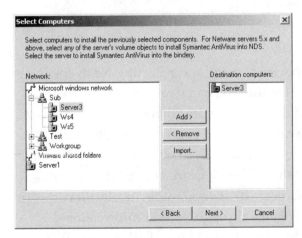

Figure 3-27 Server3 added to the list of computers targeted for installation.

As with the client installation, one or more servers can be manually added here, or a prepared listing of target IP addresses can be imported using the **Import** button.

4. After selecting **Next** again, the administrator is offered the opportunity to change the installation directory that will be used for the server application's installation on the targeted systems. Following this, the administrator can elect to create a new server group or to join an existing one (see Figure 3-28). Here, the new server will be a member of the first server group, which is currently hosted only by Server1.

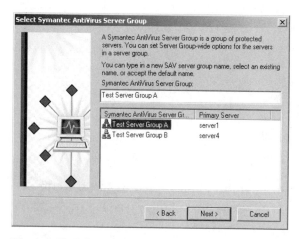

Figure 3-28 Selecting the desired server group.

5. After entering the desired server group and selecting **Next**, the administrator is prompted for the username and password that was created during the original server's installation into this server group. Following this, the administrator is given the option to configure the new server to automatically start or to require manual startup. This option is only valid for Netware servers. For Windows the Symantec AntiVirus server will always automatically start. The administrator then navigates through several informational screens before initiating the remote server installation, shown in Figure 3-29.

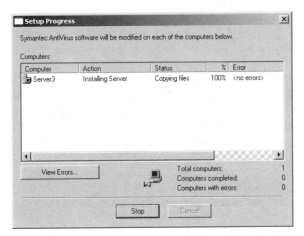

Figure 3-29 An in-process remote server installation on Server3.

6. When the installation process is finished, the administrator is reminded to restart the new server to complete the Symantec AntiVirus installation. If any errors occurred during installation, the View Errors buttons can be used to obtain additional details needed to correct them.

Remote Server Installation
Remote server installation can also be initiated from within the Symantec System Center by selecting **Tools, AV Server Rollout** from the header. The process of remote Symantec AntiVirus server installation here is identical to that of deploying from the source media.

Remote Network Client Deployment
During the installation of a Symantec AntiVirus Server, a file share named VPHOME is created, containing the files necessary for network installation. Here, we will install the Symantec AntiVirus client onto a Windows XP workstation (WS2), using the installation files found on Server1 shared as \\Server1\VPHOME\CLT-INST\WIN32\.

After logging on to the client system using an account with local or domain administrative privileges over the client, this process can be initiated by opening the Windows Explorer (double-clicking the My Computer icon opens this interface) and navigating to the shared folder location.

Figure 3-30 shows the results of accessing the file share \\Server1\ VPHOME\CLT-INST\WIN32\.

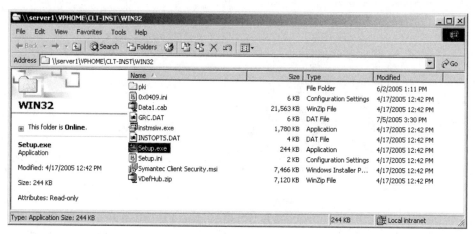

Figure 3-30 Windows Explorer showing the contents of the remote installation directory.

Selecting the **Setup.exe** file within this share initiates the Symantec AntiVirus client installation on the local computer. This installation is identical to the step-by-step client installation detailed earlier in this chapter, with the single exception that no option is available to install an unmanaged client. The newly installed client is managed, and has the installation source server as its parent.

Web-Based Client Deployment

During Symantec AntiVirus server installation, an additional set of files is created for use in Web distribution of the Symantec AntiVirus client. These files are located within the VPHOME file share as well and can be accessed within the example network by the path \\Server1\VPHOME\CLT-INST\ WEBINST\ (see Figure 3-31). This WEBINST folder can be shared as a virtual directory within an IIS Web site on the host server, or these files can be copied to another Web server altogether for use in Web-based installation of the managed Symantec AntiVirus client.

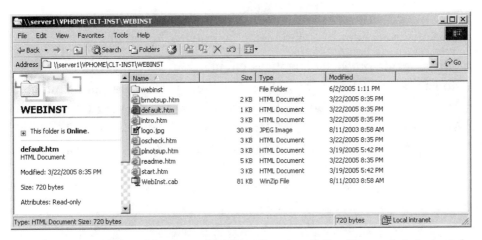

Figure 3-31 The Web-based Symantec AntiVirus client installation files, ready to be copied to an existing Web server.

The Example Web site

Here, we have copied this directory to Server2 to demonstrate that the Web host need not be a Symantec AntiVirus server itself. We have given Server2 an additional alias within the DNS service, allowing webserver.local to refer to the same IP address as server2.test.local. We could just as easily use the host name for resolution, but we take the extra step here to demonstrate that this functionality works just as well within a Web site identified by host headers. Remember that Server2 is not itself a Symantec AntiVirus server; it is merely a Web server to which the Web installation files have been copied.

The files used in the previous demonstration of file share installation (located in \\Server1\VPHOME\CLT-INST\WIN32\ in the example network) must then be copied into the newly created \WEBINST\webinst\ folder on the Web server. The Start.htm file should be modified to specify the correct ServerName and VirtualHomeDirectory values to match your new Web site, and then the installation package files should be added to the \webinst\

files.ini configuration file. When this process has been completed, remote Symantec AntiVirus client installation can be initiated using the new Web site.

1. After logging on to the client system using an account with local or domain administrative privileges, the Web installation can be initiated by opening the Internet Explorer browser and navigating to the target Web server's URL. Figure 3-32 shows the web installation welcome screen located at `http://webserver.local/WEBINST/` within the example network.

Figure 3-32 The Web-based Symantec AntiVirus client installation welcome screen.

2. Selecting the **Install Now** button initiates installation of a managed instance of the Symantec AntiVirus client on the local computer. The

parent server associated with this new installation is the server that provided the files copied to the Web site. Because the Web-based installation uses a Microsoft Active-X component, it is necessary to accept the installation of this control on Windows XP systems with Service Pack 2 and later. Figure 3-33 illustrates the ActiveX control authorization prompt.

Figure 3-33 Installing the Symantec AntiVirus Client Web Installer ActiveX control.

3. After the ActiveX component has been installed, the installation files are downloaded from the Web server (see Figure 3-34). When the download completes, installation begins and proceeds as in previous demonstrations of the client installation process.

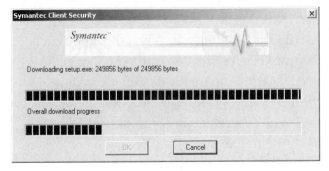

Figure 3-34 Downloading installation files from the Web server.

Logon Script Symantec AntiVirus Client Installation

You can automate client installations in an Active Directory environment by using the logon script files that the Symantec AntiVirus server installation program copies to each Symantec AntiVirus server. The Logon directory contains the script files. For successful automation, you must copy the Symantec AntiVirus logon scripts to the Netlogon shared directory on a computer that is an Active Directory domain controller.

You control how automated installation works by editing the Vp_Login.ini file, which is located in the Logon directory. The default Vp_Login.ini file contents are as follows:

```
[Installer]
Win32=\\SERVER-NAME\VPHOME\CLT-INST\WIN32\Setup.exe
[InstallOptions]
WinNT=NONE
[ClientNumber]
BuildNumber=012F03E8
```

The SERVER-NAME and BuildNumber values are automatically populated after Symantec AntiVirus server installation. The default InstallOptions value for WinNT=NONE specifies that no automated installation occurs. The other two InstallOptions WinNT values are OPTIONAL and FORCE. OPTIONAL prompts the user to install Symantec AntiVirus client software, and FORCE automatically installs Symantec AntiVirus client software without user intervention.

Once configured, the logon script files (Vplogon.bat and Nbpshpop.exe) should be copied from the C:\Program Files\Symantec AntiVirus\Logon directory on the parent server to the NETLOGON share (by default, C:\Winnt\Sysvol\Sysvol\<Domain>\Scripts on Windows 2000/XP/2003computers). This volume is automatically replicated to all other domain controllers by Windows 2000 and Windows 2003 servers configured in an Active Directory.

> **Note**
> Logon scripts perform default installations only. You cannot customize installations with logon scripts.

The new logon batch file (Vplogon.bat) can then be associated with user accounts using Group Policy, or by specifying this batch file within the Profile tab of either a local user or domain user account, as shown in Figure 3-35. When this user performs a logon event on any client system within the Active Directory, the logon script will perform as configured before; however, it is possible to associate the Vplogon.bat script with only a single Symantec AntiVirus server, so all systems that run this script will have the same parent server.

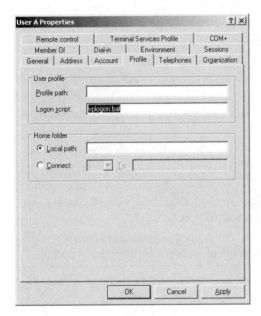

Figure 3-35 Specifying the Symantec AntiVirus client installation logon script, Vplogon.bat.

Configuring Installer (.msi) Options

Symantec AntiVirus uses the Microsoft Windows Installer (.msi) to perform client and server installations, regardless of the mechanism by which the package is transferred to the installation target computer. It is possible to

Table 3-4

Windows Installer Command-Line Options

Element	Description
Msiexec	Specifies the Windows Installer executable to be used for installation.
Symantec AntiVirus.msi	Specifies the Symantec AntiVirus installation file to be used.
/i "*<filename>*"	Command-line option that specifies an installation using "*<filename>*".
/x	Command-line option that specifies an uninstallation (removal).
/qn	Specifies to silently install, without providing an interface for user interaction with the installation process.
/qb	Allows user interaction with the installation process, as in the logon script example.
/l*v *<filename>*	Specifies that a verbose log be created as the specified filename.
INSTALLDIR=*<path>*	Specifies the installation directory on the target computer where files will be installed.
REBOOT=*<value>*	Specifies whether the computer should reboot after installation. *<value>* may be one of the following: Force, Suppress, or ReallySuppress.
ADDLOCAL=*<feature>*	Allows custom features to be installed by specifying the feature or a list of features for installation.
REMOVE=*<feature>*	Allows custom removal of installed programs or features, without requiring a complete uninstall, as with the /x option.

When path and filename entries include spaces, enclose the value using quotation marks.

modify the settings used during installation by configuring available options. Table 3-4 lists several options that can be used when configuring the command-line installation parameters for an installation of Symantec AntiVirus.

When performing an installation, a number of properties can be specified to configure the installation process for a specific environment. Table 3-5 lists many of the available properties for client and server installation.

Table 3-5

Symantec AntiVirus Properties

Property	Description
INSTALLSERVER=<value>	A <value> of 1 indicates a server installation, while a <value> of 0 indicates a client installation.
ENABLEAUTOPROTECT=<value>	Determines whether Symantec AntiVirus Auto-Protect is automatically enabled after installation. A <value> of 1 enables Auto-Protect, while any other integer value disables Auto-Protect. The default is to enable Auto-Protect.
RUNLIVEUPDATE=<value>	Specifies whether LiveUpdate will be automatically performed after installation. A <value> of 1 enables LiveUpdate, while 0 disables automatic LiveUpdate. LiveUpdate is enabled by default.
NETWORKTYPE=<value>	Used in client installations to specify the management state. A <value> of 1 indicates a managed client installation, 2 indicates an unmanaged client installation (the default).
SERVERNAME=<server>	Used in client installations to specify the parent server a managed client will join.
SERVERGROUPNAME=<group>	Used in server installations to specify the server group the new server will join.
SERVERGROUPLOGON=<name>	Used in server installations to specify the logon used when joining the new server to its server group.
SERVERGROUPPASS=<password>	Used in server installations to specify the password used when joining the new server to its server group.

When entries include spaces, enclose the value using quotation marks.

Example Command-Line Installation

An example command-line configuration for a silent managed Symantec AntiVirus Client with Auto-Protect enabled, using Server1 as its Parent server, with a custom install path of C:\Symantec AntiVirus, and configured to perform LiveUpdate but not to reboot after installation, would look like this:

```
msiexec /i "Symantec AntiVirus.msi" INSTALLSERVER=0 INSTALLDIR= "C:\Symantec
AntiVirus" NETWORKTYPE=1 SERVERNAME=Server1 ENABLEAUTOPROTECT=1
RUNLIVEUPDATE=1 REBOOT=Suppress /qn
```

Migrating from Previous Versions

Symantec AntiVirus provides a seamless upgrade from earlier versions of Symantec AntiVirus products. This section includes information on the supported and unsupported migration paths when upgrading to the current version of Symantec AntiVirus.

Migration occurs by overinstalling the new version of Symantec AntiVirus management servers and clients on computers that run the old version. You do not need to uninstall management servers and clients before you install the new version. The overinstall process saves legacy settings, uninstalls the legacy software, and then installs the latest version. Furthermore, server group migration will fail if you uninstall migration-supported legacy management servers and clients.

An exception to this is the process for upgrading the Symantec System Center console. Before installing the current version, you need to uninstall the legacy version and then install the new version. This process is called upgrading. When you upgrade the first instance of the Symantec System Center console in your network, you must uninstall the Symantec System Center console, overinstall one or more management servers in a server group, and then reinstall the Symantec System Center console.

When you migrate a primary or secondary management server, the overinstall automatically detects the server's role, and migrates and configures it appropriately when you install from the CD and select Install Symantec AntiVirus.

When you migrate a client, the overinstall automatically detects the client, and migrates and installs it appropriately.

Migrating your entire network to the current version rather than managing multiple versions of Symantec AntiVirus is strongly recommended.

Migrating to the current version of Symantec AntiVirus includes the following steps:

1. If legacy Quarantine Console or Server is installed on any server or client that you plan to migrate, uninstall the legacy software first.

2. Upgrade the Symantec System Center. The first step in migration is to install at least one new version of the Symantec System Center in the server group that contains the computer that runs the Symantec

System Center. This process involves uninstalling the legacy version of the Symantec System Center, upgrading the primary management server to the new version, upgrading the Symantec software that protects the computer that runs the Symantec System Center, and then installing the new version of the Symantec System Center.

3. After you upgrade the initial instance of the Symantec System Center, you migrate secondary management servers in the server group that contains the computer that runs the Symantec System Center.

4. When all management servers in the server group are migrated, deploy the new version of Symantec AntiVirus to clients.

5. Migrate servers and clients in other server groups by migrating the primary management server first and then migrating the secondary management servers and then migrating the clients. You can perform this server migration remotely from the new version of the Symantec System Center.

Supported and Unsupported Server and Client Migration Paths

The following section lists the platforms that are supported and unsupported when migrating to the current version of Symantec AntiVirus. If the migration of a program is supported, the Symantec AntiVirus setup program automatically detects the software, removes the legacy components and Registry entries, and installs the new version. If the migration from a previous product is not supported, you must uninstall the program before you run the Symantec AntiVirus installation program.

Supported Migration Paths

Symantec AntiVirus migrates seamlessly over the following products:

- Symantec AntiVirus Corporate Edition 8.0 and later
- Norton AntiVirus™ Corporate Edition 7.6 and later
- Symantec Client Security, all versions

Unsupported Migration Paths

Symantec AntiVirus migration is not supported for the following products:

- Symantec AntiVirus 64-bit client, version 9.0
  Symantec AntiVirus 64-bit client version 10.0 does not support Intel® Itanium® 2 processors, which were supported in version 9.0
- Symantec™ Client Firewall Administrator
- Norton AntiVirus
- Norton Internet Security™
- Antivirus products from other vendors

Unsupported Migration of Administrator Tools

Symantec AntiVirus migration is not supported for the following administrator tools:

- Symantec System Center™
- LiveUpdate Administrator
- Quarantine Server and Quarantine Console

You must uninstall previous versions of these tools and then install the latest version.

Migrating Management Servers

Before you migrate management servers, you should ensure that any legacy versions of the Symantec System Center, Quarantine Console, or Quarantine Server are uninstalled. You also need to make sure that the time clocks on all computers that you plan to migrate are within 24 hours plus or minus of the time on the primary management server.

You must migrate the first primary management server in the first server group that you want to migrate by installing the antivirus server software from the Symantec AntiVirus CD. If the initial instance of the Symantec System Center runs on a computer that is protected by Symantec AntiVirus client software and has a secondary management server as a parent, the installation procedure also applies to that secondary management server.

> **Note**
> Do not install multiple management servers in a server group before you install and configure one primary management server in a server group.

After you have migrated your first primary management server in your first migrated server group and accessed the primary management server in the Symantec System Center, you can migrate subsequent primary servers by using the Deploy feature from the Symantec AntiVirus CD or by using the AV Server Rollout feature from the Symantec System Center. If you migrate a primary management server in another server group, migrate that server individually. You can then migrate multiple secondary management servers with deployment, but you must select Upgrade instead of Install.

Migrating Client Software

There are several ways to install the Symantec AntiVirus client software, as previously discussed in this chapter. When used to overinstall previous versions of Symantec AntiVirus client software, all of these methods will migrate these clients to the current version. Uninstalling previously existing clients is not required.

Conclusion

Many different options exist for installing Symantec AntiVirus in server and client configurations, including unmanaged (stand-alone) as well as managed options to meet the needs of many different configurations. Server groups can be used to manage multiple servers with common configuration settings, with a single server configured as the primary server within this environment (see Figure 3-36).

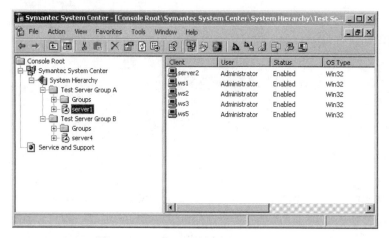

Figure 3-36 An example of multiple Symantec AntiVirus servers within the same server group. Note that Server2 here is a Symantec AntiVirus client, not a Symantec AntiVirus server, even though it is a computer running the Windows 2003 Server operating system. The term *server* within a Symantec AntiVirus environment reflects the role a system is performing rather than the type of operating system on which it resides.

By allowing managed clients to obtain updates from their designated parent server, administrators can alleviate the WAN bandwidth consumption that would be required to allow large numbers of unmanaged clients to obtain updates directly from Symantec.

Chapter Review Questions

Question 3-1

Within a managed environment with at least two computers, one of which is configured as a managed client, which two of the following will be present? Select the best two answers from those provided.

- ❏ A. Primary server
- ❏ B. Secondary server
- ❏ C. Parent server
- ❏ D. Windows 2003 server
- ❏ E. Quarantine server

Question 3-2

Of the following server types, which one is directly responsible for providing updates to a managed client? Select the best answer from those provided.

○ A. Primary server

○ B. Secondary server

○ C. Parent server

○ D. Server group

○ E. LiveUpdate server

○ F. Quarantine server

Question 3-3

Which of the following Symantec AntiVirus components can be used to deploy a new Symantec AntiVirus server to a remote computer? Select the best two answers from those provided.

❑ A. Symantec System Center

❑ B. AMS² console

❑ C. AV Server Rollout tool

❑ D. ClientRemote Install tool

❑ E. LiveUpdate Administration Utility

Question 3-4

Which one of the following update methods is supported on 64-bit operating systems? Select the best answer from those provided.

○ A. VDTM

○ B. LiveUpdate

○ C. Central Quarantine polling

○ D. Intelligent Updater

Question 3-5

You have the following computers available to install Symantec AntiVirus Server:

- ServerA: Windows NT4.0 SP6a, 128 MB RAM, 200 MB HDD space, IE 4.0

- ServerB: Windows 2000 Enterprise, 256 MB RAM, 150 MB HDD space, IE 6.0

- ServerC: Windows 2003 Standard, 256 MB RAM, 100 GB HDD space, IE 6.0

- ServerD: Windows 2003 Datacenter, 2 GB RAM, 100 MB HDD space, IE 6.0

- WorkstationA: Windows XP SP2, 96 MB RAM, 100 GB HDD space, IE 6.0

How many systems could accept a Symantec AntiVirus Server installation? Select the best answer from those provided.

○ A. 1   ○ D. 4

○ B. 2   ○ E. 5

○ C. 3

Question 3-6

Which of the following installation methods would be the best way to install a Symantec AntiVirus client on a computer that is not connected to the network? Select the best answer from those available.

○ A. File share   ○ D. Symantec System Center

○ B. Web installation   ○ E. Original media

○ C. Logon script

Question 3-7

Which of the following .msi command-line options would be used to specify a silent Symantec AntiVirus client installation? Select the best two options from those provided.

❑ A. /i   ❑ D. /qn

❑ B. /l*v   ❑ E. /x

❑ C. /qb

Question 3-8

Which value is appropriate for the NETWORKTYPE command-line option if you want to perform a Symantec AntiVirus managed client installation? Select the best answer from those provided.

○ A. 1   ○ D. 4

○ B. 2   ○ E. 5

○ C. 3

Chapter Review Answers

Answer 3-1

Answers **A** and **C** are correct. Within a managed environment, there will always be at least one Symantec AntiVirus server configured as a parent server for the managed Symantec AntiVirus client. The first server must also be configured as the primary server within its server group. Although there can be other secondary Symantec AntiVirus servers or a Central Quarantine Server, these are not mandatory within a small managed network. Although Windows 2003 Server can be used to host a Symantec AntiVirus server instance, the Symantec AntiVirus server could have been installed on one of many different possible operating systems.

Answer 3-2

Answer **C** is correct. The parent server is directly responsible for providing updates to a managed client. Primary and secondary servers within a server group can be configured as the parent server for one or more managed clients. Although a managed client can also obtain updates from a LiveUpdate Server or through Central Quarantine polling, the client obtains its updates most often from its parent.

Answer 3-3

Answers **A** and **C** are correct. The Symantec System Center and the AV Server Rollout tool can be used together to deploy a new Symantec AntiVirus server on a remote computer. The Symantec System Center cannot deploy servers unless the AV Server Rollout tool is installed. The AMS^2 console is used to manage AMS^2 alerts, while the LiveUpdate administration utility is used to manage a local LiveUpdate server. The ClientRemote tool can be used to deploy the Symantec AntiVirus client to remote computers, but it is not used for remote server installation.

Answer 3-4

Answer **B** is correct. Only the LiveUpdate method is available for 64-bit operating system clients to obtain updates to the Symantec AntiVirus client or virus definitions.

Answer 3-5

Answer **C** is correct. Only three systems (ServerB, ServerC, and WorkstationA) meet the minimum requirements for installation of the Symantec AntiVirus server. ServerA is an NT 4 system, while ServerD has insufficient file storage space available on its hard drive.

Answer 3-6

Answer **E** is correct. For a computer that is not network connected, it is necessary to provide the client installation package through some form of media. All other listed options for installation rely on network connectivity.

Answer 3-7

Answers **A** and **D** are correct. To specify a Symantec AntiVirus client installation, the /i switch is used. The /x switch would be used to specify a removal. Silent installation is specified by the /qn switch, and the /qb switch allows user interaction with the installation process. The unrelated /l*v switch is used to specify a verbose-mode log to be created during installation.

Answer 3-8

Answer **A** is correct. The command-line value NETWORKTYPE=1 specifies a Symantec AntiVirus managed client installation. A value of 2 would indicate an unmanaged client installation.

CHAPTER 4

Symantec AntiVirus Management

Terms and Techniques to Remember

- Symantec System Center™
- Server groups
- Client groups
- Creating server groups and client groups
- Symantec AntiVirus™ configuration priority
- Local and remote deployments
- Configuring settings for a manual scan

Introduction

By using the centralized policy management of Symantec AntiVirus, you can manage clients and servers that are assigned to logical groups. In addition, you can create, deploy, and lock down security policies and settings to keep systems up-to-date and properly configured at all times.

The central management console enables you to audit the network, identify unprotected nodes, and apply the appropriate security protection before a threat occurs. This chapter provides you with information on the management functions necessary to deploy and manage Symantec AntiVirus in a small business environment.

Unmanaged Environment

Symantec AntiVirus clients deployed in an unmanaged state can only be configured locally on the client. To configure options, open the Symantec AntiVirus client by selecting **Start**, **All Programs**, **Symantec AntiVirus**, **Symantec AntiVirus**. Figure 4-1 illustrates the configuration settings within the client interface, showing both left-navigation and drop-down navigation options. Both methods access the same configuration interface shown.

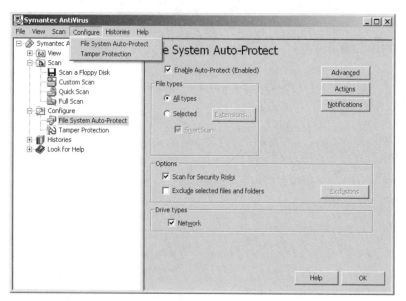

Figure 4-1 Configuration screen for an unmanaged Symantec AntiVirus client.

Symantec AntiVirus client configuration options for an unmanaged client are not discussed here as the focus is on a managed environment, although most of the client protection concepts discussed are valid for an unmanaged client, but the method of configuration is slightly different.

Managed Environment

As discussed briefly in the previous chapter and shown here in Figure 4-2, the Symantec System Center is used to manage your Symantec AntiVirus managed environment. This component is built using the Microsoft Management Console (MMC) standard and includes support for plug-ins allowing management of multiple Symantec products. The Symantec System Center console's use in deploying client firewall settings within Symantec Client Security is covered in Chapter 7, "Symantec Client Security Management."

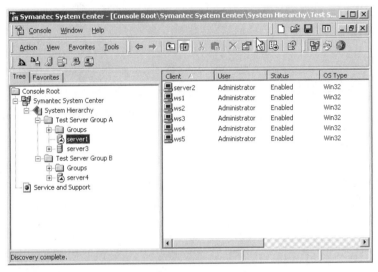

Figure 4-2 The Symantec System Center console.

> **Note**
> Figure 4-2 displays the clients assigned to Server1 as their parent Symantec AntiVirus server—including Server2, which is a Symantec AntiVirus client installed on a Windows® 2003 Server computer. If the distinction between the Symantec AntiVirus server role and a server operating system is unclear, please review the previous chapter.

The Symantec System Center can be used to configure server and client groups, initiate virus scans, configure antivirus policies, update virus definitions, and respond to identified viral threats. The settings changed using the Symantec System Center are written to a server and then distributed to affected clients through a new Grc.dat file. Settings affecting client groups are sent to the parent server in a Grcgrp.dat file and then distributed to clients through the Grc.dat file.

> **Tip**
>
> Settings in the new Grc.dat file overwrite the settings on a client, even if no changes were made before closing option configuration dialog boxes within the Symantec System Center. If you access any of the configuration settings dialog boxes and then click OK to close them, network activity is expected as the new Grc.dat file is transferred to the managed clients.

Server and Client Groups

Within the Symantec System Center, server groups are configured just below the System Hierarchy node and contain one or more Symantec AntiVirus servers sharing a common configuration set. Within Figure 4-2, two server groups can be seen:

- **Test Server Group A**—This server group consists of two Symantec AntiVirus servers (Server1 and Server3), with a number of managed clients associated with the highlighted parent server displayed.

- **Test Server Group B**—This server group resides on a single stand-alone server (Server4).

An additional Groups node is present within each server group. This node is used to configure Symantec AntiVirus client groups, which are logical groupings of Symantec AntiVirus clients that share a common set of configuration settings. Each client group can be configured with different settings than its peers within the same server group, allowing greater granularity in control of the settings that will be applied to different clients within larger or more complex implementations. A managed Symantec AntiVirus client is assigned to a particular parent server but can be assigned to a client group as well.

When clients groups are not used, all settings applied to the server group or parent server are propagated to all client systems of that parent. When client groups are implemented, clients of the same parent server can have configurations different from other clients of the same server, provided that both are members of different client groups. Assigned clients obtain their settings from the client group rather than from the parent server, as with unassigned clients. Symantec AntiVirus clients are categorized as follows:

- Assigned clients have been assigned to a client group. They receive virus and security risk definitions files from the parent server to which they are physically attached, but receive configuration settings and updates based upon the client group to which they are assigned.

- Unassigned clients have not been assigned to a client group. They receive configuration settings and updates from their parent management server.

Mixing Clients Within a Parent Server
It is possible to have a mixture of assigned and unassigned clients managed by a single parent server, but this is not considered a best practice for implementation. If client groups are used, the best practice is to assign all clients to client groups, to avoid unnecessary complexity and unexpected results.

Configuration Priority

When settings are configured within a managed environment, they can be overridden by settings configured at a higher level within the managed system hierarchy. Table 4-1 details the levels within the Symantec System Center where settings can be configured.

Locking and Unlocking Server Groups

Each server group can be individually locked or unlocked within the Symantec System Center. This allows settings to be applied individually or throughout the organization by applying settings at the system hierarchy level. When multiple server groups are unlocked at the time the higher-level settings are applied, these settings are applied to all systems within the unlocked groups. Figure 4-3 illustrates the difference between the unlocked Server Group A and the locked Server Group B.

Table 4-1

Symantec System Center Levels

Level	What Can Be Configured
System hierarchy	Settings configured here are applied to all unlocked server groups and the clients they manage, regardless of client group membership. The number of configuration options available here is extremely limited.
Server group	Settings configured here are applied to all servers and clients within the server group, including clients in client groups if the client group is configured to inherit server group settings (which is the default setting for client groups).
Server	Settings applied here are applied to the server and its clients. Both assigned and unassigned clients can be configured with the following settings: ■ Virus Sweep ■ Update definitions now ■ History configurations The server and its unassigned clients can also be configured with these settings: ■ Scheduled and manual scans ■ Definitions updating, including LiveUpdate ■ Quarantine options ■ Auto-protect options ■ Administrator-only options ■ Roaming options ■ Update client policy now ■ View/clear threat status
Client group	Settings applied here are applied only to the clients assigned to the client group. The types of settings include those settings listed for unassigned clients at the Server level.
Client	Within a managed environment, configuration settings, by default, are read-only at the client level; however a Symantec System Center option is available to allow configuration of managed clients at the client level.

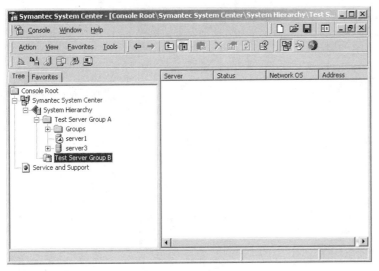

Figure 4-3 The Symantec System Center console showing both locked and unlocked server groups.

Unlocking a Server Group

A server group can be unlocked by right-clicking on the target server group within the Symantec System Center console and then selecting **Unlock Server Group** from the options provided in the drop-down list. The administrator is prompted to enter a valid Symantec AntiVirus user name and password with the necessary permissions to access the designated server group.

Once unlocked, the servers and all other items within the target server group become navigable within the Symantec System Center console, and all settings applied at the system hierarchy level also are applied within the unlocked server group. Figure 4-4 illustrates the now-unlocked Test Server Group B and its single Symantec AntiVirus server (Server4).

Locking a Server Group

To lock a server group, right-click the target unlocked server group within the console and then select **Lock Server Group** from the options provided in the drop-down list. Server groups are automatically locked by default each time you start the Symantec System Center, unless you configure to automatically unlock the server group when you start the Symantec System

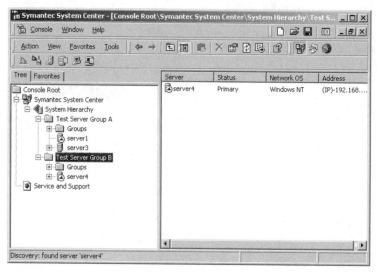

Figure 4-4 The Symantec System Center console showing both server groups unlocked.

Center. Figure 4-5 shows the Unlock Server Group dialog box with the options to remember the username and password, and to perform automatic unlock when the Symantec System Center is started. Usernames and passwords are not saved unless you explicitly configure this option.

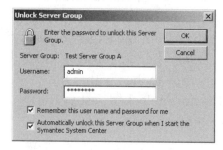

Figure 4-5 The Unlock Server Group dialog box.

New Server Groups

The Symantec System Center also can be used to create new server groups, allowing an administrator to reconfigure the Symantec AntiVirus architecture to meet emergent requirements for management. This can be done to restrict administration over a specific set of servers and clients so that only author-ized logons for the new server group can modify the settings for servers and clients within the server group.

Changing Server Groups

A new server group can be created by right-clicking on the System Hierarchy node and selecting New, Server Group from the options provided. Figure 4-6 illustrates the New Server Group creation dialog box, being used to create a new server group named New Server Group Z. Note that an initial adminis-tration username (here, admin) and password for this new server group are required.

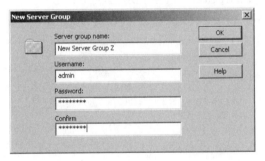

Figure 4-6 The New Server Group dialog box.

> **Note**
> When the new group is created, the administrator can drag and drop Symantec AntiVirus servers into the new server group. Managed clients can also be moved between parent servers, as examined later in this chapter.

Deleting a server group requires that all servers first be moved to another server group. Right-clicking on the empty group now provides the option to delete this group. It is necessary to right-click on the System Hierarchy node and click Refresh before the deleted server group is no longer displayed. The primary server for a server group can also be changed here by right-clicking on the new primary server and selecting the option **Make Server a Primary Server** from the list provided. The administrator is prompted to verify the new assignment before the transfer occurs.

Managing Symantec AntiVirus User Accounts

Although deploying the Symantec AntiVirus client, server, and Symantec System Center console requires a system or domain user logon with the necessary access permissions for installation, Symantec AntiVirus also provides control over each server group by creating an initial administration username/password combination as each server group is created. This username/password combination represents an account designated within the Symantec AntiVirus server group and is not related to any Windows logon account or the administration accounts used in other Symantec AntiVirus server groups.

The Configure Server Group Accounts option (see Figure 4-7) can be accessed by right-clicking the desired server group and selecting **Account Management** from the options provided.

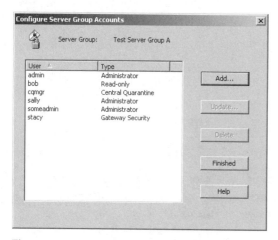

Figure 4-7 Configure Server Group Accounts for Server Group A showing several accounts.

Existing Symantec AntiVirus accounts are displayed here, along with the role to which each has been assigned. Accounts can be deleted or updated here by selecting the appropriate account and then the desired action button. Adding accounts can also be performed by first selecting the **Add** button and then providing the name, password, and account type for the new account within the Account Setup dialog box, shown in Figure 4-8.

Figure 4-8 Account Setup used to create
an Administrator account named
NewAdminUser.

Note
The capability to have multiple accounts for a server group is new
in Symantec AntiVirus 10.0. Users of version 9 and earlier might
recall that each server group had a single administrative password,
which had to be shared by administrators responsible for managing
Symantec AntiVirus settings. This new functionality makes it possible
to have both administrative and read-only accounts within the same
server group.

Using the Symantec System Center

Within managed Symantec AntiVirus scenarios, the Symantec System Center
is used to configure common settings that will be applied to server and client
groups and all servers and clients within. This avoids the need to manually
configure settings on each system throughout a company's network. The various configuration options available within the Symantec System Center can
be accessed by right-clicking on the desired node and then selecting **All
Tasks**, **Symantec AntiVirus**. This expands the list of available configuration
options for that node, as shown in Figure 4-9.

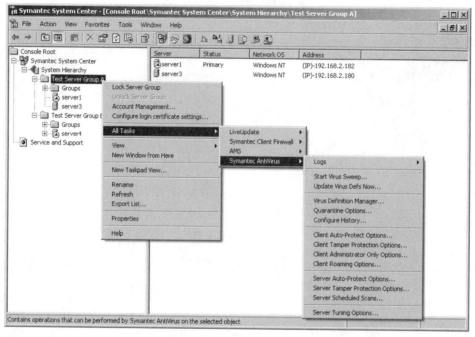

Figure 4-9 Accessing configuration options within the Symantec System Center.

The same method can be applied to the System Hierarchy node, to individual server group nodes, to individual servers and to individual clients using the Symantec System Center. Configuration settings applied at a higher level override those specified at lower levels, as discussed earlier in this chapter.

Auto-Protect

Selecting an option within this listing allows the configuration of settings to be applied to all servers and clients within the selected containing node. If **Client Auto-Protect Options** is selected (see Figure 4-10), the client behavior can be configured for what to scan for and how to react as desired when a security risk or threat is detected.

Auto-Protect scans files as they are accessed or modified, and can scan email attachments as they are sent and received. When Auto-Protect is enabled and configured, the configured Symantec AntiVirus clients will automatically detect security risks and threats. When a security risk or threat is found, a user on the infected computer sees a notice similar to that shown in Figure 4-11.

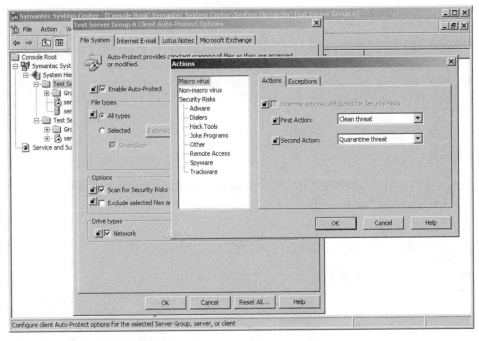

Figure 4-10 Client Auto-protect options.

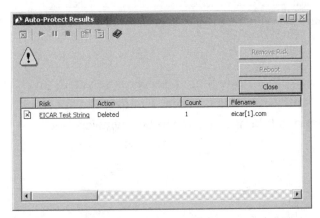

Figure 4-11 Auto-Protect message that the Eicar standard antivirus test file has been found.

Eicar Standard AntiVirus Test File
The file used to test the proper functionality of Symantec AntiVirus is provided by www.eicar.org. This test file is not a "real" virus, so it poses no harm to the target system—it is merely identified by the antivirus client to validate its operation.

Symantec Logs

Within the Symantec System Center, the same event is highlighted on the appropriate client, as seen in Figure 4-12.

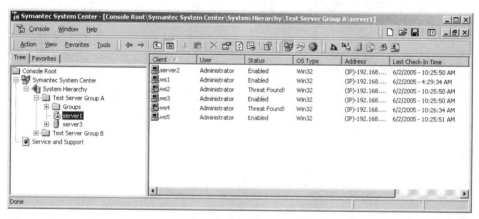

Figure 4-12 The Symantec System Center showing offline clients and those with detected threats.

By right-clicking on a client or other node (here a server is selected) and following **All Tasks**, **Symantec AntiVirus**, **Logs**, **Threat History**, the specific viruses encountered and the actions taken for each can be reviewed (see Figure 4-13).

Note
Some viruses that were left alone can be deleted or quarantined by selecting the entry and then the Delete or Quarantine keys, as appropriate. Not all viruses can be handled in the same way, so the results of these actions will vary by virus.

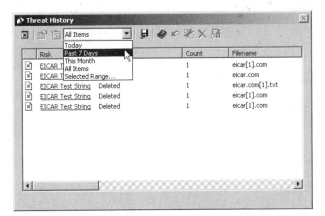

Figure 4-13 The Threat History log showing filter-by-date
options available.

Additional Symantec AntiVirus event logs are available, along with
histories of virus scans and sweeps. By selecting the desired history of a
containing node, the administrator can audit the history of Symantec
AntiVirus operations on all systems within the container. Figure 4-14
illustrates an example of the scan history for Server Group A.

	Computer	Status	Total files	Infected	Logged By
	ws4	Scan Complete	172	0	Defwatch Scan
	server3	Scan Complete	172	0	Defwatch Scan
	ws2	Scan Complete	172	0	Defwatch Scan
	server2	Scan Complete	172	0	Defwatch Scan
	ws4	Scan Complete	18616	1	Manual scan
	server3	Scan Complete	20277	0	Manual scan
	ws2	Scan Complete	18610	0	Manual scan
	server2	Scan Complete	18550	0	Manual scan
	server1	Scan Complete	176	0	Defwatch Scan
	server1	Scan Complete	22372	0	Manual scan
	ws3	Scan Complete	172	0	Defwatch Scan
	ws3	Scan Complete	18596	0	Manual scan

Figure 4-14 Symantec AntiVirus scan history for Server
Group A.

Additional logs and settings can be reviewed within the **All Tasks, Symantec
AntiVirus** options available at each level of the Symantec AntiVirus hierarchy.

Tamper Protection

Additional protective features can be configured, such as the Auto-Protect
or Tamper Protection options available within Symantec AntiVirus.

Figure 4-15 displays several of the settings that can be configured for Tamper Protection on Server1.

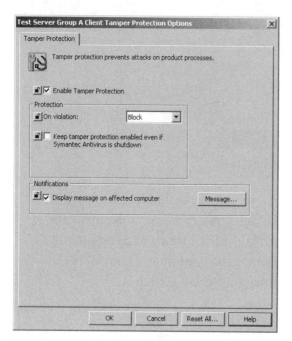

Figure 4-15 Tamper Protection options configured for Server1 and its clients. By performing this configuration within the Symantec System Center, the Reset All button allows the application of all clients of Server1. This capability to perform a mass update of configuration settings makes the Symantec System Center a key element in your company's antivirus-management process.

What Is Tamper Protection?

Tamper Protection is an optional protection Symantec AntiVirus can perform to protect processes used by Symantec AntiVirus. These settings are accessed through **All Tasks, Symantec AntiVirus, Client Tamper Protect Options** and also **All Tasks, Symantec AntiVirus, Server Tamper Protect Options**. The settings can be configured to ignore, block, or log events that attempt to attack Symantec processes.

Other Configuration Tasks

Additional tasks can be performed here, such as clearing acknowledged and resolved threat status from a client. By selecting **All Tasks**, **Symantec AntiVirus**, **Clear Threat Status**, the threat status can be cleared for the selected client. This should be done after any investigative work by the administrator, and it stops highlighting the client in the view. Additional options for client behavior, such as the forwarding of quarantined items to a central quarantine server (see Figure 4-16), can be configured within the **All Tasks**, **Symantec AntiVirus** list of options.

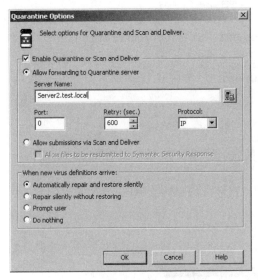

Figure 4-16 Quarantine options configured to forward quarantined options to a center server.

Managing Alerts

With the Alert Management System (AMS[2]) installed, an administrator can configure for alerts to be generated through the following means:

- Message Box
- Broadcast
- Send Internet Mail
- Send Page

- Run Program
- Write to Event Log
- Send SNMP Trap
- Load an NLM

These events can be configured to generate alerts:

- Configuration Change
- Default Alert
- Symantec AntiVirus Startup/Shutdown
- Scan Start/Stop

- Risk Repair Failed
- Risk Repaired
- Virus Definitions File Update
- Virus Found

If alerts have been configured for any of these events, when they occur on the client, a risk information block is created and forwarded to the client's parent server. The parent server enters this into its AMS[2] log and then forwards it on to the primary server, where it is passed to the AMS[2] server. The action taken by the AMS[2] server depends on the configuration set by the administrator. The configuration for AMS[2] is done at the server group level from **All Tasks**, **AMS**, **Configure**, as shown in Figure 4-17.

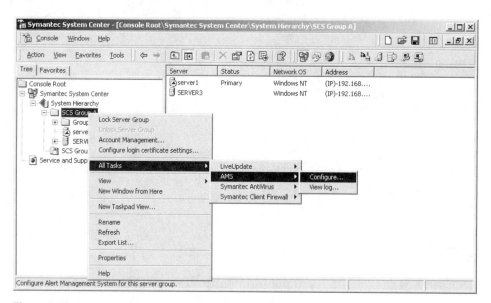

Figure 4-17 Accessing configuration options for the AMS[2] server within the Symantec System Center.

Once in the configuration, you can set the alerts for the various event types listed previously and shown in Figure 4-18.

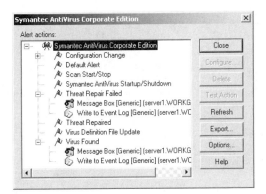

Figure 4-18 Configure AMS[2] alerts.

Multiple alerts can be configured for each event. For example, an administrator might want to get a message when a virus is detected and also want the information written to the Windows Event Log for later viewing.

Client Management

Modern corporate scenarios can present challenges for administration over a large number of widely distributed clients. By configuring servers within server groups, control is gained over the collection of settings that will be applied to servers and their clients. As discussed earlier in this chapter, client systems can also be assigned to client groups to gain even greater control over the settings that will be applied to a particular group of clients.

Client Groups

Right-clicking on the **Groups** node within a server group allows a new client group to be created by selecting **New Client Group** from the options provided. As shown in Figure 4-19, the administrator is prompted to provide a name for the new client group and to select an existing client group as a template, if desired. This allows rapid configuration of the settings for a new client group based on those of an existing already-configured group.

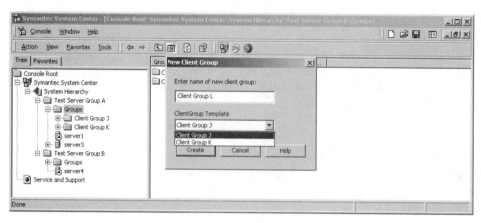

Figure 4-19 Adding a new client group (Client Group L) using Client Group K as a template.

Adding clients to a client group can be accomplished by selecting the target client or clients, and dragging them to the desired group. The parent server setting remains the same for each client, but the client also is assigned to the appropriate client group, as seen in the client interface shown in Figure 4-20.

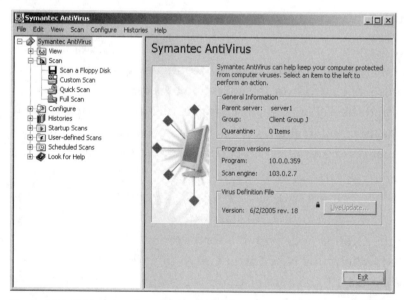

Figure 4-20 WS1 assigned to Client Group J, with Server1 as its parent server.

The membership of a client group can also be viewed within the Symantec System Center by expanding the desired server group and then the client group within the Groups node. As Figure 4-21 shows, members of a client group can be parented to any Symantec AntiVirus server within the same server group. The Microsoft Windows 2003 Server (Server2) is a client of the Symantec AntiVirus server (Server3), while WS1 and WS2 are clients of the primary Symantec AntiVirus server (Server1), yet all three are members of the client group (Client Group J).

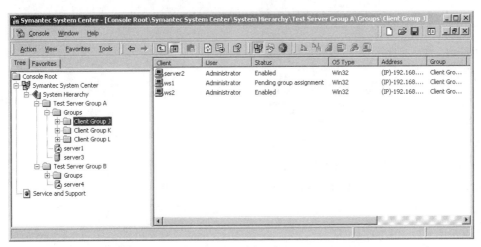

Figure 4-21 WS1 assigned to Client Group J, along with WS2 and Server2.

The Symantec System Center allows an administrator to rapidly identify the status of all client systems (here, showing group membership status). Other views show the last time each was scanned for viruses, the version of the antivirus definitions currently in use by each client, the parent server of each, the client's most recent IP address, and a wealth of other data that can be used to sort the listing of managed clients for review. Configuration settings applied to a client group are transferred to all assigned clients. As before, selecting **All Tasks**, **Symantec AntiVirus** reveals available options for configuration, such as the LiveUpdate Configuration settings shown in Figure 4-22.

Not all configuration settings available at the server group level are present at the client group level. One example of this is the option to manually trigger an update of virus definitions by selecting **All Tasks**, **Symantec AntiVirus**, **Update Virus Defs Now** within the options for a Symantec AntiVirus server and its clients. This option is not listed among

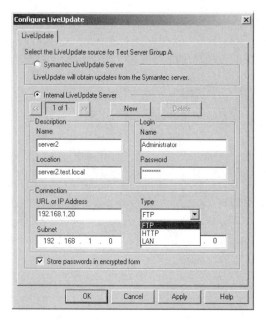

Figure 4-22 LiveUpdate Configuration settings for Client Group J.

those available when selecting **All Tasks**, **Symantec AntiVirus** for a client group.

Client Migration

As demonstrated previously in this chapter, the parent server and client group assignments for managed clients can be changed by simple drag-and-drop operations within the Symantec System Center. It is also possible to change the parent server configuration of a managed client by placing a copy of the new parent server's Grc.dat file within the configuration folder on a managed client. By default, this is as follows:

```
C:\Documents and Settings\All Users\Application Data\Symantec
\Symantec AntiVirus Corporate Edition\7.5
```

The client automatically reconfigures itself to use the new server as its parent, as defined by this line within the Grc.dat file:

```
Parent=S<server name>
```

Changing Client Management State

The same process detailed for client migration can be used to change an unmanaged client into a managed client. Simply place the Grc.dat file in the above location on the unmanaged client, and the Symantec client associates the specified parent server with the now-managed client. The process to change a managed client to an unmanaged state is slightly more involved:

1. Uninstall Symantec AntiVirus from the client.

2. Delete the Registry subkey: HKLM\Software\Intel\LANDesk\ VirusProtect6.

3. Reinstall Symantec AntiVirus as an unmanaged client.

Client Scans

The Symantec System Center can also be used to configure clients for scheduled antivirus scans, to trigger client scans manually, or to initiate a virus sweep. Manual scans can be conducted on a client or server by right-clicking on the target system and selecting **All Tasks**, **Symantec AntiVirus**, **Start Manual Scan**. Manual scans can be configured for the following:

- **QuickScan**—Symantec AntiVirus quickly scans only the system memory and common virus and security risk infection locations.

- **Full**—Symantec AntiVirus scans the memory, boot sector, and storage devices in search of any possible threats.

- **Custom**—This option allows the selection of specific files, folders, or drives for scanning.

As Figure 4-23 illustrates, the manual scan can be configured to scan particular locations, to exclude certain folders, and even to adjust its operation based on system utilization, to avoid impacting performance too greatly while in use. By selecting **All Tasks**, **Symantec AntiVirus**, **Scheduled Scans**, the administrator can configure scans to occur at regular intervals, as seen in Figure 4-24. Here a new daily full scan is being configured in addition to several pre-existing scheduled scans already configured.

In addition to individual client scans, it is possible to trigger multiple systems to scan for viruses using a virus sweep, which can be scheduled to

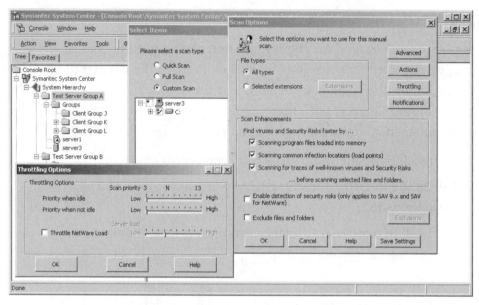

Figure 4-23 Configuring a manual scan.

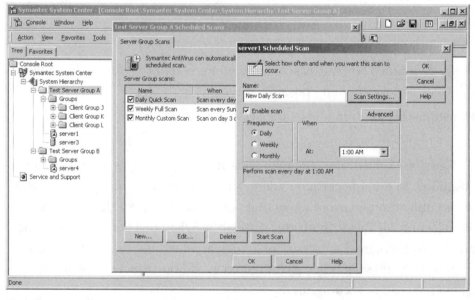

Figure 4-24 Configuring a scheduled scan.

run on your entire network, a server group, or an individual server. This should be performed with caution as a virus sweep can create considerable network traffic, the amount and duration of which depend on the size of your network. Once you start a virus sweep it must complete; you cannot stop it. A sweep is initiated by selecting **All Tasks**, **Symantec AntiVirus**, **Start Virus Sweep**. The administrator is prompted to provide a name used to identify the results of this sweep, as shown in Figure 4-25.

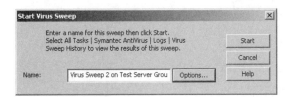

Figure 4-25 Initiating a virus sweep of all systems within Server Group A.

The options available for virus sweeps and scheduled scans are the same as those available when configuring a manual scan. As detailed earlier in this chapter, the results of scans and sweeps are available within the Scan History and Virus Sweep History options accessed through All Tasks, Symantec AntiVirus.

Removal of Symantec AntiVirus

Occasionally, it is necessary to remove Symantec AntiVirus from a computer, as in the case of migration from a managed to an unmanaged client configuration. Symantec AntiVirus can be removed by initiating the setup process using the installation media or network source, selecting to remove the installation, as shown in Figure 4-26.

An alternative to this method of removal is to follow **Start**, **Control Panel**, **Administrative Tools**, **Add or Remove Programs**. Removal can then be initiated by highlighting Symantec AntiVirus within the list of installed programs and selecting to remove the program, as shown in Figure 4-27.

To safeguard against users uninstalling Symantec AntiVirus and leaving the computer vulnerable the uninstall will ask for a password before removal. The password that is required to uninstall can be changed using the

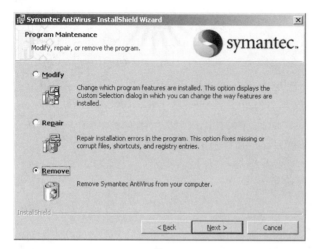

Figure 4-26 Removing Symantec AntiVirus using the installation media.

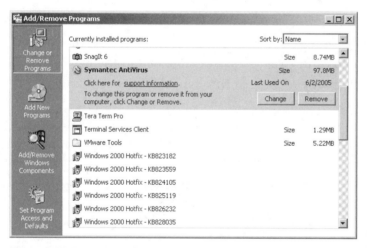

Figure 4-27 Removing Symantec AntiVirus using Add/Remove Programs.

Symantec System Center by selecting the server, server group, and then clicking **All Tasks**, **Symantec AntiVirus**, **Client**. After verifying the removal request, Symantec AntiVirus is removed from the host. To remove Registry settings left behind, it is necessary to delete the Registry subkey, HKLM\ Software\Intel\LANDesk\VirusProtect6.

Conclusion

In this chapter you learned how to use Symantec System Center to manage antivirus protection on networked computers in a small business environment. The centralized capabilities provide extensive administrative funtionality enabling the configuration of multiple antivirus protection policies, reporting and alerting functions. This centralized management is critical in providing a complete and secure solution, allowing you to set the appropriate controls to customize to the secuirty needs of the specific environment.

Chapter Review Questions

Question 4-1

All of the servers listed here are assigned to one or more roles within the Accounting server group. Within the Symantec System Center, which of the following would be listed in the left navigation pane? Select the best two answers from those provided.

- ❑ A. Server1, a Windows 2003 Server configured as the primary server for Accounting
- ❑ B. Server2, a Windows 2003 Server hosting the Symantec System Center console used to administer Accounting
- ❑ C. Server3, a Windows 2003 Server parented to Server1
- ❑ D. WS1, a Windows XP sp2 workstation configured as a parent within Accounting
- ❑ E. WS2, a Windows XP sp2 workstation parented to Server1

Question 4-2

Auto-protect configuration settings applied to which of the following containing levels within the Symantec System Center will not be applied to managed clients assigned to a client group? Select the best two answers.

- ❑ A. System hierarchy
- ❑ B. Server group
- ❑ C. Server
- ❑ D. Client group
- ❑ E. Client

Question 4-3

Which of the following steps are required to delete an existing server group named Finance, using the least amount of administrative effort? Finance has a single server named FinSrv1. Select the best two answers from those provided.

❑ A. Delete the Finance server group using the Symantec System Center

❑ B. Delete the Registry subkey HKLM\Software\Intel\LANDesk\ VirusProtect6 on FinSrv1

❑ C. Place the Grc.dat file from the new server group's primary server into C:\Program Files\All Users\Application Data\Symantec\ Symantec AntiVirus Corporate Edition\7.5\ on FinSrv1

❑ D. Drag and drop FinSrv1 into its new server group

❑ E. Set FinSrv1 as a primary server using the Symantec System Center

Question 4-4

Which of the following Auto-Protect virus-response actions will not generate log entries that can be reviewed later using the Symantec System Center? Select the best answer from those provided.

○ A. Delete infected file

○ B. Quarantine infected file

○ C. Clean infected file

○ D. Leave alone

○ E. None—all can generate Symantec AntiVirus log entries

Question 4-5

Which of the following information about a managed client is not listed within the Symantec System Center interface? Select the best answer from those provided.

○ A. Offline/online status

○ B. IP address

○ C. Last scan date/time

○ D. Definitions version

○ E. Parent server

○ F. Last user logon account

○ G. XP sp2 firewall settings

Question 4-6

Which of the following client manual scan options will check for viruses within system memory (RAM)? Select the best answer from those provided.

    ○ A. QuickScan   ○ C. Custom

    ○ B. Full   ○ D. All of the above

Chapter Review Answers

Answer 4-1

Answers **A** and **D** are correct. Within the Symantec System Center, Server1 and WS1 would be listed within the left navigation pane as Symantec AntiVirus Servers. Only these two are configured with the Symantec AntiVirus Server service.

Answer 4-2

Answers **C** and **E** are correct. Auto-protect configuration settings applied at the server levels within the Symantec System Center are not applied to clients assigned to a client group—only to the server's own protection configuration and that of its unassigned clients. Within a managed environment, these client-level settings are read-only.

Answer 4-3

Answers **A** and **D** are correct. To delete an existing server group using the least amount of administrative effort, all servers (here, only FinSrv1, as the only server within the Finance server group) must be removed from the server group before deletion.

Answer 4-4

Answer **E** is correct. Viruses identified by Symantec AntiVirus generate log entries that can be viewed using the Symantec System Center, regardless of the actions specified in client Auto-Protect configurations.

Answer 4-5

Answer **G** is correct. Of the options listed, only the XP sp2 firewall settings are not available within the Symantec System Center interface when examining clients of a server or client group.

Answer 4-6

Answer **D** is correct. QuickScan and full scans both include system memory tests automatically, while custom scans may include this option as well. All provided options can perform this test.

CHAPTER 5

Symantec AntiVirus Policies

Terms and Techniques to Remember

- LiveUpdate
- Virus Definition Transport Method
- Fully/Lightly/Sometimes managed and unmanaged clients
- Actions taken when threats and security risks are found
- Excluding files from scans

Introduction

A strong set of policies is the foundation for any effective information security program. Without a clear definition of the security program's objectives, it's difficult to ensure compliance. When working in the area of client security, it's essential that your information security program include an effective antivirus policy.

In this chapter, we begin by looking at the elements of an effective antivirus policy and then explore the technical options available to you within Symantec AntiVirus to implement policy decisions within the small business environment.

Defining an Antivirus Policy

You should build effective policies to protect your network for four main reasons:

- To protect confidential data from loss and/or damage from malicious code.

- To preserve network bandwidth and resources from overconsumption in the event of a security incident through effective architecture design.

- To prevent losses of employee productivity from the impact of a malicious code incident. An improperly managed incident could have a detrimental impact on productivity through the time required to restore data and resources and time lost during periods of resource unavailability.

- To limit legal liability and negative publicity in the face of a security incident. This is especially critical in industries that depend upon customer trust, such as financial services and health care. A single negative incident could destroy years of cultivated trust and irreparably harm a business's reputation.

Components of Antivirus Risk Management

Symantec recommends that you consider four components when developing an antivirus risk-management policy:

- The methods you use to secure the network against malicious code

- The tools you use to detect and log malicious code incidents

- The methods you use to train end users in the use of antivirus products

- The way you communicate your antivirus policy to constituents in a clear and concise manner

Policy Outline

The best way to start development of an antivirus security policy is to develop an outline of the policy's contents. You can then work with other members of your organization's information security and management teams to flesh out the specific items within each policy area. You might want to consider adding these elements to your policy:

- An explanation of the policy's importance
- Specific user and administrator responsibilities for abiding by the policy
- A list of the people involved in policy development
- Approval authority for the policy (it's best to have this authority as high as possible within the organization)
- A statement of the policy's organizational scope
- The effective date of the policy and any revisions, if applicable
- Resources to be protected against malicious code
- Methods used for installing software on workstations
- Antivirus software-configuration guidelines
- Sanctions for policy violations
- Authority and responsibility for policy enforcement
- Procedures for reporting, responding to, and investigating malicious software security incidents
- The procedure for granting exceptions to the policy, when necessary

Ensuring Policy Effectiveness

When you have a formal antivirus policy, you're halfway there. As with any guidance, the policy is good only if it's well known and enforced consistently. Here are a few guidelines that you can follow to ensure that your policy is effective:

- Put it in writing. Putting your policy in writing forces you to ensure that you have a coherent approach to antivirus management and provides you with a resource when questions arise.
- Distribute the policy widely. Everyone in your organization who is subject to the policy should have easy access to a copy. This might involve distributing printed copies or making the policy available on the corporate intranet.

- Promote your policy vigorously. Take every opportunity you can get to remind people of the policy's existence and its requirements. Repetition ensures awareness.

- Enforce your policy consistently. If you don't stick by the letter of the policy on a consistent basis, you'll lose effectiveness as well. This is a good reason to ensure that the written policy is reasonable and enforceable.

- Teach. Use every opportunity to broach the subject of antivirus policy. When users are infected and need their systems restored, use this as a golden opportunity to educate them on what happened and how they can prevent it from recurring.

Choosing a Management Hierarchy

As you learned in Chapter 4, "Symantec AntiVirus Management," the Symantec System Center enables you to organize your antivirus deployment into server groups and client groups. You can choose to manage your environment using either, or a combination of these two group types. In this section, we examine the advantages and disadvantages of each approach. Later in the chapter, we look at the specific types of policies that can be applied to systems using these hierarchies.

Server Groups

Server groups enable you to easily administer multiple Symantec AntiVirus™ servers throughout your organization. You can create server groups using the Symantec System Center™, shown in Figure 5-1.

Each server group contains a primary server that is responsible for the configuration and management functions associated with the server group. The remaining servers in the group are secondary servers, and receive their configuration information from the group's primary server and share it with their clients.

Server groups are especially useful in larger environments, especially those that are geographically distributed. You can use server groups to maintain a centralized configuration management for your entire organization

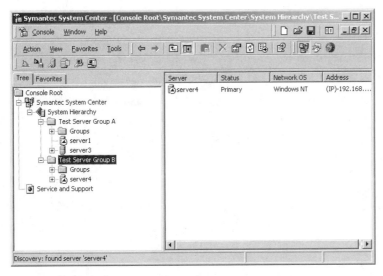

Figure 5-1 Symantec System Center.

while allowing the distribution of server workload according to geographical or organizational boundaries.

For example, assume that you work for Acme Widgets Corporation at its corporate headquarters in Miami, Florida. You have regional offices in Des Moines, Iowa; South Bend, Indiana; and Los Angeles, California. The three regional offices are connected to the Miami headquarters via WAN links. The LANs within each office are wired for gigabit-speed communication. You could run a single server out of the Miami headquarters and configure clients nationwide to use the centralized server. However, this approach has several disadvantages:

- It wastes expensive bandwidth. Clients will need to individually contact the Miami office and retrieve bulky update files each time new virus definitions become available. This could place a tremendous burden on your WAN links, reducing their availability for other business needs.

- It presents a single point of failure. If the Miami server goes down, no client anywhere in the organization will be able to retrieve updates.

- It makes the network more vulnerable to attack. If an incident renders the WAN link inaccessible, clients will be unable to retrieve the antivirus updates that might be necessary to remedy the situation.

The use of separate servers at each location is a far better solution. Placing secondary antivirus servers in Des Moines, South Bend, and Los Angeles greatly reduces the need for WAN bandwidth. When the Miami primary server receives an update, it distributes it to each of the secondary servers over the WAN links. The secondary servers then use LAN links to spread the updates to client systems.

This configuration is shown in Figure 5-2:

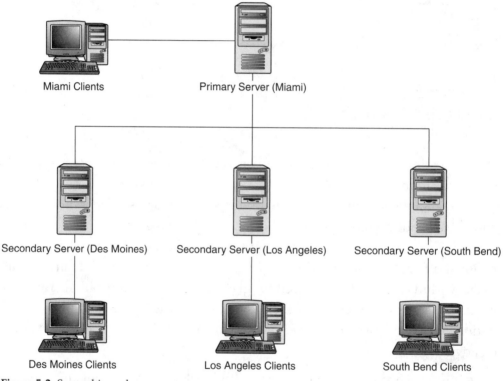

Figure 5-2 Server hierarchy.

Curious about the bandwidth savings? Let's assume that each of the three remote offices has 5,000 workstations and a new 5 MB virus definitions file becomes available. This would require a total of 15,000 5 MB transfers, for a total of 75 GB of data transfer without the use of secondary servers. With secondary servers, after the first transfer of all the definitions when the servers joined the group, this update would need only three 5 MB transfers.

The use of secondary servers significantly reduces the bandwidth requirements of an antivirus update.

Client Groups

Client groups are another useful strategy for managing antivirus installations in the organization. The goal of client groups is to enable you to manage clients with similar security requirements. You can create client groups by expanding the Groups tree under a server group and adding a new group.

> **Tip**
> If you choose to manage your antivirus environment using client groups, it is recommended that all clients are members of a client group. Attempting to manage a mixture of clients with group assignments and clients without group assignments could cause inconsistencies in the clients' configurations.

Client groups are useful in any situation in which different systems have different security requirements. For example, a company might use the following client groups to manage its antivirus solution:

- **Desktop group**—Consists of workstations that are always connected to the network
- **Mobile group**—Consists of laptops and other mobile devices that are used off the network regularly or occasionally
- **General server group**—Consists of general servers attached to the network
- **Mail server group**—Consists of mail servers attached to the network
- **Database server group**—Consists of database servers attached to the network

This arrangement gives you a good deal of flexibility. For example, you could configure mail servers and database servers to have a completely different security policy from other systems on the network. You could also configure always-connected desktops to conduct scans at night, but force laptops to scan during the day when they are on.

Client-Management Strategies

Symantec AntiVirus enables you to pursue a number of different client-management strategies, depending upon your organizational needs. In this section, we examine the four general classes of client management:

- Fully managed clients
- Sometimes-managed clients
- Lightly managed clients
- Unmanaged clients

Fully Managed Clients

Fully managed clients are systems that are always connected to the network and are capable of remaining in constant contact with the Symantec AntiVirus server. These systems retrieve updates as they become available and quickly obtain configuration changes from the primary or secondary servers.

Clients in the fully managed state check in with the server according to their configured Check-In Frequency. By default, clients are configured to check in every 60 minutes. When a client checks in with its parent server, it sends the date of its most recent definitions file along with a configuration ID. The parent server then sends any necessary updates to the antivirus client.

Sometimes-Managed Clients

Sometimes-managed clients are clients that are sometimes, but not always, connected to the network. The typical sometimes-managed client is a mobile laptop. When these clients are connected to the network, they behave in exactly the same manner as a fully managed client.

When sometimes-managed clients leave the network, they stop receiving updates from the parent server. The antivirus server tracks the client for three days. If the client doesn't return to the network during that period, the server drops the record until it again hears the client on the network.

Sometimes-managed clients can be configured to use Symantec LiveUpdate™ to retrieve definition updates from the Symantec central server. If LiveUpdate is not configured, the client continues using the update file that was last received from the parent server until it reconnects to the network and receives a new update.

Lightly Managed Clients

Lightly managed clients are unmanaged. These clients are initially configured manually using a GRC.DAT configuration file. Lightly managed clients are not managed in any other way and never receive updates from a Symantec AntiVirus server. If a configuration change must be made to a lightly managed client, administrators must generate a new GRC.DAT file and apply it manually.

Unmanaged Clients

As the name implies, unmanaged clients are under no centralized configuration control. To receive definition file updates, unmanaged clients must use LiveUpdate to contact a Symantec update server via HTTP or FTP. All configuration changes to an unmanaged client must be performed locally by the user.

Antivirus Security Policy Recommendations

When you've defined your antivirus security policy and determined an appropriate architecture for your antivirus server environment, it's time to put those policies to work. You can implement these policies at either the server group or the client group level by using the Symantec System Center.

General Recommendations

In general, Symantec recommends several best practices to ensure the efficient and effective management of your antivirus infrastructure:

- Consolidating all managed antivirus deployments underneath a single management infrastructure. This does not mean that all clients need to receive updates from the same server, but rather that all servers in an organization fall under the same management hierarchy.

- Developing standard configurations and using them throughout the organization. Very few templates should be used for antivirus deployments. The more configurations you have, the more difficult it becomes to manage and maintain them, and the more likely it becomes that maintenance tasks will be neglected.

- Using client groups to manage high-risk and sensitive systems. Two core groups require special attention: mobile users and telecommuters.

- Implementing effective antivirus policies, publicizing them throughout the organization, and enforcing them. It is impossible for an antivirus program (or any information security program) to be effective if it isn't grounded in a firmly supported and enforced policy. Get senior management support for your program, and take advantage of that support while promoting antivirus management throughout the organization.

- Training users on the antivirus program in addition to general information security principles and practices. Users cannot comply with policy if they're not aware of both their responsibilities and the appropriate procedures for complying with those responsibilities.

Virus-Mitigation Strategy

Your antivirus strategy needs to address the action that will be taken when threats or security risks are detected on a system. Symantec AntiVirus provides you with four options for handling these events:

- Clean the infected file. This attempts to remove the threat and restore the file to its uninfected state. This option is not available for security risks.

- Quarantine the file. If this action is selected, Symantec AntiVirus moves the file to the specified quarantine location.

- Delete the infected file. This action might be a bit extreme in many circumstances because it deletes the file without administrator intervention.

- Leave it alone. The incident is logged, but no further action is performed.

Symantec AntiVirus enables you to specify a primary and secondary action to take after discovery of a threat or security risk The secondary action occurs only if the primary action fails to successfully complete. A common strategy, illustrated in Figure 5-3, is to specify Clean as the primary action and Quarantine as the secondary action for viruses and other threats, and specify Quarantine as the primary action and Leave Alone as the secondary action for security risks such as adware and spyware.

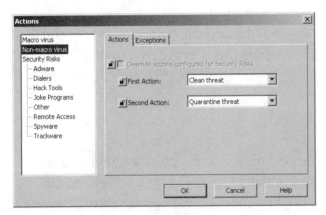

Figure 5-3 Virus-mitigation strategy.

As shown in Figure 5-4, you can also configure clients to automatically forward quarantined files to a dedicated quarantine server for further analysis.

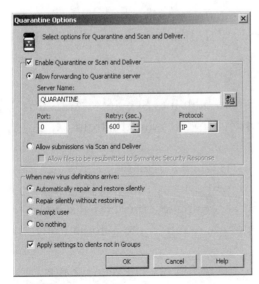

Figure 5-4 Quarantine server configuration.

Scan Frequency

You should configure scheduled scans according to your antivirus policy. As a general rule, many organizations perform a full system scan on a weekly basis for desktops and a daily basis for mobile computers. Additionally, Auto-Protect should be configured to provide real-time protection against email- and Internet-borne threats. Auto-Protect should also be enabled (it is by default) so it can continuously scan files and email data for viruses and for security risks, such as spyware and adware, as they are read from or written to a computer.

Scan Exclusions

It might be necessary to exclude certain files or directories from the scan, such as when you are configuring antivirus scanning for a server and the server contains large data files used by applications running on the server (such as a database or mail server). Scanning these files would take a long time and cause an inordinate consumption of server resources.

Distributing Definitions

You have two choices for distributing virus definitions in a managed environment: Virus Definition Transport Method (VDTM) and Symantec LiveUpdate.

LiveUpdate

LiveUpdate is the familiar update mechanism built into Symantec AntiVirus and other Symantec applications that retrieve updates directly from Symantec.

This method is a pull operation that starts when a Symantec AntiVirus client or server uses LiveUpdate to request new virus definitions. LiveUpdate can be initiated manually or automatically according to a predefined schedule. LiveUpdate recognizes what, if any, updates are required and automatically downloads and installs them.

LiveUpdate uses microdefs, which are the difference between what is currently on the computer and the current update. If the computer has an

Internet connection, the computer is automatically connected to the Symantec LiveUpdate server for new definitions.

To reduce internet bandwidth required, an internal LiveUpdate server can be set up to download all LiveUpdate virus-definitions files. You can then configure your managed servers and clients to update from the internal server, eliminating many concurrent Internet downloads.

Virus Definition Transport Method (VDTM)

VDTM is a fully automated method of downloading virus-definitions updates to all servers and clients. Only primary servers access a Symantec LiveUpdate server directly; all other computers update from the primary servers.

Use the Virus Definitions Transport Method when you want to control virus-definitions file updates from the Symantec System Center.

The use of VDTM is one of the main advantages of working in a managed environment. VDTM enables you to distribute updates throughout the antivirus hierarchy. Here's how the process works:

1. The primary server receives an updated definitions file from Symantec.

2. The primary server pushes the update to all secondary servers located in its server group.

3. The primary server pushes the update to all clients for which it is responsible.

4. Secondary servers push the update to all clients for which they are responsible.

In an emergency, it's possible to force an immediate push of new virus definitions throughout the hierarchy. For example, if a new worm is detected on your network and Symantec supplies an updated definitions file designed to eradicate that worm, you would want to force an immediate update to clean your network.

In such a situation, the process is quite simple. Right-click on the primary server; select **All Tasks**, **Symantec AntiVirus**; and force the update by selecting **Update Virus Defs Now**, as shown in Figure 5-5. This forces the primary server to download the latest definitions from Symantec's LiveUpdate servers and push them out to all secondary servers and managed clients.

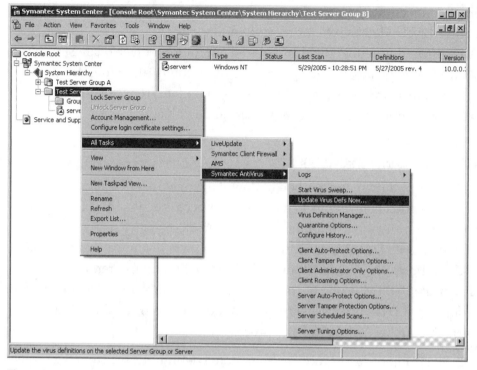

Figure 5-5 Emergency virus-definition update.

Using LiveUpdate: Advantages and Disadvantages

When considering LiveUpdate as the choice for distributing definitions files there are various factors that should be taken into account. Here is a list of some of the main advantages and disadvantages to be considered.

Advantages:

- It can be used to apply program updates.

- Connected clients can be configured to update themselves whenever an Internet connection is available.

- LiveUpdate is the only method for updating virus definitions files that is supported on 64-bit computers.

- Microdefs are used, so Internet access time is reduced.

Disadvantages:

- More configuration is required.

- External LiveUpdate requires all computers to have Internet access.

- Internal LiveUpdate servers must download more megabytes than a Symantec AntiVirus parent server would.

- A full definition download periodically must be performed.

- The full package is downloaded to every client.

- In large environments LiveUpdate generates significantly more traffic than VDTM. This is because the microdefs for LiveUpdate grow bigger in a 4-week cycle. Every fourth LiveUpdate is a full update. Then the definitions are recompiled, which makes the LiveUpdate microdefs small again. Also, every PC gets the full package; whereas, using VDTM, only primary servers get the full package, and those servers strip the packages down for their clients.

Using VDTM: Advantages and Disadvantages

As with LiveUpdate, there are factors that should be taken into account when considering VDTM for distributing definitions. Here is a list of some of the main advantages and disadvantages to be considered.

Advantages:

- The process is fully automated. It is necessary to update only one server to update all managed computers in the network.

- Minimal configuration is required.

- Client updates happen immediately following the server update.

- One mouse-click update can update an entire Symantec AntiVirus network worldwide.

- Uses microdefs to minimize network bandwidth.

Disadvantages:

- Program software updates are not downloaded.

- VDTM cannot be used to update unmanaged clients.

Best Practice: Using Both LiveUpdate and VDTM

You can use the Virus Definition Transport Method and LiveUpdate together. Using LiveUpdate allows for updates to the software components of Symantec AntiVirus. Using the Virus Definition Transport Method lets you schedule and push virus-definitions files updates from the Symantec System Center. In addition, you can use VDTM as an emergency system for distributing new virus-definitions files quickly when a new outbreak threatens the network.

Policy Deployment

Earlier in this chapter, we discussed the difference between fully managed, sometimes-managed and lightly managed clients. You might recall that the distinction among them is that fully managed and sometimes-managed clients depend upon communication with a Symantec AntiVirus server, whereas lightly managed clients do not.

When deploying policies, you have two options for transferring configuration settings. The majority of this chapter focused on automated deployment using the Symantec AntiVirus server hierarchy. If you need lightly managed clients within your organization, you can implement this arrangement by importing a GRC.DAT file from the Symantec AntiVirus server and manually placing it in the C:\Documents and Settings\All Users\Application Data\ Symantec\Symantec AntiVirus Corporate Edition\7.5 folder on the client.

Conclusion

Symantec AntiVirus provides an efficient and effective means for managing a company's antivirus policy. In this chapter, the importance of developing an effective antivirus policy was discussed. Symantec AntiVirus enables you to deploy multiple protection strategies based on the risks associated with the differing needs of a small business environment.

Chapter Review Questions

Question 5-1

Which four of the following are items Symantec recommends you consider when developing an antivirus policy? (Select four correct answers.)

❏ A. The way you communicate your antivirus policy to constituents in a clear and concise manner

❏ B. The methods you use to secure the network against malicious code

❏ C. The types of malicious code prohibited

❏ D. The tools you use to detect and log malicious code incidents

❏ E. The methods you use to train end users on the antivirus products

Question 5-2

You are the antivirus administrator for Giant Bolt Corporation. You have four major regional sites and a corporate headquarters. All locations have a large number of workstations and are connected via expensive WAN links. You are concerned with limiting bandwidth usage on the WAN links. What is the minimum number of antivirus servers you should consider? (Select the correct answer.)

○ A. One

○ B. Two

○ C. Three

○ D. Four

○ E. Five

○ F. Ten

Question 5-3

Which of the following client types receive updates automatically from a Symantec AntiVirus server? (Select two correct answers.)

❏ A. Unmanaged client

❏ B. Sometimes-managed client

❏ C. Fully managed client

❏ D. Partially managed client

❏ E. Lightly managed client

Question 5-4

In a managed environment configured to distribute virus-definitions files using VDTM, which one of the following describes the update process? (Select the correct answer.)

○ A. All clients need to be configured manually to receive updates.

○ B. All clients receive updates from the Symantec LiveUpdate server.

○ C. All clients receive updates from their parent server.

○ D. All clients receive updates from the primary server.

Question 5-5

You are the administrator in a mixed environment consisting of managed and unmanaged clients. Which of the following scenarios will keep bandwidth to a minimum and keep all clients up-to-date with virus-definitions files?

- ○ A. Configure all clients to receive updates using VDTM
- ○ B. Configure managed clients to receive updates using LiveUpdate and unmanaged clients to receive updates using VDTM
- ○ C. Configure managed clients to receive updates using VDTM and unmanaged clients to receive updates using LiveUpdate
- ○ D. Configure all clients to receive updates using LiveUpdate

Question 5-6

Which two of the following server types provide virus-definitions updates to desktop systems? (Select two correct answers.)

- ❏ A. Primary server
- ❏ D. Backup server
- ❏ B. Update server
- ❏ E. Tertiary server
- ❏ C. Secondary server

Question 5-7

You want to deploy several clients in lightly managed mode. Which file do you need to place on each client? (Select the correct answer.)

- ○ A. SYM.DAT
- ○ D. SYM.CFG
- ○ B. AV.DAT
- ○ E. AV.CFG
- ○ C. GRC.DAT
- ○ F. GRC.CFG

Question 5-8

Which of the following client types do not receive updates automatically from a Symantec AntiVirus server? (Select two correct answers.)

- ❏ A. Unmanaged client
- ❏ B. Sometimes-managed client

❑ C. Fully managed client

❑ D. Partially managed client

❑ E. Lightly managed client

Question 5-9

What is the default time interval that managed clients check in with their parent server to check for new updates?

❑ A. 10 minutes   ❑ C. 30 minutes

❑ B. 60 minutes   ❑ D. 1 minute

Chapter Review Answers

Answer 5-1

Answers **A, B, D,** and **E** are correct. Symantec recommends that you consider the way you will communicate your antivirus policy to your constituents, the methods you will use to secure the network against malicious code, the tools you will use to detect and log malicious code incidents, and the methods you will use to train end users.

Answer 5-2

Answer **E** is correct. You should have a minimum of one server per site to minimize the use of WAN links.

Answer 5-3

Answers **B** and **C** are correct. Fully managed clients are always connected to the network and check in with the antivirus server for updates on a regular basis. Sometimes-managed clients check in whenever they are connected to the network.

Answer 5-4

Answer **C** is correct. When updates are available, the primary server pushes the update to all secondary servers located in its server group and to all clients for which it is responsible. The secondary servers then push the update to all clients for which they are responsible. Clients always receive updates from their designated parent server.

Answer 5-5

Answer **C** is correct. To keep bandwidth to a minimum, all managed clients should be configured to use VDTM to receive their updates. Unmanaged clients cannot use VDTM because they are not assigned to any server group or parent server and, therefore, would need to receive updates using LiveUpdate.

Answer 5-6

Answers **A** and **C** are correct. Primary and secondary servers are both capable of providing updates to client systems.

Answer 5-7

Answer **C** is correct. The GRC.DAT file can be taken from the Symantec AntiVirus server and used to configure lightly managed clients.

Answer 5-8

Answers **A** and **E** are correct. Unmanaged clients and lightly managed clients will not receive updates from a Symantec AntiVirus server and must be configured to use LiveUpdate to retrieve updates directly from Symantec.

Answer 5-9

Answer **B** is correct. The default check-in time for client to see if there are new updates is 60 minutes, although this time can be modified by the administrator using the Symantec System Center.

PART II

SYMANTEC CLIENT SECURITY

CHAPTER 6

Symantec Client Security Installation

Terms and Techniques to Remember

- Primary server
- Secondary server
- Symantec System Center™
- Quarantine server
- Preinstallation requirements for Symantec™ Client Security
- Installation of Symantec Client Security using local, Web-based, and command-line deployment options
- Components available during Symantec System Center installation

Introduction

Symantec™ Client Security combines the antivirus management and protection capabilities of Symantec AntiVirus with the added protection of a client firewall and intrusion prevention. The firewall, intrusion prevention, and antivirus capabilities work together to defend against blended threats. The purpose of this chapter is to provide a detailed step-by-step approach to the installation of Symantec Client

Security. In addition to client-installation techniques, this chapter covers several different types of server installations. Not all server technologies will be necessary in all scenarios, but you should at least be familiar with the use of each before taking the exam.

Before Beginning

Before beginning installation, it is important to understand the various components of Symantec Client Security as well as the different types of installation that can be performed. This section is very similar to the introduction to Symantec AntiVirus™ earlier in this book, although it includes details that extend Symantec AntiVirus to include the client firewall and intrusion prevention capabilities integrated into Symantec Client Security.

The client firewall component adds stateful inspection by tracking information about current connections such as source and destination IP addresses, ports, and applications. This ensures that inbound traffic is a legitimate reply to outbound traffic. The firewall component also secures ports known to be used by Trojan horses, both inbound and outbound, never triggering firewall rulebase inspection. The client firewall also cloaks inactive ports to protect against port scans.

The intrusion prevention component adds an additional layer of security by scanning each packet that enters and exits the computer for attack signatures, arrangements of information that identify an attacker's attempt to exploit a known operating system or program vulnerability. In addition to blocking known variants of attacks, intrusion prevention checks for possible variations of attacks and blocks them as well. For example, a hacker can modify an attack by changing the information that an attack signature uses to identify the intrusion attempt. Firewalls that rely on exact signature matches do not detect this attack. Intrusion prevention blocks this type of intrusion attempt by anticipating as many conceivable variants in the attack signature as possible.

Managed and Unmanaged Clients

Symantec Client Security can be installed as a standalone client, protecting an individual computer without centralized control over protection policy options. Such stand-alone installations are referred to as *unmanaged* clients, which are not associated with a particular parent server from which their updates are acquired. Unmanaged clients can still receive regular updates to their antivirus definitions files directly through the LiveUpdate service, as long as the client's subscription has not expired.

> **Note**
> Because unmanaged clients must individually download updates from the Symantec LiveUpdate server, large numbers of these clients configured to download updates at the same time can place a heavy load on LAN connectivity.

Managed clients receive configuration and definition file updates from a designated parent server. The server obtains updates through either Symantec LiveUpdate or by use of the Intelligent Updater pushes out updates directly to other servers in the group and direct to any clients associated with it. This can improve network utilization and avoid saturating low-bandwidth WAN channels, although large numbers of managed clients might need to be distributed across multiple parent servers to balance the load further. Figure 6-1 illustrates the basic differences between these options.

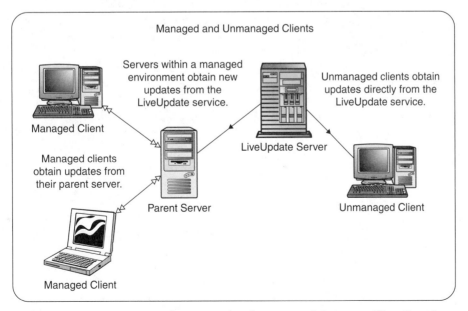

Figure 6-1 The update process for managed and unmanaged Symantec Client Security clients.

Symantec Client Security Servers

Within a managed environment, several types of server installations can be implemented. Table 6-1 details the different server roles that can be implemented within a managed Symantec Client Security scenario.

Table 6-1

Symantec Client Security Server Roles	
Role	**Purpose**
Primary server	Responsible for downloading new updates and then distributing these updates to secondary servers within the same server group, as well as to any clients that are configured with this as their parent server.
Secondary server	An optional server type that obtains updates from the primary server within its server group and distributes these updates to clients configured with the secondary server as their parent server.
Server group	Not a specific server role, but rather a logical grouping of servers in which a primary server and potentially one or more secondary servers can better manage the distribution of updates, antivirus policy settings, and firewall policy settings.
Quarantine server	An optional server type that provides a secure data store for threats that are identified by clients but for which no specific remedy has yet been developed. Clients can forward suspicious code to the Symantec Central Quarantine so that later updates can be used to attempt to clean infected files.
Parent server	Any server to which a particular managed client has been assigned. A client's parent server provides updates and policy settings. Both primary and secondary servers can be configured as the parent server for one or more antivirus clients.

Symantec Client Security Components

Symantec Client Security allows the installation of only those components that are necessary for a given host or function. These components are available within a Symantec Client Security installation:

- **Symantec AntiVirus client**—This component is installed on workstation and server hosts to scan and monitor for threats and security risks. The

Symantec Client Security a virus client is installed on workstation and server operating systems, in either a managed or unmanaged configuration, to provide protection against these threats.

- **Symantec™ Client Firewall**—This component is installed on workstations to provide firewall protection of the individual system. It provides an additional barrier against network-based attacks beyond that provided by a boundary firewall defense.

- **Symantec Client Security server**—This service supports the central management of firewall and antivirus protections within a managed Symantec Client Security environment. This service also provides protection for the hosting server and enables an authorized administrator to push out updates and settings to managed clients.

- **Symantec System Center**—This console utility allows centralized management of clients, servers, client groups, and server groups within a managed environment. The Symantec System Center provides a single unified interface for management tasks, including update and policy management as well as server and client rollout.

- **Alert Management System[2] (AMS[2]) console**—This console enables the configuration of enhanced alert options provided by AMS[2]. The Alert Management System supports notifications generated by Symantec Client Security servers and clients.

- **Symantec AntiVirus snap-in**—This is a Microsoft Management Console (MMC) snap-in used to centrally manage antivirus protection settings.

- **Symantec Client Firewall snap-in**—This is a Symantec System Center snap-in used to centrally manage firewall protection settings.

- **AV Server Rollout tool**—This utility enables the remote installation of a Symantec Client Security server to be pushed out from the Symantec System Center. This utility can also be run from the installation media for Symantec Client Security, as discussed later in this chapter.

- **ClientRemote Install tool**—This utility is responsible for pushing out the Symantec Client Security client installation to remote computers running supported Microsoft Windows operating systems. Like the AV Server Rollout tool, this utility can be run from the Symantec Client Security installation media or from within the Symantec System Center.

- **Symantec Central Quarantine**—The Central Quarantine Server and Quarantine Console are required for automatic response to heuristically detect new threats or unrecognized viruses. If cleaning or removal options become available for infected files secured within this service, Symantec Central Quarantine automatically repairs infected files submitted by Symantec Client Security clients and servers.

- **LiveUpdate administration utility**—This utility allows the setup of an internal LiveUpdate server.

Windows Server vs. Symantec Client Security Server

A Symantec Client Security server is defined by its role within the managed protection environment, not by the operating system on which it is installed. Windows Server 2000/2003 can host the Symantec Client Security server, but it might also be configured as only a Symantec Client Security client within the managed environment. When we refer to a Symantec Client Security server, this refers to a system based on its role as a computer running the Symantec Client Security server software.

Symantec Client Security Update

Antivirus-definitions files and client security updates can be updated through several means, depending on the type of operating system hosting the Symantec Client Security client. Table 6-2 details the available methods for updating virus files.

Central Quarantine uses VDB files, which are larger than XDB/IDBs. Using Central Quarantine polling can potentially use more bandwidth than other methods.

Table 6-2

Symantec Client Security Update Methods	
Update	**Description**
Virus Definition Transport Method (VDTM)	Primary servers use VDTM to push updates obtained from a LiveUpdate server to secondary servers; parent servers use it to push updates to managed clients. This method is not supported in 64-bit operating systems.
LiveUpdate	The primary server, unmanaged clients, and internal LiveUpdate servers use this method to obtain new updates from the Symantec LiveUpdate service. This is the only method supported on 64-bit operating systems.
Central Quarantine polling	This method relies on a Central Quarantine server to pull updates from the Symantec Digital Immune System Gateway. These updates are then pushed out to managed clients using VDTM, so this method is also not supported on 64-bit operating systems.
Intelligent Updater	This method relies on downloading executable files that can update antivirus definitions. The executable file is downloaded from the Symantec Security Response site and then distributed via network or removable media. This method is not supported on 64-bit operating systems.

Preinstallation

Before installing Symantec Client Security, it is important to perform a few simple preinstallation steps that are appropriate to most application installations:

1. Log in as a user with the appropriate privileges.

2. Close all open applications.

3. Ensure that mobile devices are plugged in, to prevent installation failure because of exhausted batteries.

4. Make sure that scheduled processes such as full-system virus scans or system automatic updates will not occur during the installation.

System Requirements

Before installing the various components of Symantec Client Security, it is important to ensure that all host computer systems meet the minimum requirements for the installation. The amount of memory and storage required for installation varies by component, depending on the options selected.

Time Synchronization

Because Symantec Client Security makes use of SSL encryption when transmitting settings between clients and servers, it is important to ensure that all system clocks are synchronized to that of the primary server. The threshold for this synchronization is 24 hours plus or minus that of the primary server.

Required Protocols

Symantec Client Security uses TCP and UDP for its communications. If client firewall software is already installed on target computers, it is necessary to open ports 1024–4999 (TCP) and 2967 (TCP) for both console and support operations. For remote installation, TCP ports 137, 138, and 139 must also be opened, and Server Discovery requires opening port 38293 (UDP).

Windows XP® with Service Pack 2 and later, as well as Microsoft Windows 2003® Server, include a basic firewall installed by default. To deploy Symantec Client Security to these hosts, it is necessary to manually configure all necessary ports or to simply turn off the basic firewall during installation. This can be performed by accessing the Windows Firewall MMC through **Start**, **Control Panel**, **Security Center**, **-Windows Firewall**. Here, simply select the **Off** option, as shown in Figure 6-2, and then close the console.

> **Tip**
> The Windows Firewall can also be turned off for all clients within an Active Directory using Group Policy.

Windows XP systems with Service Pack 2 or later must also be configured to allow remote software installation if configured in a workgroup rather than as members of an Active Directory domain. This can be accomplished by accessing the Local Security Policy console through **Start**, **Control Panel**, **Administrative Tools**, **Local Security Policy**. By navigating through Local Policies, Security Options, the Network Access: Sharing and Security Model for Local Accounts setting can be located (see Figure 6-3). This setting should

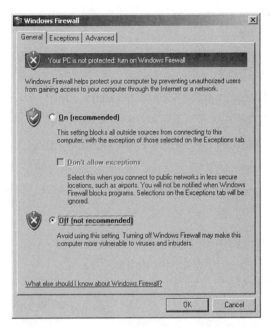

Figure 6-2 The update process for managed and unmanaged Symantec Client Security clients.

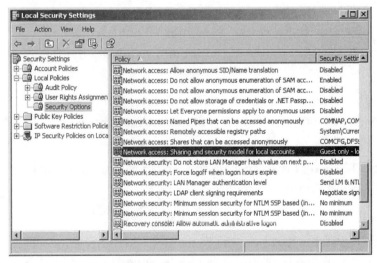

Figure 6-3 The Local Security Settings management console.

be changed from **Guest Only** (the default) to **Classic**. After this is applied, this console can be closed.

Symantec Client Security Client Requirements

Thirty-two-bit workstations that host the Symantec Client Security client component must meet the following minimum requirements for installation:

- Windows® 2000 Professional, Windows XP Home/Professional/Tablet PC
- 128 MB RAM and 115 MB of disk space available
- IE 5.5 with SP2 or later

Sixty-four-bit workstations and servers hosting the Symantec Client Security client require slightly reduced resources for Symantec Client Security client installation:

- Windows XP 64-bit Edition version 2003, Windows Server 2003 Enterprise/Datacenter 64-bit
- 80 MB RAM and 55 MB of disk space available
- IE 5.5 with SP2 or later

Symantec Client Security Server Requirements

Microsoft Windows systems that host the Symantec Client Security server component must meet the following minimum requirements for installation:

- Windows 2000 Professional/Server/Advanced Server, Windows XP Professional, Windows Server 2003 Web/Standard/Enterprise/ Datacenter
- 64 MB RAM and 140 MB of disk space available (15 MB of additional drive space required if AMS^2 is installed)
- IE 5.5 with SP2 or later

Novell® NetWare® systems that host the Symantec Client Security server component must meet the following minimum requirements for installation:

- NetWare 5.1 with SP 3 or higher, NetWare 6.0 with SP 1 or higher, NetWare 6.5

- 15 MB RAM available
- 116 MB of disk space available (70 MB for server files, 46 MB for client disk images, 20 MB of additional disk space required if AMS2 is installed)
- 15 MB of additional drive space required if AMS^2 is installed

Central Quarantine Server Requirements

Microsoft Windows systems that host the Central Quarantine Server service must meet the following minimum requirements for installation:

- Windows 2000 Professional/Server/Advanced Server, Windows XP Professional, Windows Server 2003 Web/Standard/Enterprise/Datacenter
- 128 MB RAM
- 40 MB of disk space available for the quarantine server service (500 MB or more disk space minimum recommended to store quarantined items)
- 250 MB minimum swap file
- IE 5.5 with SP2 or later

> **Tip**
> If you are running the Central Quarantine Server service on Windows XP systems, the System Restore option can increase disk space and throughput utilization.

Symantec System Center and Snap-In Requirements

The Symantec System Center and the Symantec MMC snap-ins require the following minimum requirements:

- Windows 2000 Professional/Server/Advanced Server, Windows XP Professional, Windows Server 2003 Web/Standard/Enterprise/Datacenter
- 64 MB RAM
- 36 MB of disk space available for the Symantec System Center (snap-ins can be individually selected and require additional space for each)
- 6 MB of disk space for the Symantec AntiVirus snap-in (if selected)

- 1 MB of disk space for the Symantec Client Firewall snap-in (if selected)
- 35 MB of disk space for the Quarantine Console snap-in (if selected)
- 24 MB of disk space for the AMS_2 snap-in (if selected)
- 130 MB of disk space for the AV Server Rollout tool
- 2 MB of disk space for the ClientRemote Install tool
- Microsoft Management Console (MMC) version 1.2 or later (if not already installed, 10 MB of disk space is necessary to install MMC)
- IE 5.5 with SP2 or later

Installation Methods

Symantec Client Security uses Microsoft Windows Installer (.msi) technology for installation and deployment of its various components. Packages can be deployed in several different ways:

- Local installation using the installation media
- Remote installation using the Rollout tools provided on the installation media
- Symantec System Center, to roll out client and server installations
- Web-based installation
- Network-based logon scripts
- Third-party deployments (such as Microsoft Systems Management Server, Tivoli, or ZenWorks)
- The Symantec Packager deployment tool

Caveats to SSC Client Rollout

The Symantec System Center cannot be used to roll out client installations on Windows server operating systems running any of the following services:

- Terminal Server
- Fast Switching
- Remote Assistance
- Remote Desktop

Administrative Rights

To install Symantec Client Security, the account used must have administrative rights to the computer or the Windows domain of which the computer is a member. These rights can be directly assigned to the account, inherited through its group membership, or assigned using Windows Group Policy settings. For Novell NetWare installations, the account used must be an administrator or supervisor.

File sharing must also be enabled on computers that will host a Symantec Client Security server installation. The installation package makes use of administrative shares (such as c$ and admin$) during installation; these might need to be enabled if the domain or local Group Policy settings have been configured to disable standard administrative shares.

Installation

Symantec Client Security can be installed in a managed or unmanaged configuration, and the Symantec Client Security management components can be installed as needed on either Symantec servers or Symantec client systems that meet the minimum necessary requirements for installation. Installation can be performed using the source media for local or remote installations, or across the network using Web-based or network file-sharing deployment methods. We explore each of these alternatives throughout the rest of this chapter. Although you are provided with clear step-by-step walkthroughs of each installation procedure, you are encouraged to perform various types of installation on a test network, if at all possible.

Local Installation

The most basic form of installation relies on the source media, which must be transported to the target system or shared on a LAN in a manner that allows direct access from the target computer. This scenario is typically not used beyond small workgroup settings, but it can still be used in remote locations, when creating deployment system images, or when necessary because of other considerations. Within the example network detailed in Chapter 3,

"Symantec AntiVirus Installation," we will configure a Windows XP worksta-tion (WS6) as an unmanaged Symantec Client Security client and the Windows 2003 Server (Server1) as a Symantec Client Security server using the local installation methods.

Local Client Installation

To install Symantec Client Security locally, the administrator should insert the installation medium into the CD-ROM drive. If auto-play is enabled, the welcome screen (shown in Figure 6-4) will appear; otherwise, you should navigate to the proper drive and select **SETUP** from the root folder.

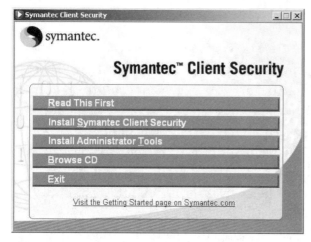

Figure 6-4 The Symantec Client Security welcome screen.

From this location, the user can choose to install Symantec Client Security or the Administrator Tools alone, to browse the installation media's contents, or to exit and abort the installation. Follow these steps to start an installation.

 1. Selecting the option to **Install Symantec Client Security** begins the installation process, displaying the installation options screen shown in Figure 6-5.

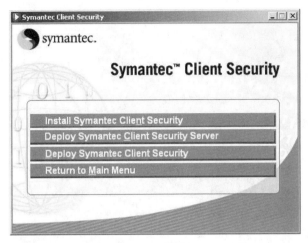

Figure 6-5 The Symantec Client Security installation
options screen.

> **Note**
> The Deploy options will be used later when performing remote rollouts to
> nonlocal installations.

2. Click the **Install Symantec Client Security** button to advance to the
   InstallShield Wizard screen, followed by the licensing agreement
   screen. Clicking the **Next** button for each enables the administrator
   to select the type of installation to be performed (client or server), as
   shown in Figure 6-6.

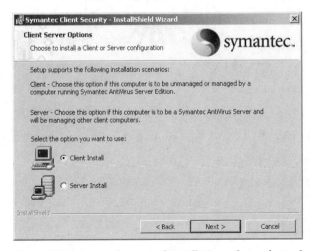

Figure 6-6 Selecting the type of installation to be performed.

3. The administrator can select a client installation and then click the
Next button to select a complete or custom installation. The complete
installation installs all normal components of the Symantec Client
Security client, whereas the Custom installation option allows more
granular selection of individual components (see Figure 6-7).

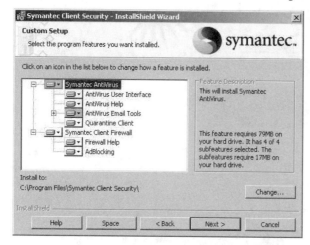

Figure 6-7 Selecting components for a custom installation.

4. After selecting a complete or custom installation and then pressing
the **Next** button, the administrator is prompted to select a managed or
unmanaged client installation, as shown in Figure 6-8. Here, an
unmanaged client is being installed.

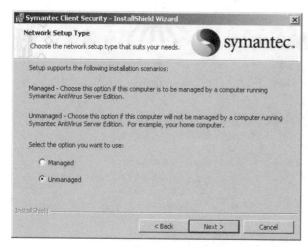

Figure 6-8 Selecting the client type for installation.

5. In the following screen, the administrator is prompted to select configuration options for the client, including whether to enable Auto-Protect or whether the client should immediately run LiveUpdate following installation. After selecting the desired options and advancing to the next screen, the option to install the client initiates the Symantec Client Security client-installation process. Depending on system resources and speed, this process can take several minutes to complete; a progress bar is displayed during this time (see Figure 6-9).

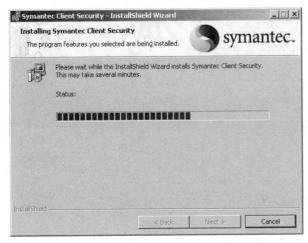

Figure 6-9 Installation showing progress during the setup process.

6. When installation has completed, the administrator is prompted to finish the installation process. If the client computer is connected to the Internet and LiveUpdate was selected to execute following installation, the LiveUpdate screen is displayed (see Figure 6-10).

7. After the administrator clicks **Next**, the client contacts the LiveUpdate service and begins to install any available updates. When this is complete, selecting **Finish** concludes the installation process.

The Symantec Client Security AntiVirus user interface can now be accessed by **Start**, **All Programs**, **Symantec Client Security**, **Symantec AntiVirus** (see Figure 6-11). Here you can see that no parent server is present, identifying this as an unmanaged client.

Figure 6-10 Initial LiveUpdate of the new unmanaged client.

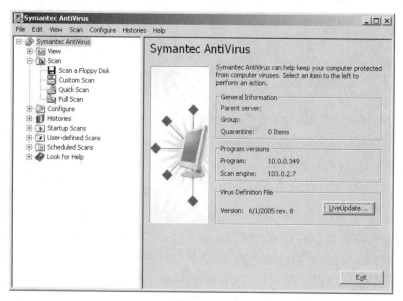

Figure 6-11 Administering the unmanaged Symantec Client Security AntiVirus client settings.

The Symantec Client Firewall local user interface can be accessed through **Start**, **All Programs**, **Symantec Client Security**, **Symantec Client Firewall** (see Figure 6-12). The following chapters detail how to configure these clients to provide the best protection.

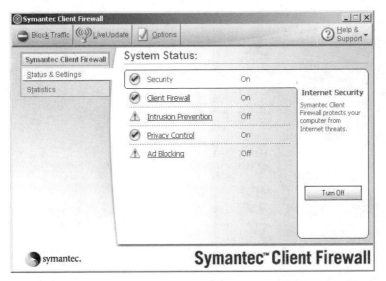

Figure 6-12 Administering the unmanaged Symantec Client Security
client firewall.

Local Server Installation

During a local Symantec Client Security server installation, steps 1 through 3
are the same as those just taken, except that a server installation is selected
in step 2.

1. After selecting a complete or custom installation and then pressing
   the **Next** button, the administrator is prompted to provide a name and
   password for the new server group that will have the new server as its
   initial member (shown in Figure 6-13). Here, the group has been
   named SCS Group A.

2. After selecting **Next**, the administrator is prompted to verify the password once more. Then the installation process continues by asking for
   client-configuration options, as in step 5 of the client installation
   process. Because the Symantec Client Security server also includes
   antivirus and firewall protections for its host computer, the installation process continues exactly as before.

After installation, the server's local user interface can be accessed by
following the same paths as those used to access the client-management
consoles. Figure 6-14 provides an example of the Symantec Client Security

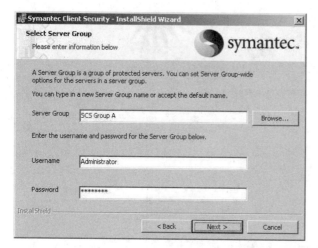

Figure 6-13 Creating the new Symantec Client Security server group.

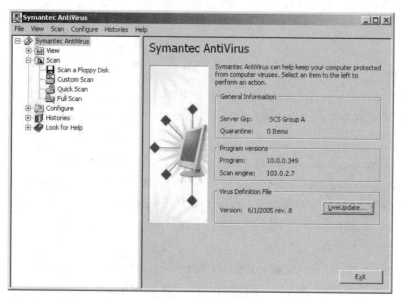

Figure 6-14 Managing the server's local protection settings.

AntiVirus local user interface showing that this server belongs to the SCS Group A server group.

Local Symantec System Center Installation

To effectively configure the new managed environment, we will now install the Symantec System Center. In this demonstration, the administrative console is installed to a separate server (Server2) within the example network. This is done only to show that the console can be used on other servers to configure the managed environment as well; the Symantec System Center could also be installed on Server1 just as easily.

1. Selecting the option **Install Administrative Tools** at the initial setup screen brings up the option Install Symantec System Center. Selecting this option begins the process of installation, as before navigating through an introductory InstallShield screen and license agreement before presenting the component-selection screen, shown in Figure 6-15.

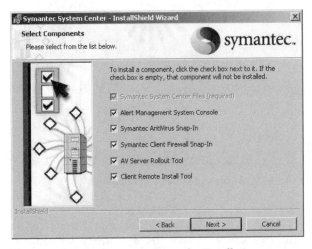

Figure 6-15 Selecting components for installation.

2. After selecting all components desired and selecting the **Next** button, the administrator is prompted for an installation location (C:\Program Files\Symantec\Symantec System Center\ by default). After specifying a new location or accepting the default location, the administrator should confirm the installation to begin installing all selected components. A reboot is required after this process has completed.

The Symantec System Center console can be accessed through **Start**, **Programs**, **Symantec System Center Console**, **Symantec System Center Console**. When first opened, the console displays icons for the various components selected during installation, as shown in Figure 6-16. Had some

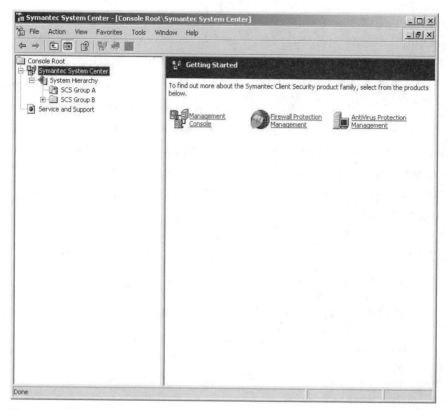

Figure 6-16 The Symantec System Center console showing available component snap-ins.

of the available snap-in components been deselected, those options would not be present here.

The newly created server group (SCS Group A) is displayed with a small lock icon, which illustrates that the group is currently locked. Right clicking on the server group and selecting **Unlock Server Group** causes a prompt to appear in which the user name and password provided during setup should be entered.

Before using the Symantec System Center to configure the managed environment, it is necessary to configure the first server as the primary server for the new server group. By right-clicking SERVER1, the drop-down menu provides the option **Make Server a Primary Server.** Selecting this option configures SERVER1 as the primary server for the test server group. You can then use the Symantec System Center to perform remote installation tasks in the next portion of this chapter.

Local Symantec Client Firewall Administrator Installation

To create custom policies for the firewall component, the Symantec Client Firewall Administrator (see Figure 6-17) should be installed on a system also configured with the Symantec Client Firewall. This facilitates the easy importing of policies created in the Symantec Client Firewall.

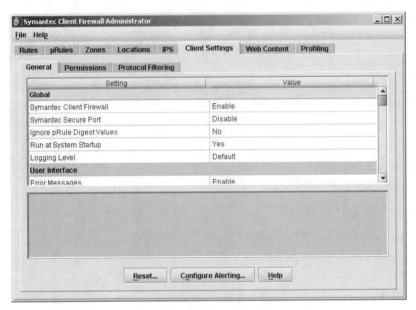

Figure 6-17 The Symantec Client Firewall Administrator.

Selecting the option **Install Administrative Tools** at the initial setup screen brings up the option Install Symantec Client Firewall Administrator. Selecting this option begins the process of installation, as before navigating through an introductory InstallShield screen and license agreement, and allowing selection of the target folder for the installation.

An option to place an icon for the new console on the desktop is provided before beginning the installation process itself. This is a relatively short process that includes the automatic installation of the Java Runtime Environment (JRE) required by Symantec Client Firewall Administrator. After installation, the desktop icon can be used to open the console, or it can be accessed through **Start**, **Programs**, **Symantec Client Security**, **Symantec Client Firewall**

Administrator. This console will be used extensively in Chapter 8, "Symantec Client Security Policies," to create custom client firewall policies.

Remote Installation

To support larger networks, Symantec Client Security includes a number of remote installation options. The installation media can be used to deploy remote Symantec Client Security client and server installations. This functionality is also included within the Symantec System Center, if selected, and allows easy deployment to multiple clients or servers from this convenient interface. Client installation can also be performed using network file sharing and Web-based distribution points. The .msi installation package can also be distributed via Group Policy, or through SMS or another third-party tool used for package distribution. Command-line installations can also be used to specify options during scripted installation.

Deploying Symantec Client Security Client

By selecting the option **Deploy Symantec Client Security** from the Install Symantec Client Security screen from the original medium's welcome screen, it is possible to begin a remote installation. Here, the Symantec Client Security client will be installed onto a remote Windows XP workstation (WS1) and a remote Windows 2003 Server (Server2), using the installation files found on Server1.

1. After initiating the remote installation process, the administrator is prompted for a source location where the client installation files can be found (see Figure 6-18). By default, this is the clt-install directory within the VPHOME network share created during server installation, although an alternate location can be provided at this time, if desired.

2. After specifying a source location and selecting **Next**, the administrator is prompted to select one or more clients to be targeted for client installation and to select the server that will be assigned as the parent server for the newly installed clients. In Figure 6-19, you can see the Windows XP workstation (WS1) selected for Symantec Client Security client installation. Server 1, the primary server for the first server

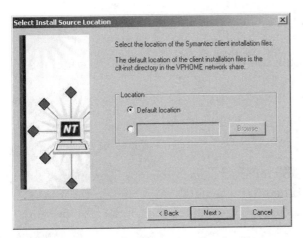

Figure 6-18 Selecting the source location for client-installation files.

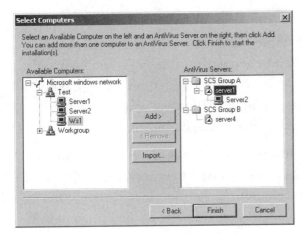

Figure 6-19 Selecting client-installation targets and a parent server.

group, has been selected as the parent server for the new clients installed on WS1 and Server2.

3. When one or more clients and a parent server have been highlighted, selecting the **Add** button adds the target computers to the list for client installation. If a listing of IP addresses for target installation has been created as a .txt file, the **Import** button can be used to select this file to mass-configure a large number of systems at one time.

4. After adding and importing all clients for installation, selecting **Next** begins the client-installation process for each client. When this is completed, the administrator can click the Done button to conclude the process.

Remote Client Installation
Remote client installation can also be initiated from within the Symantec System Center by selecting **Tools, ClientRemote Install** from the header. The process of remote client installation here is identical to that of deploying from the source media.

Remotely Deploying Symantec Client Security Server

By selecting the option **Deploy Symantec Client Security Server** from the original medium's installation screen, it is possible to begin a remote installation of the Symantec Client Security server on a targeted remote computer. Here, the server will be installed onto a remote Windows 2003 Server (Sever3), joining the server group currently managed by Server1 alone.

1. After initiating the remote installation process, the administrator is prompted to identify whether this will be a new server installation or an update of an existing installation. The option **Install** should be selected here. After selecting **Next** and agreeing to the licensing statement, the administrator is prompted to select the components to be installed to the remote server, as shown in Figure 6-20.

2. After selecting **Next**, the administrator is prompted to add the computer(s) that will be targeted for server installation (see Figure 6-21). As with the client installation, one or more servers can be manually added here, or a preprepared listing of target IP addresses can be imported to speed the addition of multiple computers.

3. After selecting **Next** again, the administrator is given the opportunity to change the installation directory that will be used for the server application's installation on the targeted systems. Following this, the

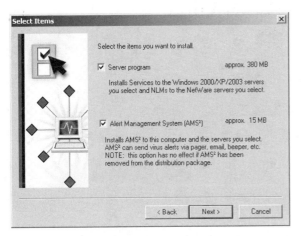

Figure 6-20 Components selected for remote server installation.

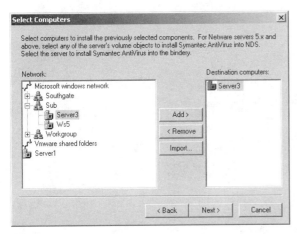

Figure 6-21 Server3 added to the list of computers targeted for installation.

administrator can elect to create a new server group or to join an existing one (see Figure 6-22). Here, the new server will be a member of the SCS Group A, which is currently hosted only by Server1.

4. After entering the desired server group and selecting **Next**, the administrator is prompted for the user name and password that was created during the original server's installation into this server group. The

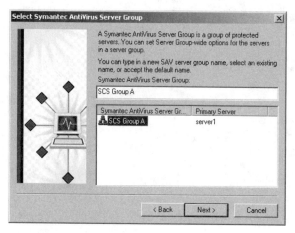

Figure 6-22 Selecting the desired server group.

administrator then navigates through several informational screens before initiating the remote server installation, shown in Figure 6-23.

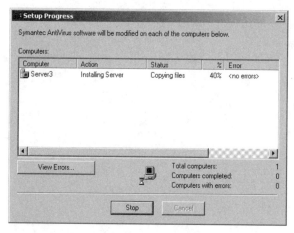

Figure 6-23 An in-process remote Symantec Client Security server installation on Server3.

5. When the installation process is finished, the administrator is reminded to restart the new server to complete the Symantec Client Security server's installation. If any errors occur during installation, the View Errors option can be used to obtain additional details needed to correct them.

Remote Server Installation

Remote server installation can also be initiated from within the Symantec System Center by selecting **Tools, AV Server Rollout** from the header. The step-by-step process of remote Symantec Client Security server installation initiated within the Symantec Client Security console is identical to that used when deploying from the source media.

Remote Network Client Deployment

During the installation of a Symantec Client Security server, a file share named VPHOME is created, containing the files necessary for network installation. In the next example, the Symantec Client Security client will be remotely installed onto a remote Windows XP workstation (WS2), using the installation files found on Server1 and shared within \\Server1\VPHOME\CLT-INST\WIN32\.

After logon to the client system using an account with local or domain administrative authority over the client, this process can be initiated by opening the Windows Explorer (double-clicking the My Computer icon opens this interface) and navigating to the shared folder location. In Figure 6-24, you can see the results of accessing the file share \\Server1\VPHOME\CLT-INST\WIN32\.

Selecting the **Setup.exe** file within this share initiates the Symantec Client Security client installation on the local computer. This installation is identical to the step-by-step client installation detailed earlier in this chapter, with the single exception that no option is available to install an unmanaged

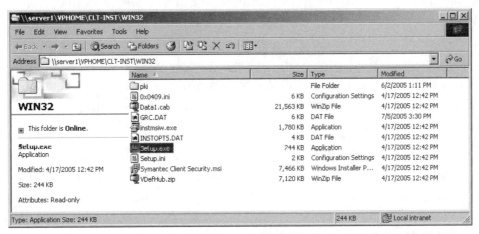

Figure 6-24 Windows Explorer showing the contents of the remote installation directory.

client. The newly installed client is automatically configured as a managed client to use the installation-source server as its parent.

During Symantec Client Security server installation, an additional set of files is created for use in Web distribution of the Symantec Client Security client. These files are located within the VPHOME file share as well and can be accessed within the example network by the path \\Server1\VPHOME\ CLT-INST\WEBINST\. This WEBINST folder can be shared as a virtual directory within an IIS Web site on the host server, or these files can be copied to another Web server altogether for use in Web-based installation of the managed Symantec Client Security client.

The Example Web Site

For this example, we have copied the Web files to Server2 to demonstrate that the Web host can be a different system. Server2 has a CNAME (alias) within the DNS database, allowing webserver.local to refer to the same IP address as server2.test.local. Remember that Server2 is not itself a Symantec Client Security server; it is merely a Web server to which the Web installation files have been copied.

The files used in the previous demonstration of file share installation (located in \\Server1\VPHOME\CLT-INST\WIN32\ in the example network) must then be copied into the newly created \WEBINST\webinst\ folder on the Web server. The Start.htm file should be modified to specify the proper ServerName and VirtualHomeDirectory values to match your new Web site, and then the installation package files should be added to the \webinst\file.ini configuration file. When this process is complete, remote Symantec Client Security client installation can be initiated using the new Web site.

1. After logging on to the client system using an account with local or domain administrative authority over the client, open Internet Explorer and navigate to the target Web server's URL. Figure 6-25 illustrates the Web installation welcome screen, located at `http://webserver.local/ WEBINST/` within the example network.

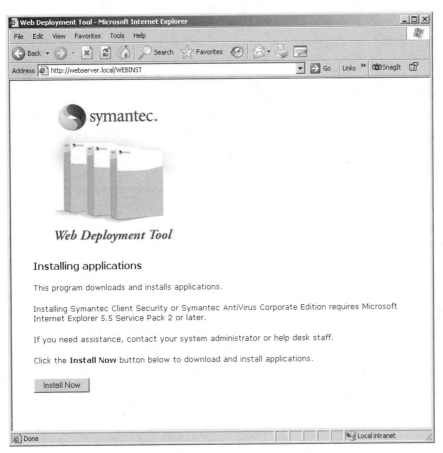

Figure 6-25 The Web-based Symantec Client Security client installation welcome screen.

2. Selecting the **Install Now** button initiates installation of a managed instance of the Symantec AntiVirus client on the local computer. The parent server associated with this new installation is the server that provided the files copied to the Web site. Because the Web-based installation uses a Microsoft Active-X component, it is necessary to accept the installation of this control on Windows XP systems with Service Pack 2 and later.

3. After the Active-X component has been installed, the installation files are downloaded from the Web server. When the download completes,

installation begins and proceeds as in previous demonstrations of the client-installation process.

Logon Script Symantec Client Security Client Installation

During the installation of a Symantec Client Security server, the files necessary for client logon script installation are created. This process within Symantec Client Security is identical to that presented within Chapter 3, "Symantec AntiVirus Installation."

Configuring Installer (.msi) Options

Symantec Client Security uses the Microsoft Windows Installer (.msi) to perform client and server installations, regardless of the mechanism by which the package is transferred to the installation target computer. It is possible to modify the settings used during installation by configuring available options, as in logon scripted installations. Although these options are similar to those available during Symantec AntiVirus installation, Symantec Client Security includes additional entries. Table 6-3 lists several options that can be used when configuring the command-line installation parameters for an installation of Symantec Client Security.

When performing an installation, a number of properties can be specified to configure the installation process for a specific environment. Table 6-4 lists many of the available properties for Symantec Client Security installation.

When performing a Symantec Client Security installation on a client, several properties can be specified to configure the installation process to interact with the Windows® Security Center (WSC) running on Windows XP systems with Service Pack 2 or later. Table 6-5 lists the properties for WSC configuration.

Because the firewall component installed is more robust than the basic firewall installed by Windows XP in Service Pack 2, Symantec Client Security includes options for installation to configure the process to interact with the Windows Firewall running on Windows XP systems with Service Pack 2. Table 6-6 lists the properties for Windows Firewall configuration.

Table 6-3

Windows Installer Command-Line Options

Element	Description
Msiexec	This specifies that the Windows Installer executable be used for installation.
Symantec Client Security.msi	This specifies that the Symantec Client Security installation file should be used.
/i *<filename>*	This command-line option specifies an installation using *<filename>*.
/x	This command-line option specifies an uninstallation (removal).
/qn	This option specifies to silently install, without providing an interface for user interaction with the installation process.
/qb	This option allows user interaction with the installation process, as in the logon script example.
/l*v *<filename>*	This option specifies that a verbose log be created as the specified filename.
INSTALLDIR=*<path>*	This specifies the installation directory on the target computer where files will be installed.
REBOOT=*<value>*	This specifies whether the computer should reboot after installation. *<value>* can be one of the following: Force, Suppress, or ReallySuppress.
ADDLOCAL=*<feature>*	This option allows custom features to be installed by specifying the feature or a list of features for installation. To install all custom features, this can be specified as ADDLOCAL=ALL.
REMOVE=*<feature>*	This option allows custom removal of installed programs or features, without requiring a complete uninstallation, as with the **/x** option. The ALL keyword can also be used here to represent removal of all optional features.

When values include spaces, enclose the value using quotation marks.

Example Command-Line Installation

An example command-line configuration for a silent managed Symantec Client Security client with Auto-Protect enabled, using Server1 as its parent server, all optional features installed, and configured to perform LiveUpdate but not to reboot after installation, would look like this:

```
msiexec /i "Symantec Client Security.msi" INSTALLSERVER=0
NETWORKTYPE=1 SERVERNAME=Server1 ADDLOCAL=ALL
ENABLEAUTOPROTECT=1 RUNLIVEUPDATE=1 REBOOT=Suppress /qn
```

Table 6-4

Symantec Client Security Properties

Property	Description
INSTALLSERVER=*<value>*	A *<value>* of 1 indicates a server installation, whereas a *<value>* of 0 indicates a client installation. The default value is 0.
ENABLEAUTOPROTECT=*<value>*	Determines whether Symantec AntiVirus Auto-Protect is automatically enabled after installation. A *<value>* of 1 enables Auto-Protect; any other integer value disables Auto-Protect. The default is to enable Auto-Protect.
RUNLIVEUPDATE=*<value>*	Specifies whether LiveUpdate will be automatically performed after installation. A *<value>* of 1 enables LiveUpdate; 0 disables automatic LiveUpdate. LiveUpdate is enabled by default.
MIGRATESETTINGS=*<value>*	Specifies whether to automatically install firewall policy file settings from cpolicy.xml if the file is included in the distribution package. A *<value>* of 0 installs the settings if the file exists; 1 disables automatic setup using this file.
NETWORKTYPE=*<value>*	Allows the specification of a management state. A *<value>* of 1 indicates a managed client installation, 2 indicates an unmanaged client installation (the default), and 4 indicates a server installation.
SERVERNAME=*<server>*	Used in client installations to specify the parent server a managed client will join.
SERVERGROUPNAME=*<group>*	Used in server installations to specify the server group the new server will join.
SERVERGROUPLOGON=*<name>*	Used in server installations to specify the logon used when joining the new server to its server group.
SERVERGROUPASS=*<password>*	Used in server installations to specify the password used when joining the new server to its server group.
SERVERPARENT=*<server>*	Used in server installations to specify the primary server name for the server group the new server will join.

When entries include spaces, enclose the value using quotation marks.

Table 6-5

Windows Security Center (WSC) Properties

Property	Description
WSCCONTROL=<value>	A <value> of 0 (the default) indicates that the installation should not control the WSC. A <value> of 1 disables the WSC only the first time it is detected, whereas 2 disables the WSC always. Specifying a value of 3 allows the WSC to be restored if currently disabled.
WSCAVALERT=<value>	Used to configure antivirus alerts for the WSC. A <value> of 0 enables WSC alerts, 1 disables WSC antivirus alerts (the default), and 2 is used to specify no control over WSC antivirus alerts.
WSCFWALERT=<value>	Used to configure firewall alerts for the WSC. A <value> of 0 enables WSC alerts, 1 disables WSC firewall alerts (the default), and 2 is used to specify no control over WSC firewall alerts.
WSCAVUPTODATE=<value>	Used to configure the WSC out-of-date period for antivirus definitions. <value> specifies the number of days before antivirus definitions are considered out-of-date (default is 30).

When entries include spaces, enclose the value using quotation marks.

Table 6-6

Windows Firewall Configuration Properties

Property	Description
ICFCONTROL=<value>	A <value> of 0 (the default) indicates that the installation should not control the Windows Firewall. A <value> of 1 disables the Windows Firewall only the first time it is detected, whereas 2 disables it always. Specifying a value of 3 allows the Windows Firewall to be restored if currently disabled.
ICFDISABLENOTIFY=<value>	Used in configure the Windows Firewall notification message. A <value> of 0 does not disable the notification, whereas a value of 1 (the default) disables the notification message.

When entries include spaces, enclose the value using quotation marks.

Conclusion

Symantec Client Security extends the power of Symantec AntiVirus by including the additional security of a client firewall and intrusion prevention. The firewall, intrusion prevention, and antivirus capabilities work together to defend against blended threats. Like Symantec AntiVirus, Symantec Client Security includes many different options for client and configurations, including unmanaged as well as managed options to meet the needs of many different organizational configurations. Server and client groups can be used to manage multiple systems with common configuration settings, with a single server configured as the primary server within this environment (see Figure 6-26).

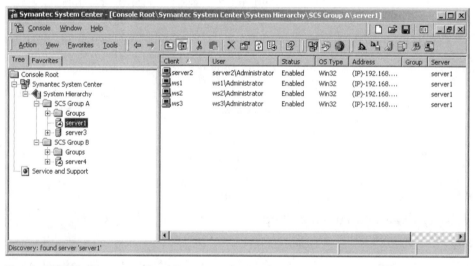

Figure 6-26 The Symantec Client Security managed environment we have created during this chapter. Note that Server2 is a Symantec Client Security client and not a Symantec Client Security server, even though it is a computer running the Windows 2003 Server operating system. As with Symantec AntiVirus, the term *server* within a Symantec Client Security environment reflects the role a system is performing rather than the type of operating system within which it resides.

By allowing managed clients to obtain updates from their designated parent server, administrators can alleviate the WAN network bandwidth consumption that would be required to allow large numbers of unmanaged clients to obtain updates directly from Symantec individually.

Chapter Review Questions

Question 6-1

Which of the following components would be installed by this command-line installation?

```
msiexec /i "Symantec Client Security.msi" INSTALLSERVER=0
NETWORKTYPE=2 ADDLOCAL=ALL REBOOT=Suppress /qn
```

Select the best two answers from those provided.

❑ A. Primary server ❑ D. Firewall client

❑ B. Secondary server ❑ E. Server Rollout tool

❑ C. AntiVirus client

Question 6-2

A primary server's system clock is currently set to 12:01 p.m., December 31, 2005. Of the following system clocks, which one is outside of the maximum threshold for time synchronization within a Symantec Client Security managed environment? Select the best answer from those provided.

○ A. 12:00 p.m., December 30, 2005

○ B. 11:59 a.m., December 31, 2005

○ C. 11:59 p.m., December 31, 2005

○ D. 12:00 a.m., January 1, 2006

○ E. 12:00 p.m., January 1, 2006

○ F. 11:59 a.m. January 1, 2006

Question 6-3

Which of the following ports is required for Server Discovery within a Symantec Client Security managed network environment? Select the best answer from those provided.

○ A. 137 ○ D. 1024

○ B. 138 ○ E. 2967

○ C. 139 ○ F. 38,293

Question 6-4

Which one of the following local security policies must be altered to support remote Symantec Client Security client installation on Windows XP systems with SP2 installed? Select the best answer from those provided.

   ◯ A. Network Access: Remotely Accessible Registry Paths

   ◯ B. Network Access: Shares That Can Be Accessed Anonymously

   ◯ C. Network Access: Sharing and Security Model for Local Accounts

   ◯ D. Network Security: LAN Manager Authentication Level

Question 6-5

You have the following computers available to install Symantec Client Security server:

- ServerA: Windows NT4.0 SP6a, 128 MB RAM, 200 MB HDD space, IE 5.0

- ServerB: Windows 2000 Enterprise, 256 MB RAM, 150 MB HDD space, IE 5.0

- ServerC: Windows 2003 Standard, 256 MB RAM, 100 GB HDD space, IE 6.0

- ServerD: Windows 2003 Datacenter, 2 GB RAM, 100 MB HDD space, IE 6.0

- WorkstationA: Windows XP Home, SP2, 96 MB RAM, 100 GB HDD space, IE 6.0

How many systems could accept a Symantec Client Security server installation? Select the best answer from those provided.

   ◯ A. 1   ◯ D. 4

   ◯ B. 2   ◯ E. 5

   ◯ C. 3

Question 6-6

Which of the following administrative components requires the most available disk space for installation? Select the best answer from those provided.

○ A. Symantec Client Firewall snap-in

○ B. Symantec AntiVirus snap-in

○ C. Symantec System Center

○ D. AV Server Rollout tool

○ E. ClientRemote Install tool

Question 6-7

Which of the following command-line options would be used to enable Windows Security Center alerts when antivirus definitions are too old? Select the best option from those provided.

○ A. WSCONTROL

○ B. WSCALERT

○ C. WSCFWALERT

○ D. WSCAVUPTODATE

Question 6-8

Which value is appropriate for the NETWORKTYPE command-line option if you want to configure a command-line Symantec Client Security unmanaged client installation? Select the best answer from those provided.

○ A. 0

○ B. 1

○ C. 2

○ D. 3

○ E. 4

Chapter Review Answers

Answer 6-1

Answers **C** and **D** are correct. The Symantec Client Security antivirus client and the Symantec Client Security firewall client would be installed during a Symantec Client Security client installation (defined by the INSTALLSERVER=0 and NETWORKTYPE=2 options).

Answer 6-2

Answer **A** is correct. Only the first server's system clock is outside of the range of 24 hours +- the primary server's system clock, currently set to 12:01 p.m., December 31, 2005.

Answer 6-3

Answer **F** is correct. Port 38,293 (UDP) is required for Server Discovery within a Symantec Client Security managed network environment. TCP ports 137, 183, and 139 are required for remote installation, and TCP port 2967 is required for console and server operations, along with TCP ports 1024–4999.

Answer 6-4

Answer **C** is correct. The Network Access: Sharing and Security Model for Local Accounts local security policy must be changed from the default Guest Only value to Classic, to support remote Symantec Client Security client installation on Windows XP systems with SP2 installed.

Answer 6-5

Answer **A** is correct. Only ServerC meets the minimum requirements for Symantec Client Security server installation. ServerA and ServerB do not meet the necessary IE 5.5 SP2 browser requirement, and ServerA is also running a legacy operating system not supported by Symantec Client Security. ServerD lacks the necessary hard drive storage space available for installation, and

WorkstationA is running the unsupported Windows XP Home operating system.

Answer 6-6

Answer **D** is correct. The AV Server Rollout tool requires the most available space (130 MB) for installation of the listed administrative components. The Symantec System Center requires 36 MB, whereas all other listed options require less than 10 MB each. Only the Symantec AntiVirus snap-in requires more than 5 MB (at 6 MB).

Answer 6-7

Answer **D** is correct. The WSCAVUPTODATE command-line option would be used to manipulate when Windows Security Center considers antivirus definitions to be out-of-date.

Answer 6-8

Answer **C** is correct. NETWORKTYPE=2 specifies the installation of a Symantec Client Security unmanaged client installation. A value of 1 indicates a managed client, whereas a value of 4 specifies a server installation. The values 0 and 3 are not used with this option.

CHAPTER 7

Symantec Client Security Management

Terms and Techniques to Remember

- Symantec user account
- Firewall policy
- Lock and unlock server groups
- Manage Symantec System Center™ user accounts
- Deploy firewall policies using the Symantec System Center

Introduction

By using the centralized policy management of Symantec™ Client Security, you can manage clients and servers that are assigned to logical groups. The Symantec System Center enables the centralized distribution of Client Firewall and Intrusion Prevention policies. This chapter provides you with information on the management functions necessary to standardize and customize these policies to meet the differing needs of the small business environment and provide maximum protection.

Symantec System Center

As discussed in earlier chapters, Symantec Client Security relies on the Symantec System Center management console, shown in Figure 7-1. This component is built utilizing the Microsoft Management Console (MMC) standard and includes support for plug-ins allowing management of Symantec Client Security, along with other Symantec-managed products.

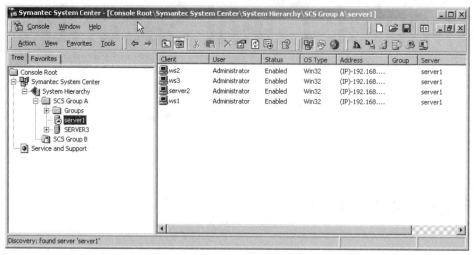

Figure 7-1 The Symantec System Center console.

The Symantec System Center can be used to configure server and client groups, initiate virus scans, configure antivirus policies, update virus definitions, and respond to identified threats. In addition, it can be used to update client firewall policies, review firewall exceptions, and manage firewall event logs. The Symantec™ Client Firewall Administrator is used to create new firewall policies to be deployed by the Symantec System Center; is examined briefly in this chapter. A detailed review of the firewall policy creation process follows in Chapter 8, "Symantec Client Security Policies."

Server and Client Groups

Within the Symantec System Center, server groups are configured just below the System Hierarchy node and contain one or more Symantec Client Security servers. Server group members can share a single Symantec Client Security configuration, and enable you to run Symantec Client Security operations on all members of the server group. Within Figure 7-1, two server groups can be seen:

- **SCS Group A**—This server group consists of two Symantec Client Security servers (Server1 and Server3).

- **SCS Group B**—This server group resides on a single stand-alone server (Server4).

An additional Groups node is present within each server group. This is used to configure client groups, logical groupings of Symantec Client Security clients that share a common set of configuration settings. Although client groups are always attached to a server group, each client group can be managed individually. Each client group can be configured with different policies from its peers within the same server group, allowing different settings to be applied to clients assigned to the same parent server.

Symantec Client Security clients are categorized as follows:

- Assigned clients are Symantec clients that have been assigned to a client group. They receive virus and security risk definitions files from the server to which they are physically attached, but receive configuration settings and updates based upon the client group to which the Symantec Client Security policies are applied.

- Unassigned clients are Symantec clients that have not been assigned to a client group. They receive configuration settings and updates from their parent management server.

Mixing Assignment Within a Single Parent Server
It is possible to have a mixture of assigned and unassigned clients within the same parent server, but this is not considered a best practice for implementation. The best practice when using client groups is to assign all clients to client groups to ensure a consistent application of settings.

When you manage using client groups, clients assigned to a group receive their configuration from their group, rather than their parent management server. Configuration changes made at the server group level or system hierarchy level have priority over client group settings, however, overriding any settings made at the client group level. To change this default priority, you can configure client groups to use their own settings instead of inheriting settings from their server group. You do this within the Symantec System Center by right-clicking the client group and unchecking **'Inherit settings from Server Group.'**

Locking and Unlocking Server Groups

Each server group can be individually unlocked within the Symantec System Center. Figure 7-1 above illustrates the difference between the unlocked SCS Group A and the locked SCS Group B.

Unlocking a Server Group

A server group can be unlocked by right-clicking on the target server group within the Symantec System Center console and then selecting **Unlock Server Group** from the options provided in the context menu pop-up. The administrator is prompted to enter a valid Symantec Client Security user name and password with the necessary permissions to access the designated server group, as shown in Figure 7-2.

Figure 7-2 Prompt for user name and password to unlock SCS Group B.

When unlocked, the servers and all other items within the target server group become navigable within the Symantec System Center console, and all settings applied at the system hierarchy level also are applied within the unlocked server group.

Locking a Server Group

To lock a server group, right-click the unlocked server group within the console and then select **Lock Server Group** from the options provided in the drop-down list. Server groups are automatically locked by default each time you start the Symantec System Center, unless you configure to automatically unlock the server group when you start the Symantec System Center. Figure 7-3 shows the Unlock Server Group dialog box with the options to remember the user name and password, and to perform automatic unlock when the Symantec System Center is started. User names and passwords are not saved unless you explicitly configure this option.

Figure 7-3 The Unlock Server Group dialog configured to remember user name and password and to automatically unlock the group when the Symantec System Center starts.

New Server Groups

The Symantec System Center can be used to create new server groups, allowing an administrator to reconfigure the Symantec Client Security architecture to meet changing business requirements.

A new server group can be created by right-clicking on the System Hierarchy node and selecting **New**, **Server Group** from the options provided. Figure 7-4 illustrates the New Server Group creation dialog box, being used to create a new server group SCS Group X-Ray. Note that an initial administration username (here, MyAdmin) and password for this server group are also required.

Deleting a server group requires that all servers first be moved to another server group. Right-clicking on the empty group now provides the option to

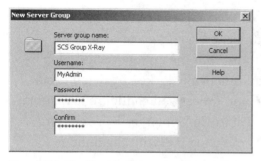

Figure 7-4 The New Server Group dialog box.

delete this group. The primary server for a server group can also be changed here by right-clicking on the new primary server and selecting the option **Make Server a Primary Server**.

Managing Symantec Client Security User Accounts

Symantec Client Security allows administrative control over each server group by creating an initial administration user name/password combination as each server group is created. This user name/password combination represents an account within the Symantec Client Security server group and is not related to a Windows® logon account or to the accounts used in other Symantec Client Security server groups.

The Configure Server Group Accounts dialog (see Figure 7-5) can be accessed by right-clicking the desired server group and selecting **Account Management** from the options provided. Existing Symantec Client Security accounts are displayed, along with the role for each account. Accounts can be added, deleted, or updated here.

> **Note**
> The capability to have multiple accounts for a server group is a change from earlier versions of Symantec Client Security. This new functionality makes it possible to have both administrative and read-only accounts within the same server group.

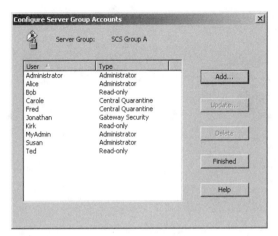

Figure 7-5 Configure Server Group Accounts for SCS Group A.

Using Symantec System Center

Within a managed Symantec Client Security environment, the Symantec System Center is used to configure common settings that will be applied to server or client groups and all servers and clients within those groups. AntiVirus configuration options available within the Symantec System Center can be accessed by right-clicking on the desired node and then selecting **All Tasks, Symantec AntiVirus**. Options for Symantec Client Firewall management are accessible through **All Tasks, Symantec Client Firewall**. The same method can be applied to the System Hierarchy node, individual server group nodes, individual servers, client groups, or registered clients using the Symantec System Center. Configuration settings applied at a higher level override those specified at lower levels.

AntiVirus

Selecting options within the provided AntiVirus listing has the same result as discussed in detail within Chapter 4, "Symantec AntiVirus Management." If the Client Auto-Protect Options are selected for example, Auto-Protect options can be configured as desired. When Auto-Protect is enabled and configured at the parent server, the Auto-Protect feature is automatically

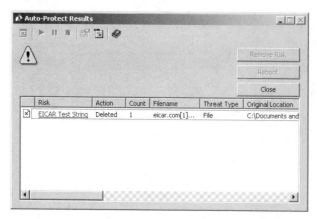

Figure 7-6 Auto-Protect message that the Eicar standard
test file has been found.

updated on the managed clients. If a threat or security risk is found, a user
on the infected host will see a notice similar to that shown in Figure 7-6.

Eicar Test file
The file used to test the proper functionality of Symantec Client Security's
antivirus protection can be obtained from www.eicar.org. This test file is not
an actual virus; it is merely identified by the antivirus client to validate its
operation. Never test the functionality of your defenses by releasing a live
virus into the enterprise.

As with Symantec AntiVirus, Symantec Client Security provides event
logs of antivirus activity within the managed environment, along with histories of virus scans and sweeps. By selecting the desired history of a group,
the administrator can audit the history of Symantec Client Security antivirus
operations on all systems within the container. In addition to antivirus logs,
Symantec Client Security includes a number of firewall log options that can
be used to review configuration changes, firewall violations, and intrusion-
detection events. Violations of configured firewall policies can also generate a
notice on the client system, allowing the user to respond where appropriate,
as shown in Figure 7-7.

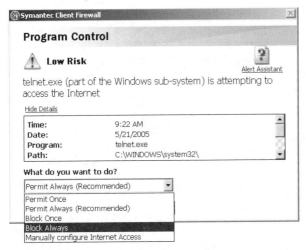

Figure 7-7 Selecting a response to a detected potential firewall violation.

Other Configuration Tasks

Additional tasks can be accessed by right-clicking System Hierarchy, selecting **All Tasks**, and then selecting either **Symantec Client Firewall** or **Symantec AntiVirus**. From here, firewall policies and virus definitions can be updated, or a virus sweep can be started on a server or server groups.

Client Management

By configuring servers within server groups, a collection of settings can be applied to specific servers and their clients within the network. Client systems can also be assigned to client groups to gain even greater control over the settings that are applied to smaller groups.

Client Groups

A new client group can be created by right-clicking the Groups node and selecting **New Client Group**. As shown in Figure 7-8, the administrator is prompted to provide a name for the new client group and to select an existing client group as a template, if desired. Using an existing configured group as a template allows rapid configuration of the settings for a new client group based on those of an existing already-configured group.

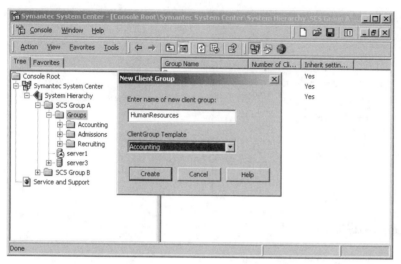

Figure 7-8 Adding a new client group (HumanResources) using the Accounting client group as a template.

Adding clients to a client group can be accomplished by selecting the target clients and then dragging them onto the desired target client group. The parent server setting remains the same for each client. If **Show Client Machines When Viewing Client Groups** is selected from **Tools**, **SSC Console Options**, the membership of a client group can be viewed within the Symantec System Center by expanding the desired server group and then the client group.

The Symantec System Center allows an administrator to rapidly identify the status of all client showing online or offline status, and systems pending in-process group assignment. In addition, the Symantec System Center details the last time each was scanned for viruses, the version of the antivirus definitions currently in use by each client, the parent server of each, the client's most recent IP address registered for each client, the last time the client checked in, whether the firewall is enabled, and a wealth of other data that can be used to sort the listing of managed clients for review.

Client Migration

As demonstrated previously, the parent server and client group assignments for managed clients can be changed with simple drag-and-drop procedures. It is also possible to change the parent server configuration of a managed client by placing a copy of the new parent server's Grc.dat file within the configuration folder on a managed client. By default, this is as follows:

```
C:\Documents and Settings\All Users\Application Data\Symantec\
Symantec AntiVirus Corporate Edition\7.5
```

The client automatically reconfigures itself to use the new server as its parent, as defined by this line within the Grc.dat file:

```
Parent=S<server name>
```

Changing Client-Management State

As with Symantec AntiVirus, the same process detailed for client migration can be used to change an unmanaged client into a managed client. Simply place the Grc.dat file in the proper location on the unmanaged client, and the Symantec client will associate the specified parent server with the now-managed client. The process to change a managed client into an unmanaged client requires the same steps as required with Symantec AntiVirus:

1. Uninstall Symantec Client Security from the client.
2. Deleted the Registry subkey: HKLM\Software\Intel\LANDesk\ VirusProtect6.
3. Reinstall Symantec Client Security as an unmanaged client.

Client Scans

Antivirus scanning remains the same as with Symantec AntiVirus, whether performed as a manual or a scheduled host scan, or as a full virus sweep. This should be performed only during low-utilization hours, to minimize the network and system impact this can have, and should be reserved for use during a virus outbreak. The options available for virus sweeps and scheduled scans with Symantec Client Security are the same as those detailed in Chapter 4: "Symantec AntiVirus Management."

Firewall Policies

Firewall polices are configured using the Symantec Client Firewall Administrator, which is installed separately from the Symantec System Center. The administration console provides a tabbed interface where individual settings can be configured, as shown in Figure 7-9.

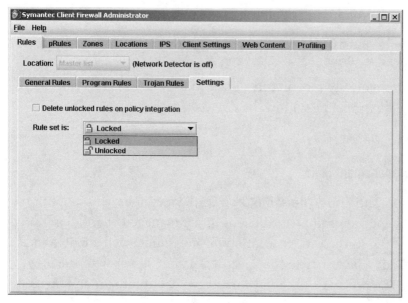

Figure 7-9 Symantec Client Firewall Administrator.

Symantec Client Firewall policies are sets of configured firewall rules and settings to govern firewall operation. Policy management lets you do the following:

- Customize Symantec Client Firewall to better accommodate your organization's needs.

- Configure Symantec Client Security clients differently for different groups, departments, or users in your organization.

- Configure Symantec Client Security clients differently, depending on client location and network connection information, by using one policy file.

- Update firewall rules to accommodate changing conditions on your corporate intranet and threats on the Internet.

Individual settings can be configured for handling general connectivity, application rules, and Trojan horse responses (see Figure 7-10). Configuring these settings is covered in detail in the next chapter.

When a policy has been completed within the Symantec Client Firewall Administrator, it is saved to an accessible location and then deployed using the Symantec System Center console. Policy deployment begins by right-clicking on the desired server or client group and selecting **All Tasks, Symantec Client Firewall, Update Client Policy Now**, as shown in Figure 7-11.

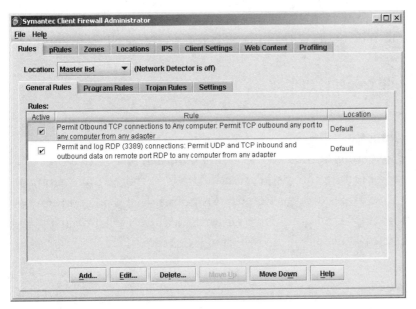

Figure 7-10 Symantec Client Firewall Administrator showing configured general network rules.

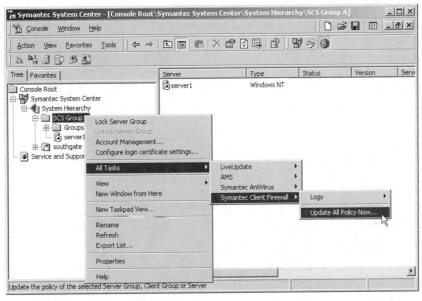

Figure 7-11 Deploying Symantec Client Firewall policy.

The administrator can then browse to the newly created policy file and select it for application to the clients within the targeted server or client group.

Removal of Symantec Client Security

If it is necessary to remove Symantec Client Security from a computer, this is achieved by initiating the setup process using the installation media or network source, and selecting to remove the installation. An alternative that does not require remounting the installation media is to follow **Start**, **Control Panel**, **Administrative Tools**, **Add or Remove Programs**. Removal can then be initiated by highlighting Symantec Client Security within the list of installed programs and selecting to remove the program (see Figure 7-12).

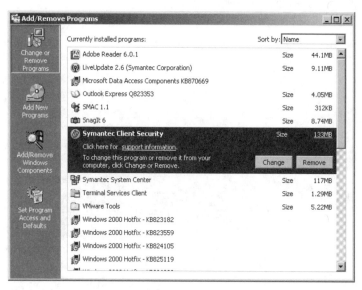

Figure 7-12 Removing Symantec Client Security.

To safeguard against users uninstalling Symantec Client Security and leaving the computer vulnerable the uninstall will ask for a password before removal, shown in Figure 7-13. After the removal request is verified, Symantec Client Security is removed from the Computer. The password that is required to uninstall Symantec Client Security can be changed using the Symantec System Center by selecting the server, server group, or client group, and then clicking **All Tasks**, **Symantec AntiVirus**, **Client Administrator Only Options**. The password option can be found on the Security tab.

Figure 7-13 Password required to uninstall Symantec Client Security.

In this example, the Symantec System Center and Symantec Client Firewall Administrator could also be individually removed in the same manner, if desired. To remove the Registry settings left behind by Symantec Client Security, it is necessary to delete the Registry subkey: HKLM\Software\Intel\LANDesk\VirusProtect6.

Conclusion

In this chapter you learned how to use Symantec System Center to manage a Symantec Client Security infrastructure providing firewall and IPS protection on networked computers in a small business environment. The centralized capabilities provide extensive administrative functionality enabling the configuration of multiple firewall policies, reporting and alerting functions. This centralized management is critical in providing a complete and secure solution, allowing you to deploy and monitor firewall protection and intrusion prevention appropriate to the security needs of the specific environment.

Chapter Review Questions

Question 7-1

Which of the follow statements are not true regarding client group assignment? Select the best two answers from those provided.

> ❑ A. All clients of a parent server must be assigned if client groups are implemented.

❑ B. Clients can be assigned to only a single parent server.

❑ C. Clients can be assigned to only a single client group.

❑ D. A client group contains assigned clients from a single parent server only.

Question 7-2

You want to configure a new server group to be named Laptops, which will contain a single Symantec AntiVirus server that is currently a member of the Workstations Server Group. Which of the following steps are required to create and configure the new server group using the minimum amount of administrative time and effort? Select the best two answers from those provided.

❑ A. Reload the existing server, specifying Laptops as the new server group to which it is assigned.

❑ B. Remove the existing server from Workstations. Use the installation media to perform a repair installation specifying the Laptops server group.

❑ C. Drag and drop the existing server from Workstations into Laptops.

❑ D. Create the new server group using the Symantec Client Firewall Administrator.

❑ E. Create the new server group using the Symantec System Center.

Question 7-3

Which of the following is not a valid Symantec Client Security user account type? Select the best answer from those provided.

○ A. Administrator

○ B. Power user

○ C. Read-only

○ D. Central Quarantine

○ E. Gateway Security

Question 7-4

You have a managed client parented to a Symantec AntiVirus server that was removed from service. You need to migrate the managed client to a new

Symantec AntiVirus parent server. Which of the following options would perform this process using the least amount of administrative effort? Select the best option from those provided.

○ A. Perform a repair client installation using the installation media, and select the new parent server when prompted.

○ B. Place the Grc.dat file from the old server in C:\Documents and Settings\All Users\Application Data\Symantec\Symantec AntiVirus Corporate Edition\7.5.

○ C. Drag and drop the client to the new server within the Symantec System Center.

○ D. Place the Grc.dat file from the new server in C:\Documents and Settings\All Users\Application Data\Symantec\Symantec AntiVirus Corporate Edition\7.5.

○ E. Delete the Registry subkey: HKLM\Software\Intel\LANDesk\VirusProtect6.

Question 7-5

Which of the following is not a valid option when configuring scheduled scans using the Symantec System Center? Select the best answer from those provided.

○ A. Hourly

○ B. Daily

○ C. Weekly

○ D. Monthly

○ E. Advanced

Question 7-6

When using client groups, what is the default order of priority for configuration changes? Select the best answer from those provided.

○ A. Changes made at the server group level take priority over client group settings

○ B. Changes made at the server level take priority over client group settings

○ C. Changes made at the client group level take priority over server group settings

○ D. Changes made at the client group level take priority over system hierarchy settings

Chapter Review Answers

Answer 7-1

Answers **A** and **D** are correct. Clients of a parent server can be mixed (assigned and unassigned), although this is not considered a best practice. Likewise, client groups can include a mixture of clients of one or more Symantec AntiVirus parent servers. Clients can be associated with only a single parent server and can be assigned to only a single client group.

Answer 7-2

Answers **C** and **E** are correct. To create and configure a new server group using the minimum amount of administrative time and effort, it is only necessary to create the new server group using the Symantec System Center and then to drag and drop an existing server into the new group. This server would then be configured as the primary server for the new server group. This avoids having to reconfigure the server's associated clients, as would be required if the server were reloaded.

Answer 7-3

Answer **B** is correct. Of the options provided, only the power user account type is not available for Symantec Client Security user accounts. Power user is a Windows account type, and Symantec Client Security user accounts are not associated with Microsoft Windows logon accounts.

Answer 7-4

Answer **D** is correct. The easiest way to migrate an existing managed client to a new parent server is to place the Grc.dat file from the new server in the

C:\Documents and Settings\All Users\Application Data\Symantec\Symantec AntiVirus Corporate Edition\7.5 folder on the client system. This can be scripted if it becomes necessary to migrate a large number of clients in this manner. If the original Symantec AntiVirus server was still available, migration could also be performed by drag-and-drop within the SSC, but without the original server, this option is not available here.

Answer 7-5

Answer **A** is correct. When configuring scheduled antivirus scans using the Symantec System Center, schedules can be configured to operate daily, weekly, monthly, or using Advanced settings. There is no hourly option, requiring the use of Advanced scheduling or multiple separate scheduled scans to scan more often than daily.

Answer 7-6

Answer **A** is correct. By default configuration changes made at the server group level or system hierarchy level have priority over client group settings, although this priority can be changed by unchecking '**Inherit settings from Server Group'** on the client group in the Symantec System Center.

CHAPTER 8

Symantec Client Security Policies

Terms and Techniques to Remember

- Client Firewall policy
- Client Firewall updates
- Rules
- pRules
- Zones
- Intrusion-prevention system
- IPS signatures
- Protocol filtering

Introduction

Symantec™ Client Security is an integral part of the Symantec desktop security solution. It provides protection from threats and security risks, repair of viral and security risk side effects, and firewall and intrusion prevention for workstations. Chapter 5, "Symantec AntiVirus Policies," explored the policies specific to the antivirus component of Symantec Client Security. This chapter focuses on those that are specific to the Client Firewall functionality.

Symantec Client Security Overview

Symantec Client Security provides firewall protection and other security services to the desktop. It runs on individual workstations and can be either configured locally or centrally managed throughout a company.

Client firewall policies enable you to do the following:

- Customize the Symantec™ Client Firewall to better accommodate your organization's needs

- Customize Symantec Client Security clients differently for different groups, departments, or users in your organization

- Configure Symantec Client Security clients differently, depending on client location and network connection information, by using one policy file

- Update firewall rules to accommodate changing conditions on your corporate intranet and threats on the Internet

Symantec Client Firewall policies are saved in two different formats. Client Firewall policy (.cfp) files contain the complete configuration information for a policy, including firewall rules and intrusion-prevention signatures. Client Firewall update (.cfu) files contain updates to the firewall rules and pRules that are to be added to an already-configured Symantec Client Firewall.

Both of these file formats are compressed to minimize the use of network bandwidth and disk space. You can also store these files in an uncompressed format using the eXtensible Markup Language (XML), which stores files with an .xml extension.

> **Note**
> Client Firewall policy (.cfp) files that are saved to XML format (.xml) do not contain Intrusion-Prevention signatures. However, Client Firewall update (.cfu) files can be saved to XML without the loss of any data.

Options

Using firewall policies enables you to flexibly configure Symantec Client Security to meet the needs of your organization. You can configure firewall policies using the Symantec Client Firewall Administrator and then deploy those policies to various clients throughout the company.

Symantec Client Firewall policies include a number of configurable components:

- The *Rules* component regulates the traffic that is allowed to traverse the client firewall. Symantec Client Security uses three types of rules. General rules apply to all TCP, UDP, and ICMP traffic passing through the firewall. Program rules are specific to individual applications. Trojan rules seek out the activity characteristic of malicious code. For example, the Accounting Department might be limited to the use of only one application for Internet access, while all other installed applications may access only the corporate intranet.

- The *pRules* component consists of potential rules. Useful in environments consisting of mixed-use systems, pRules enable you to specify the types of activity that are allowed, but in a suspended state. A pRule becomes a program rule only when the end user invokes the associated program on the client system for the first time. Suppose that certain members of the Accounting Department use a client/ server application that connects on a particular UDP port. All members of the department might be *authorized* to use the software, but they don't all use it. A pRule that applies to the entire department would enable you to convey this authorization without opening a port on the firewall of nonusers.

- The *pRule Settings* component enables you to customize the application of pRules to specific client locations. For example, mobile users might have one set of pRules available to them when connected to the corporate network, and a more restrictive set available when they're connected to a less secure home or hotel network.

- The *Zones* component enables you to classify systems into logical groups of trust. Computers placed into the Trusted Zone have unrestricted access to the protected system, and their traffic is not analyzed by the Symantec Client Firewall. Conversely, systems placed into the Restricted Zone are completely blocked and can gain no access to the client system, despite any rules that might exist. For example, you might place all systems within the Accounting Department into the Trusted Zone, while completely blocking all other systems from accessing them through the Restricted Zone.

Note

Trusted Zones should be used with care. If a system listed in a Trusted Zone is compromised, its traffic will not be analyzed or blocked by any IPS signatures or firewall rules.

- *Locations* are collections of rules, pRules, zones, and firewall settings. Locations are especially useful for organizations with mobile users who need to be subject to one firewall configuration when in the office on a protected network, and to a more stringent policy when on the road and connected to untrusted networks.

- The *IPS* componant can be used to configure the IPS signatures that apply to a specific firewall policy and to the systems subject to scrutiny by the intrusion-prevention system. IPS signatures define the behaviors characteristic of malicious network activity. The Symantec Client Firewall intrusion-prevention system (IPS) uses these signatures to recognize activity that might require a response and/or a notification to the system administrator.

- *Client Settings* allow you to enable or disable various firewall components for use in a specific policy. You can configure a number of subcategories of client settings, which include the following:

  - *Permissions* determines the authority of the system user to configure firewall settings, modify firewall policies, and view the logs of firewall activity.

- *General* contains groups of configuration settings that control overall operation of Symantec Client Firewall, and include whether to automatically generate rules, security levels for various Internet communications, configuring alerts, and any ports or IP addresses that will be blocked or filtered on the client. You can use these configuration settings for all Symantec Client Firewall clients when you roll out a policy package, or for certain groups of clients so that different client groups are configured differently.

- *Protocol Filtering* configures how the Symantec Client Firewall handles protocols other than TCP, UDP, and ICMP.

Note
It's significant to note that Protocol Filtering is a new feature of the Symantec Client Firewall. Earlier versions permitted traffic from less common protocols without any filtering.

- *Alert Customization* enables you to select the types of alerts, notifications, and messages that the firewall will generate, including the capability to customize the messages generated to system events.

- *Privacy Control* provides enhanced protection to Web browsers. You can configure Privacy Control to prevent users from entering information into insecure sites, block Web servers from retrieving information on user activity from the browser, block cookies, and permit communication using the secure HTTPS protocol.

- *Ad Blocking* modifies Web pages viewed in the browser to prevent the retrieval and display of advertisements.

- *Web Content* settings enable you to create global settings for how the firewall handles privacy issues, animated images, scripts, and

Flash content. You can also configure these settings for individual sites and customize the sites affected by the Symantec Client Firewall ad-blocking functionality.

- *Profiling* settings enable you to generate rules based upon detected network activity using firewall profile event files.

Configuration

You should now have a basic understanding of the types of customizations that you can make using Symantec Client Firewall policies. The remainder of this chapter is devoted to describing the process used for creating policies and updates.

Creating Firewall Policies and Updates

As you learned earlier in this chapter, the Symantec Client Firewall Administrator can be used to create complete Client Firewall policies (.cfp files) or Client Firewall updates (.cfu files) consisting only of rule updates. Regardless of whether you're creating or updating a firewall policy, when you first open Symantec Client Firewall Administrator, you'll see an empty screen, similar to the one shown in Figure 8-1.

At this point, you have several options to choose your starting point. From the File menu, you can choose to do the following:

- Create a **New Policy** from a blank template.
- Create a **New Update** from a blank template.
- **Open** an existing Client Firewall Policy, Client Firewall Update, or XML file.

- **Import** settings from a client firewall policy. If you choose this option, you will be able to select the specific settings that you would like to import using the dialog box shown in Figure 8-2.
- Import the settings from the active instance of the Symantec Client Firewall, using the **Import from Active Client** option.

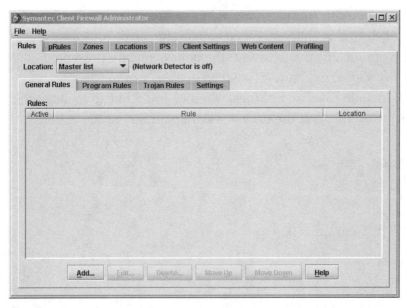

Figure 8-1 Symantec Client Firewall Administrator.

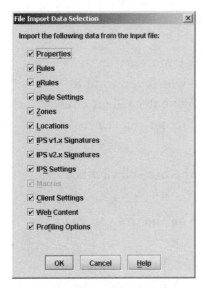

Figure 8-2 File Import Data Selection
dialog box.

From this point, you can configure the policy or update using the techniques described in this chapter. When you are finished, you can use the **Save** option from the File menu to save the policy. You are presented with the dialog box shown in Figure 8-3, which enables you to specify whether you will include rules and pRules, whether you'd like to include IPS signatures in the saved file, and the backward compatibility of the export.

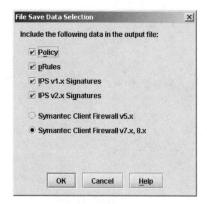

Figure 8-3 File Save Data Selection dialog box.

Distributing Policies

Policies can be distributed using the Symantec System Center by selecting the server group, client group, or parent server to which you want to distribute the policy file, then select **All Tasks > Symantec Client Firewall**, and then do one of the following depending on whether you selected a server group, client group or parent server.

- Select **Update All Policy Now** to update all the firewall clients in the server group.

- Select **Update Client Policy Now** to update all the firewall clients in the client group.

- Select **Update Client Policy Now** to update all the firewall clients that are managed by the parent server, but are not assigned to a client group.

Location Awareness and Zones

Locations and zones facilitate the administration of the Symantec Client Firewall in multiple complex environments. Instead of manually reconfiguring the firewall, locations allow clients to store multiple configurations and easily switch between them to meet the security needs of the current network environment. For example, in a mobile environment, clients might have one firewall policy when operating over a wired Ethernet connection in an office behind a hardware firewall device, and another, more stringent policy when connected to the Internet via an untrusted connection (such as a home office, hotel network, or other public Internet connectivity source).

Zones, on the other hand, enable you to organize computers on your network and the Internet into two Zones: Trusted and Restricted. The firewall permits all traffic to and from computers that are listed in the Trusted Zone and blocks all traffic to and from computers that are listed in the Restricted Zone.

Firewall policies on location are configured using the Locations tab within the Symantec Client Firewall Administrator, and zones are configured through the Zones tab. We first explore the configuration of locations and then examine the use of zones to simplify administration.

Location Settings

Figure 8-4 shows the Settings subtab within the Locations tab. Notice that there are three check box settings along with a NetSpec priority list. The check boxes have the following functionality:

- The first setting, **Enable Network Detector**, enables location awareness. If this box is not checked, the Symantec Client Firewall location functionality is disabled. This box should be checked if you intend to support different policies for users in different locations on the network.

- The second setting, **Allow user to create locations**, allows users with appropriate privilege settings to create and manage their own locations based upon the Default Location configuration.

■ The final setting, **Delete unlocked locations on policy integration**, deletes any user-created locations when the policy is installed. This is a significant setting when deploying a new policy to existing clients, enabling you to override user-configured settings with your policy.

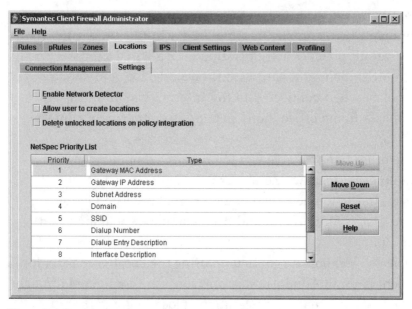

Figure 8-4 Location settings.

Symantec NetSpec technology enables you to flexibly define locations. Instead of binding policy to an IP address or physical interface, Symantec Client Security enables you to designate locations based upon the following criteria (listed in default priority order from highest reliability to lowest reliability):

■ **Gateway MAC address**—Uses the hardware address (Machine Address Code) of the network gateway's interface. This is typically considered the most reliable indicator of a system's identity.

■ **Gateway IP address**—Uses the software address (Internet Protocol address) of the network's gateway interface.

■ **Subnet address**—Uses the local network of the address assigned to the client interface to determine location.

■ **Domain**—Uses the connection-specific domain information to determine the client's location.

> **Note**
> It is important to recognize that the domain information used in a NetSpec comes from the Domain Name System (DNS). The use of the term *domain* in this case should not be confused with Microsoft's Active Directory domain.

- **SSID**—Uses the service set identifier (SSID) of wireless network to determine the client's location. The SSID is typically referred to as the "name" of the wireless network.
- **Dial-up number**—Uses the telephone number used to establish a dial-up connection to determine the client's location.
- **Dial-up entry description**—Uses the description of the remote access point for a dial-up connection to establish the client's location.
- **Interface description**—Uses the description of the network interface to determine the client's location.
- **Interface type**—Uses the type of the network interface (such as Ethernet or PPP) to identify the client's location.
- **Interface index**—Uses the hexadecimal index assigned to an interface to determine the client's current location.
- **SAV parent server**—Uses the identity of the Symantec AntiVirus™ management server stored in the client's Registry to determine location.

The Location Settings subtab enables you to adjust the priority of each characteristic by using the **Move Up** and **Move Down** buttons. You can also use the **Reset** button to restore the priority to the default order.

The Connection Management tab enables you to create and manage locations and connections. You can create a new location by clicking the Add Location button. This results in the dialog box shown in Figure 8-5.

After giving the location a name, you can identify the specific settings that apply to each location. The configurable settings include the following:

- **Rule Exception Handling** determines how the firewall reacts to traffic not covered by a rule or pRule. The **Prompt** setting asks the user whether the traffic should be allowed. The **Block** setting

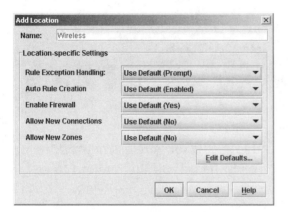

Figure 8-5 Adding a new location.

automatically drops the traffic, and the **Permit** setting automatically permits the traffic without further analysis.

- **Auto Rule Creation**, when enabled, creates a new program rule when activity matches a pRule but does not match any firewall rules. When disabled, new rules are not automatically created from pRules.

- **Enable Firewall** requires that the firewall be enabled in this location. When this setting is disabled, the firewall stays in its present state.

> **Note**
> If the client firewall is enabled and the user changes to a location where the Enable Firewall setting is set to No (disabled), the firewall will remain active.

- **Allow New Connections**, when enabled, allows users to create and clear connections for the present location.

- **Allow New Zones**, when enabled, allows users to add and delete zones for the present location.

> **Note**
> Users can modify and delete only zones and locations that they create. A user cannot modify or delete administrator-created zones and locations.

You can also use the firewall policy to modify the default location settings. Modifications made to the default settings apply to any new locations created by users, provided that users are permitted to create locations. When modifying the default location, you can work with the same settings as when modifying a specific location, with the exception of the **Allow New Connections** setting. This is not available because it is not possible to add a connection to the default location. This is also important because when Location Awareness is disabled, the default Location settings are the ones that are enforced by the firewall.

Connections

Locations can be viewed as general descriptions of a connectivity source and the places where policies are applied. Connections are the specific manifestations of locations and are defined by NetSpecs. Each connection is defined by a single NetSpec, and each connection belongs to a single location. Locations, on the other hand, can be associated with multiple connections.

The **Add Connection** dialog box, which is used to create a new connection, is shown in Figure 8-6.

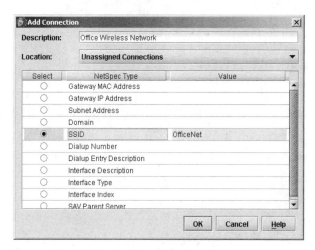

Figure 8-6 Add Connection dialog box.

The process of adding a connection is quite simple. You need only specify a description (name) for the connection, select the associated location, select the type of NetSpec used to identify the connection, and then provide the specific value for that NetSpec that identifies the location.

To create the connection, access the **Connection Management** tab, shown in Figure 8-7. Highlight the location with which you intend to associate the connection and click the **Add Connection** button. Figure 8-7 reflects the addition of the Office Wireless Connection to the wireless location.

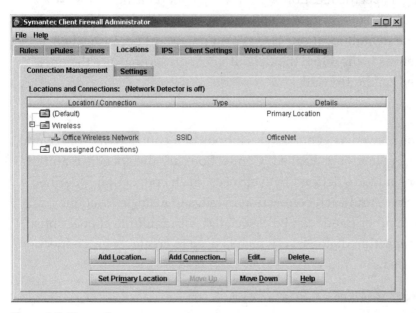

Figure 8-7 Connection management.

Zones

As mentioned earlier, zones can be used to simplify the management of remote hosts with which the client can communicate. Zones are managed through the **Zones** tab of the Symantec Client Firewall Administrator, as shown in Figure 8-8. This tab contains different settings for each location defined within the policy. You can choose to edit only the default location or create different zones for each location in your policy.

When editing zones, you first select the applicable location using the **Location** pull-down menu. Then use the **Add**, **Edit**, **Copy**, and **Delete** buttons to manage listings of hosts in each zone. There are separate tabs for **Trusted Zone, Restricted Zone, AutoBlock Exclusions**, and general Zone **Settings**.

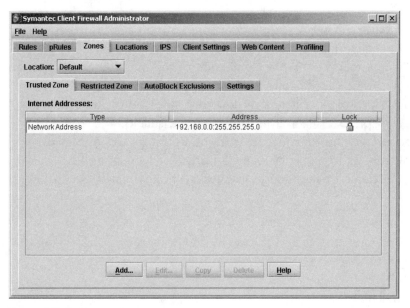

Figure 8-8 Zone management.

When you click **Add** to add a new entry to a particular zone, you are presented with the dialog box shown in Figure 8-9. It enables you to create a zone entry based upon a single IP address, the name of the host, a network address, an address range, or a named address group.

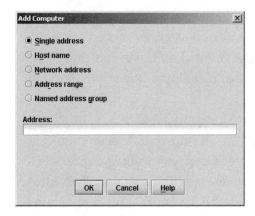

Figure 8-9 Add zone entry.

Zones and Protocol Filtering

It is important to realize that protocol filtering is not affected by zone settings that are in effect. Zones are significant for the majority of standard network traffic, specifically traffic that utilizes the TCP, UDP, and ICMP protocols. If a protocol filter is set to explicitly allow a particular type of traffic, that protocol filter overrides the zone setting. The traffic will be allowed even if the remote host is in the Restricted Zone. Similarly, if a protocol filter is set to explicitly deny a particular type of traffic, that traffic will be denied even though the host is in the Trusted Zone.

Working with Firewall Rules

Firewall rules are the core of Symantec Client Security. All traffic passing through the firewall is evaluated against the firewall rulebase (consisting of general rules, program rules, and Trojan rules). These rules are ranked in priority order, from highest to lowest, and all traffic is evaluated against each rule in priority order until a match is detected. The first rule to match the traffic is enforced and no further rules are evaluated. If no rules match, the default settings will permit traffic that is not specifically denied. To modify this default, administrators must edit the CPOLICY.XML file on the server from which the Symantec Client Firewall is deployed.

Symantec Client Firewall rules are categorized as either locked or unlocked. Locked rules are enforced by the client at all times and cannot be modified by the user. Unlocked rules can be created, modified, or deleted by users with appropriate permissions.

The priority order for rule evaluation is shown in Table 8-1.

You'll notice one entry in Table 8-1 that hasn't previously been mentioned: the firewall state table. The Symantec Client Firewall, like most modern firewalls, uses a technology known as stateful inspection. This means that any inbound traffic that is part of an established outbound connection is allowed. For example, if the user initiates a connection to a Web server and

Table 8-1

Rule Evaluation Priorities		
Priority	**Rule Category**	**Rule Type**
First	Firewall state table	—
Second	General	Locked
Third	Program	Locked
Fourth	General	Unlocked
Fifth	Program	Unlocked
Sixth	Trojan	Locked
Seventh	Trojan	Unlocked

the firewall allows the outbound connection, the firewall will then allow bidirectional communication between the two hosts for as long as the connection is actively maintained.

Let's explore the creation of a rule that allows outbound Web connections. First, from the Rules tab of the Symantec Client Firewall Administrator, ensure that **General Rules** is selected and click the **Add** button. While looking at this screen, you'll notice that the Rules tab has a location subtab. You can create rules specific to a location or apply the rule to all locations. The Master List option displays all rules associated with all locations.

When you click the **Add** button, you are presented with the dialog box shown in Figure 8-10.

The **Description** property allows you to apply a name to the rule. You should always try to use a descriptive name that will help you or another administrator understand the purpose of the rule when examining the rulebase later. This is especially important because firewall rulebases become more complex over time. We use the description Allow Outbound HTTP for the rule here. Descriptions are limited to 70 characters.

The **Action** property associated with a rule instructs the firewall on the appropriate action to take when a packet matches the rule. If the action is set to **Permit**, the traffic is allowed. If it is set to **Block**, the traffic is dropped.

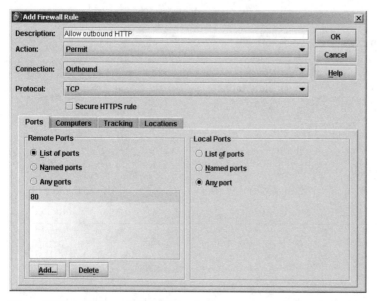

Figure 8-10 Add Firewall Rule dialog box.

If it is set to **Monitor**, an entry is automatically created in the event log to record the event. The rule here is a Permit rule.

> **Note**
> Monitor rules are not considered a match for priority purposes. Although the Symantec Client Firewall logs any matches to Monitor rules, it continues to search the rulebase for matching rules until a Permit or Block rule is discovered.

The **Connection** property specifies the direction of the rule. If the rule is an outbound rule (as most workstation rules are), the rule applies to connections initiated by the client. If the rule is an inbound rule (as some server rules are), it applies to connections with the client initiated by other hosts. Rules can be configured as applying to both inbound and outbound connections by selecting the **Both** setting. The rule here is intended to permit Web browsers installed on the client to communicate with Web servers. Therefore, the rule is an outbound rule. The rule would be an inbound rule (or both) only if we were running a Web server on the system that offered Web pages to other systems.

244

> **Note**
> It is extremely important to remember that the direction of a TCP rule applies only to the initial connection. Stateful inspection ensures that TCP packets replying to an established, permitted session are allowed through the firewall. It is not necessary to create bidirectional rules to allow a remote server to respond to a request from the client. However, because ICMP and UDP traffic do not create persistent sessions, inbound and outbound traffic are analyzed separately.

The **Protocol** property defines the protocols to which the rule applies. The available options are TCP, UDP, ICMP, and both TCP and UDP. TCP is selected in this example.

The **Ports** tab, shown in Figure 8-10, enables you to specify the ports associated with the rule. We intend to allow remote Web connections with our rule, so we set the rule to apply to traffic destined for port 80 on a remote host from any port on the local host.

The **Computers** tab, shown in Figure 8-11, allows the specification of individual systems and network interfaces impacted by the rule. You

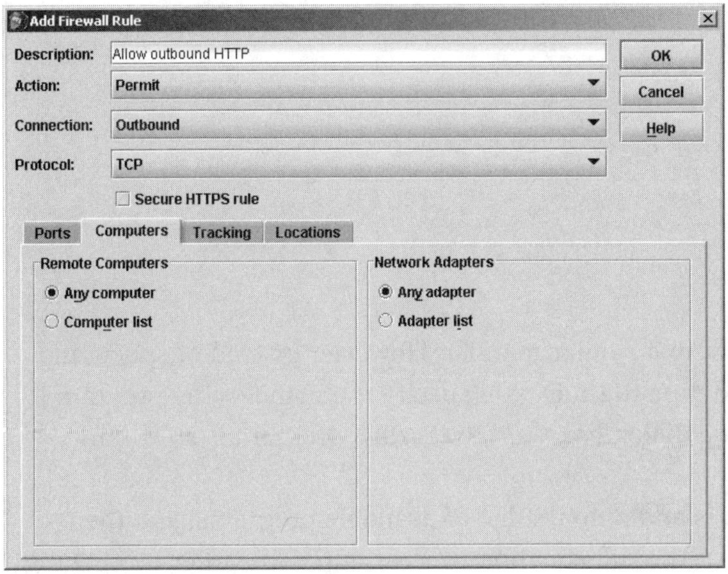

Figure 8-11 Computers tab.

can specify these by either allowing any computer/adapter or creating a list.

The **Tracking** tab enables you to order the creation of alerts and event log entries when the rule is matched. You can specify a threshold number of times the rule must be matched before creating an event log entry, and you can also specify the creation of a security alert to the end user.

The **Locations** tab enables you to specify the location(s) that will be regulated by the firewall rule by either selecting all locations or choosing from the defined locations.

When the rule is defined, click the **OK** button to add the rule to the firewall policy. The result of adding our rule is shown in Figure 8-12.

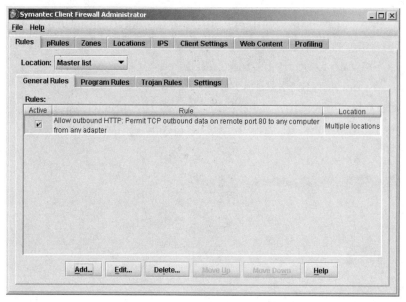

Figure 8-12 Updated rulebase.

Program rules work in a similar manner. However, instead of specifying ports and systems to define the rule, you specify the name of the program file to be regulated. The dialog box used to create a program is shown in Figure 8-13.

After the program is added to the list of available programs, you then proceed with the rest of the rule-creation process outlined earlier by clicking the **Add** button in the lower portion of the **Program Rules** tab.

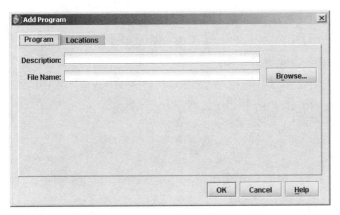

Figure 8-13 Adding a program.

> **Note**
> Symantec Client Firewall recognizes only the exact program that is
> selected. Any different version or a localized version of the program is
> not recognized.

Working with pRules

As mentioned earlier, pRules enable you to use Symantec Client Firewall on
systems with diverse, unpredictable software configurations without opening
a large number of unnecessary firewall holes. pRules are potential rules that
turn into program rules when each of three conditions is met:

- A user invokes the program for the first time
- No program rule exists for the program
- No general or Trojan rule covers the requested communication type

Symantec Client Firewall includes a large number of pRules for common
programs. You can edit these pRules or create entirely new pRules for
customized applications (such as locally developed software).

If you need to create or edit a pRule, you use the dialog box shown in
Figure 8-14. The available configuration options include these:

- The name of the file that activates the pRule
- The description of the pRule

- The options that apply to the pRule, which include allowing you to specify that the rule is never created automatically (user intervention is required) and disabling the firewall's filename checking functionality (this is not recommended unless specifically required)
- Sets of match criteria, which can include the following:
  - File version
  - Version data
  - Required digest (the unique cryptographic hash of the file)
  - File size
  - Program rules associated with the pRule

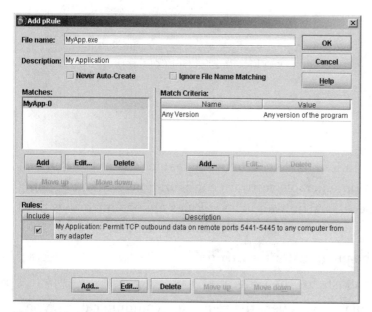

Figure 8-14 Adding a pRule.

Intrusion Prevention

The Symantec Client Firewall intrusion-prevention system (IPS) blocks malicious traffic that matches one of the predefined intrusion signatures. If network traffic matches an IPS signature and AutoBlock is enabled, the IPS drops the packet and immediately terminates the connection with the remote system to defend against the attack.

IPS Signature Versions

The current version of the Symantec Client Firewall supports only v2.x signatures. If possible, you should upgrade older clients to support v2.x signatures. This can be done by migrating legacy clients to the current version of the firewall or upgrading the engine of older firewall versions through a maintenance release. You should distribute v1.x signatures only if you cannot configure a portion of your clients to support v2.x signatures. IPS signatures are updated using the same process described earlier in this book for updating AntiVirus signatures.

You can also decide to exclude specific signatures from your IPS policy, if necessary. For example, if an IPS rule prevents the legitimate execution of a corporate application, you might need to exclude it for users of that application. You do this by using the **IPS** tab in the Symantec Client Firewall Administrator. Figure 8-15 shows an exclusion for the Invalid TCP Source Port signature.

This same tab enables you to lock IPS rules, which prohibits users from modifying the include/exclude status of the rule. Figure 8-15 also shows the

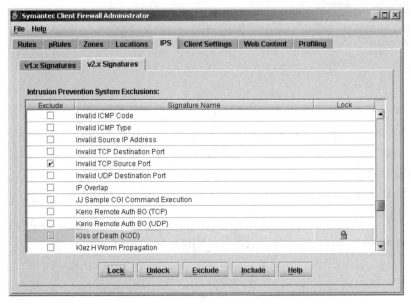

Figure 8-15 IPS Signatures.

locking of the Kiss of Death (KOD) rule. This rule blocks a specific attack, known as the Kiss of Death, which exploits a vulnerability in the way unpatched versions of Windows® 95, 98, and 2000 process the Internet Group Management Protocol (IGMP).

AutoBlock can be configured by using the **Intrusion Prevention–AutoBlock** setting in the Client Settings tab of the firewall administrator. This is shown in Figure 8-16.

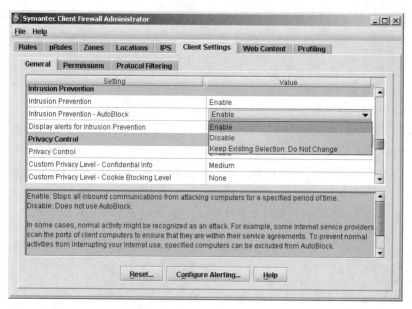

Figure 8-16 Configuring AutoBlock.

Web Content

The **Web Content** tab of the Symantec Client Firewall Administrator enables you to configure settings related to the firewall's treatment of online content, advertising, and privacy-related concerns.

The **Global Settings** subtab, shown in Figure 8-17, enables you to configure the following options:

- **Information about your browser**—Blocking this traffic prevents Web servers from receiving information about your Web browser and computer.

- **Information about visited sites**—Blocking this traffic prevents Web servers from obtaining information about the last site you visited.

- **Animated images**—Blocking this traffic prevents the execution of animated images and renders them as still images.

- **Scripts**—Blocking this traffic disallows Java and Visual Basic scripts.

- **Flash animation**—Blocking this traffic prevents content created with Macromedia Flash.

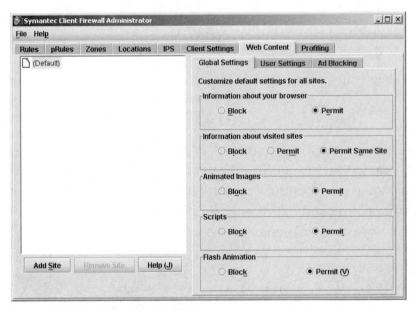

Figure 8-17 Web Content Global settings.

The **User Settings** subtab enables you to create customized settings for the handling of cookies, Java applets, ActiveX controls, and pop-up ads for specific Web sites. The **Ad Blocking** tab allows the regulation of advertisements.

Client Settings

We've already briefly looked at the **Client Settings** tab as an avenue for enabling and disabling intrusion-prevention AutoBlock. This same tab can be used to configure a variety of settings, permissions, and protocol filters.

General Settings

The **General Settings** tab includes a large number of settings, all of which are configured in a manner similar to the AutoBlock setting explored earlier in this chapter. These are some of the more significant settings you can configure here:

- Enabling/disabling the various Symantec Client Security components
- Setting the logging level for the system (either default or the more informative verbose mode)
- Integrating with Windows Firewall and Windows Security Center
- Customizing privacy control
- Customizing alert messages
- Configuring alerting

Permissions

The **Permissions** subtab, shown in Figure 8-18, enables you to specify the specific permissions granted to users of the client system. This includes general administrative tasks, such as opening the user interface and viewing logs, as well as specific firewall functions, such as enabling and disabling Symantec Client Security components and configuring zones.

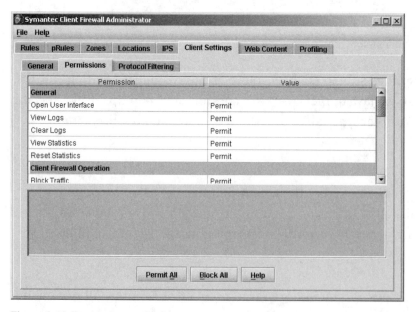

Figure 8-18 Permissions subtab.

Protocol Filtering

As you learned earlier, the Symantec Client Firewall rules apply only to TCP, UDP, and ICMP traffic. If you need to enable traffic for other protocols, you must do so using a protocol filter. Protocol filters are enabled using the **Protocol Filtering** subtab of the **Client Settings** tab. Protocol filters can be created for any extended IP protocol in use simply by using the IANA assigned protocol number (0–255).

Figure 8-19 shows the use of protocol filters to allow traffic using the Encapsulating Security Payload protocol and the Authentication Header protocol. Both of these protocols are members of the IPSec suite and are commonly used for establishing virtual private network (VPN) connections. It is not possible to allow IPSec tunnels through the firewall without using these protocol filters.

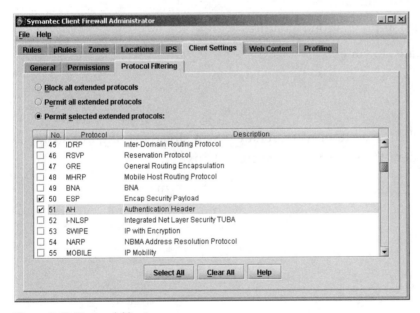

Figure 8-19 Protocol filtering.

Conclusion

Symantec Client Security offers an unprecedented degree of flexibility to administrators seeking to apply consistent policies within a small business environment with minimal administrative overhead. Features such as zones, locations, and pRules simplify administrative tasks, while providing strong centrally administered firewall and Intrusion Prevention security at the desktop.

Chapter Review Questions

Question 8-1

Which of the following items are included in a Client Firewall Policy file when exported to uncompressed XML format? Select two answers.

- ❑ A. Firewall rules
- ❑ B. Configuration information
- ❑ C. Antivirus signatures
- ❑ D. Intrusion-prevention signatures
- ❑ E. Updates to zones

Question 8-2

What type of file is used to provide updates to an already-configured instance of Symantec Client Firewall? Select the correct answer.

- ○ A. .cfp
- ○ B. .tmp
- ○ C. .upd
- ○ D. .sym
- ○ E. .cfu

Question 8-3

Which two of the following zones contain hosts that can be allowed to communicate with the client? Select the two correct answers.

- ❑ A. Restricted Zone
- ❑ B. Trusted Zone
- ❑ C. Untrusted Zone
- ❑ D. AutoBlock Exclusions
- ❑ E. DMZ

Question 8-4

Which one of the following rule types has the highest priority of those listed? Select the correct answer.

○ A. Locked program rules

○ B. Unlocked general rules

○ C. Locked Trojan rules

○ D. Unlocked Trojan rules

○ E. Unlocked program rules

Question 8-5

Which one of the following objects must be created to establish communications with the Authentication Header (AH) protocol? Select the correct answer.

○ A. Program rule

○ B. General rule

○ C. Protocol filter

○ D. Trojan rule

○ E. Network rule

Question 8-6

What is the maximum number of locations that can be associated with a single connection? Select the correct answer.

○ A. 0

○ B. 1

○ C. 2

○ D. 256

○ E. 1,024

Question 8-7

What type of directory information is used in a NetSpec? Select the correct answer.

○ A. LDAP

○ B. Active Directory

○ C. EDS

○ D. RADIUS

○ E. DNS

Question 8-8

What will happen if the client firewall is enabled and the user changes to a location where the Enable Firewall setting is set to No?

- ○ A. The client firewall will deactivate.
- ○ B. The client firewall will remain active.
- ○ C. The user will be asked whether the client firewall should be activated or deactivated.

Question 8-9

How many rules are required to allow a user to connect to a Web site and allow that site to answer the user's requests?

- ○ A. 0
- ○ B. 1
- ○ C. 2
- ○ D. 3
- ○ E. 4

Chapter Review Answers

Answer 8-1

Answers **A** and **B** are correct. Client Firewall Policy (.cfp) files contain firewall rules, configuration information, and intrusion-prevention signatures. When these files are exported to uncompressed XML format, they no longer contain intrusion-prevention signatures.

Answer 8-2

Answer **E** is correct. Client Firewall Update (.cfu) files contain updates for already-configured instances of Symantec Client Firewall.

Answer 8-3

Answers **B** and **D** are correct. Hosts in the Trusted Zone are allowed unrestricted access to the client. Hosts in the AutoBlock Zone are allowed to communicate with the client if appropriate rules are in place.

Answer 8-4

Answer **A** is correct. Of the rule types listed, locked program rules have the highest priority. Locked general rules and the firewall state table do have higher priorities than locked program rules, but they are not included in this question.

Answer 8-5

Answer **C** is correct. The Authentication Header protocol (part of IPSec) does not use TCP, UDP, or ICMP, so it must be enabled using a protocol filter instead of a firewall rule.

Answer 8-6

Answer **B** is correct. Each connection can be associated with only a single location.

Answer 8-7

Answer **E** is correct. NetSpecs use DNS directory information.

Answer 8-8

Answer **B** is correct. The client firewall will remain active in this scenario.

Answer 8-9

Answer **B** is correct. A single rule allows the required bidirectional communication.

PART III

NORTON ANTISPAM

CHAPTER 9

Spam Threats

Terms and Techniques to Remember

- Spam
- Phishing
- Address mining
- Allowed and Blocked Lists
- The different types of spam

This chapter examines the evolution of electronic mail and its physical junk-mail equivalent, which is known as spam. This type of email threatens to overwhelm businesses with advertisements, scams, and other forms of unsolicited and undesirable "junk" filling inboxes everywhere. We review various types of spam and briefly discuss the strategies that can be used to defend a client's network against the veritable flood of undesirable email.

Spam

Like physical mail, email is increasingly exploited by advertisers sending "virtual" junk mail. Physical mailboxes were once stuffed full of fliers, advertisements, product samples, and other unsolicited materials intended to encourage the recipient to purchase a new product or service. Physical mass mail often carries a high cost per item and so remains limited to a geographic region or targeted lists of individuals.

SPAM vs. Spam

The nickname *spam* refers to unsolicited commercial email and can be written in lower case or mixed case. Hormel Foods has trademarked the product SPAM™, which is always written in upper case when referring to the canned luncheon meat product.

Although email spam is the most common form of spam, the term *spam* is also used to refer to mass advertising postings on USENET groups and over instant-messaging systems. Spam is not simply an unsolicited email, but a mass mailing of such.

Defining Spam

Unlike physical mail, email generally carries no cost per-item associated with transmission, nor does it take time to individually package and address. As a result, the amount of unsolicited email that can be sent each day has no real limit beyond the capacity of the network and the email server's file storage system. *Spam* is the colloquial term for unsolicited commercial email (UCE) or unsolicited bulk email (UBE). (The cost is borne by the recipient's mail service, whether an Internet service provider (ISP) or a corporation that hosts its own mail server.)

With the global nature of the Internet, sending an email across the world is no more difficult or expensive than sending an email across the street. As such, spam has no regional limitations. Because so much spam can be sent so cheaply, only a tiny percentage must get a positive response (whether a product sale or a user following a link to a Web site) for the spammer to profit.

Putting Spam into Perspective

Researchers estimate that by 2007, the rate of spam email generation will be 23 billion messages per day. In 2004, various research groups reported that the percentage of email messages received in the United States that was spam was between 50 and 80 percent, with some estimates placing the true percentage at more than 90 percent.

U.S. government agencies, including the Federal Trade Commission, along with the Center for Democracy & Technology and other groups such as the Anti-Spam Research Group (ASRG) of the Internet Research Task Force (IRTF), have researched spam and released the following results:

- 86% of email addresses that are posted on Web sites or newsgroups receive spam.

- 63% of list-removal requests are not honored.

- 18% of spam is advertisement for adult entertainment, such as sexually explicit Web sites or dating services. Of that number, 17% contain explicit images and 40% have subject or sender information that is not indicative of the content.

- 20% of spam is solicitation for investment or business opportunity such as work-at-home offers, franchises, or chain letters.

- 17% of spam is solicitation for credit cards, loans, insurance, and other financial services.

- 66% of spam has some type of falsity, whether an obscured sender, a misleading subject, or false/fraudulent text (such as miracle weight loss pills, get-rich-quick schemes, chain letters, and other scams).

Email

To understand the evolution of spam, it is helpful to briefly examine the development of electronic mail. Electronic mail, or email, was originally developed to allow system operators to leave messages for one another on a single large mainframe system. At that time, personal-computing devices did not exist; later, the first entrants into the personal computing market were not interconnected into the globally distributed Internet we have today. Only mainframe systems supporting multiple users needed this type of functionality.

In the Early Days

As internetworking connections were developed under the Defense Advanced Research Projects Agency's ARPANET project, email became a means of communication between systems operators located in disparate geographic areas. Transfer of email throughout these early network projects was typically managed through manual route addressing to the proper destination node. Such routing was managed using the machine names of all intervening nodes so that, for example, !firstcomp!nextcomp!mycomp!userA would allow an administrator to route email through each computer in the order specified (see Figure 9-1).

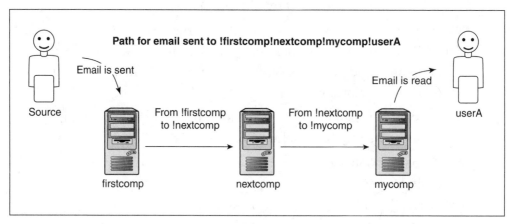

Figure 9-1 An example of electronic mail transfer using fixed route addressing.

One disadvantage of this type of routing was that a single node could hold up all email routing until the node was available and the operator directed batch email transfer to occur with another node. Electronic mail was not considered a "rapid" means of communication at this point; delivery delays of days or weeks were not uncommon and required human intervention for each batch of data transferred.

Later other networking solutions, such as the BITNET and UUCP implementations, were developed. These solutions contributed to the growing need for interoperability and interconnection between networks that relied on proprietary protocols for system-to-system communication. A group of communications protocols evolved from the ARPANET project, resulting in the TCP/IP protocol suite that forms the basis of the modern global Internet.

SMTP

Within the TCP/IP protocol suite, the Simple Mail Transfer Protocol (SMTP) specification provides the fundamental basis for modern automatic (or "dynamic") electronic mail transfer. Dynamic mail routing is an outgrowth of the introduction of many millions of new Internet addresses, each of which might potentially be the source or destination host for an email transmission. Without the capability to automatically redirect mail based on the target email server, it would be impossible to route millions of individual messages to their proper destination.

The SMTP protocol, together with the Post Office Protocol (POP), allows the transfer of electronic mail messages between systems utilizing the lingua franca, or common language, provided by the SMTP protocol. Individual messages are formatted according to the specifications provided by RFC 2822 (an RFC of this type is a standards document adopted by the Internet Society, ISOC, for use throughout the global Internet).

Modern Email Routing

With the adoption of a standard network protocol for email transfer, many vendors' products could communicate across the growing Internet network. Common email systems within the small business environment include Microsoft® Exchange Server and Novell® GroupWise®, although many other packages perform similar tasks.

These packages allow automated email transfer between Internet subnets using the hierarchical address resolution provided through the domain name system (DNS). DNS provides Internet routing by allowing a human-readable address such as userA@bigcorp.com to be automatically translated to send the email to userA at the bigcorp.com email server, which might be defined by the Mail Exchange (MX) record as IP address 128.192.191.5. Through this service, a client no longer needs to manually configure the specific route that the email will take to reach the intended target address.

The Evolving Threat

In recent years, email use has grown to such a degree that it is now considered a mission critical application for business. When trying to understand the extent of this growth, a few illustrations prove useful:

- In the 1960s, electronic mail was used to communicate between administrators sharing a single mainframe computer.

  Today almost a billion electronic mail messages are sent around the world every year.

- In the 1970s, early electronic mail was transferred in batches between network nodes by human operators.

  Today automated systems can generate more than a million messages in a day.

- Networked electronic mail was originally sent between large, fixed servers.

  Today electronic mail can be received on cellphones, pagers, and PDAs.

- Early electronic-mail addressing was uniquely assigned to individual system operators.

  Today disposable or one-use electronic-mail addresses are freely available.

- Before the development of the Internet, electronic-mail addresses could be obtained only from individual system registries.

  Today automated agents mine the Internet for email-formatted addresses.

- Early electronic mail systems were isolated and not available to commercial data mining.

  Today electronic mail systems can customize offerings based on the client's past habits.

Now that you have an understanding of the origins of email and spam, we examine the types of spam you might encounter and then follow with a review of the defenses you can aid your clients in developing.

Types of Spam

Because of the subjective nature of spam, it is difficult to automatically assess whether a particular email message is unsolicited and undesirable by the individual recipient. Spam comes in many forms and includes materials ranging from merely nuisance items to messages containing offensive and potentially illegal materials.

The purpose of most spam is to advertise products and services such as diet pills, casino gambling, software, inkjet cartridges, matchmaking services, or adult entertainment Web sites. Many of the products are illegal (such as pirated software) or harmful (such as counterfeit prescription drugs), and images associated with adult entertainment Web sites might be, at best, offensive or, at worst, illegal. Spam has been used for noncommercial purposes as well. For example, political or religious groups might use spam as a tool to get their message to a wider audience.

Spam can also be used as a form of harassment. In this type of spam, the spam appears to originate from the person or company that the spammer wants to harass. This typically causes a backlash of angry emails or telephone calls to the unfortunate victim of the harassment, who, in most cases, was in no way involved in the email generation. Pretending to send from an address other than the actual original address is referred to as spoofing and is a common propagation mechanism for email carrying viruses and spam.

Social Engineering

Unfortunately, the Internet provides the ideal medium for scams. Door-to-door scams take time, and the perpetrators risk being identified. The Internet gives the perpetrators access to the global market via spamming. These are only a few of the myriad Internet email scams:

- Offers of free products such as game consoles or computer equipment. In these scams, the victim might be asked to pay shipping charges with a credit or debit card to receive a product that is never sent. In other free product scams, the victim might be required to sign up for additional bulk emails or to purchase other products or services.

- Advance-fee fraud scams, such as the infamous Nigerian 419 scam. These scams tempt victims with the promise of multimillion-dollar sums for helping wealthy foreigners move large sums of money out of their country of origin. The originator of the mail might also appear to be a government official, foreign royalty, or a bank official, making the scam seem more plausible.

- Business opportunities that promise great wealth for little work. These can be illegal pyramid schemes or other illegal scams intended to defraud the targeted client, or they can simply require much more time, effort, and cost than the victim is willing to dedicate to correct after the fact. This type of risk includes the Ponzi scheme and other such money-shuffling processes, all intended to take money from the unwary network user.

- Work-at-home opportunities, such as product assembly or envelope stuffing. The victim often pays a fee for supplies or the privilege to work, but is never paid for the work performed.

Phishing

Phishing is another type of spam. Typically, these emails appear to come from a reputable business with which the recipient might even have an account. They attempt to trick the recipient into revealing bank account or credit card information. It is difficult to train users to recognize a phishing email because they appear to come from the organization, use the organization's graphics and language, and, in many cases, might have valid links to the organization's real Web site. In those cases, pop-up windows with no visible Web address are often used to gather the recipient's personal information.

An example of a phishing email received by the author recently (verbatim):

```
Subject: Important Online Banking Alert

From: *** Bank <support@***bank.com>

To: [recipient's email address]
```

```
[Legitimate bank graphic]

Dear valued *** Bank member,

Due to concerns for the safety and integrity
of the online banking community, we have
issued the following warning message.
```

It has come to our attention that your account information needs to be confirmed due to inactive customers, fraud, and spoof reports.

If you could please take 5-10 minutes out of your online experience and renew your records, you will not run into any future problems with the online service.

However, failure to confirm your records may result in your account suspension.

Once you have confirmed your account records, your Internet banking service will not be interrupted and will continue as normal.

To confirm your bank account records, please click here.

Thank you for your time,

*** Bank Billing Department

[Legitimate graphic]

© 2004 *** Bank. All rights reserved.

Privacy | Security | Terms of Use | Site Map

When victims follow the provided clickable link, they are prompted to provide their name, address, credit card, banking account, and other similar details that can be used to commit various crimes, including identity theft. The victim remains unaware that their confidential details have not been provided to the seemingly legitimate site claimed in the phishing email message.

In the previous example, the Privacy, Security, Terms of Use, and Site Map links at the end of email all point to the bank's legitimate Web site, and the graphics used are from the bank's site. The email headers have been spoofed to show the bank's mail server as the sender. Although careful perusal of the headers shows the mail server from which the phishing mail actually originated, most users will not have the knowledge to decode mail headers.

Phishing is typically performed to perpetrate credit card fraud or identity theft, but an attacker (particularly a current or former employee) might target a company directly using knowledge of internal procedures, personnel, and other key details. In such circumstances, the attacker could send an email that appears to be from an internal department such as IT or Human Resources, to trick employees into revealing corporate passwords, to delete accounts or file stores, or to disrupt business operations in many other ways.

Additional Threats

Spammers also take advantage of viruses, Trojan horses, and worms as a means to distribute spam. Following is a partial list detailed on the Symantec Security Response list (`http://securityresponse.symantec.com/`) found to be capable of relaying spam from infected computers to hide the true source of these messages:

- W32.Sobig.E@mm (6/2003)
- Backdoor.DMSpammer (10/2003)
- Backdoor.Hogle (10/2003)
- Trojan.Kalshi (10/2003)
- Backdoor.Dister (11/2003)
- Trojan.Bedrill (11/2003)
- Trojan.Naldem (11/2003)
- Trojan.Benuti (12/2003)
- W32.HLLW.Gaobot.DK (12/2003)
- W32.HLLW.Gaobot.EE (12/2003)
- W32.Bobax.A (5/2004)
- W32.Bobax.D (5/2004)
- Trojan.Mitglierder.L (6/2004)
- Trojan.Spabot (7/2004)

In addition, spam can be the medium used to distribute threats and security risks, to infect systems both directly and indirectly. Spam emails often contain attachments or links that lead to the installation of viruses or other security risks. After being installed on the recipient's computer, these programs might allow further exploitation in the form of executing malicious code, downloading additional software, carrying out browser redirection (also known as hijacking), or turning over control of the computer to the attacker for use in Denial-of-Service (DoS) attacks.

Spam-Borne Threats

An example of a threat distributed via spam is the Downloader.Mimail.B Trojan horse. When executed, it downloads and installs the W32.Mimail. P@mm mass-mailing worm. This worm, in turn, attempts to collect financial data from the victim and send it to the attacker's host agent. This is a mass-mailing worm that can distribute itself from infected systems via its own built-in SMTP server, spoofing the origin address to protect its operation from easy discovery and eradication.

How Spam Works

A typical spammer obtains a large number of email addresses and access to one or more SMTP servers capable of sending email (see Figure 9-2).

Although some mass mailings are perfectly legitimate, the sheer volume of spam that an individual can receive can be staggering. Spam costs little or nothing to the originator, so each spammer can generate hundreds or even thousands of different emails each day to each of the recipient addresses being targeted. Profitable spamming requires a large number of targets, and the spammers have developed a wide variety of ways to acquire email addresses.

Brute-Force Spam

Some spammers go so far as to simply attempt to send an email to all addresses at a given site, using every possible combination of characters and numbers in a "dictionary" or brute-force effort. Systems such as this can include auto-response agents capable of monitoring for returned

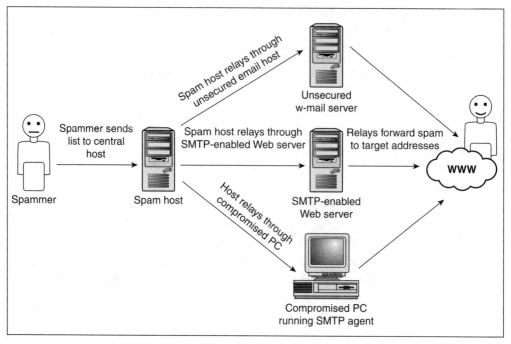

Figure 9-2 An example of a typical spamming setup.

(or "bounced") email addresses, building a list of all combinations that did not bounce as a list for later targeted advertising. Such brute force operations can slow network connectivity and consume significant amounts of email server resources simply trying to evaluate each item coming in to see if the address is valid.

Partnerships

When clients sign up for access to services and accounts at commercial sites, the End-User Licensing Agreement (EULA) that they must agree to in order to be granted access often contains the provision that a business may provide users' information to select partner agencies. Unfortunately, these agencies can then transfer your information to their own "partners," which could be a loosely defined association, at best, and so on, until your information is essentially public. Email addresses traded between spamming partners can suddenly increase the amount of spam reaching a client's inbox even years after the original account was created.

Address Harvesting

Spammers make use of automated agents capable of scanning newsgroups, Web sites, Web journals (also called blogs), and other Internet-based means of communication. These agents look for any entries that are formatted as an email address (example: `SomeUser@SomeCorp.com`); the spammer compiles these and sells targeted email advertisements to these addresses. Without any action on their part to opt in, users might start to receive spam messages each day merely because their blog signature block or a resumé posted to a job site contained an email address.

Open Records Act

Spammers do not always depend on shady means to obtain lists of email addresses. Many times, directory information stored in public databases such as those of universities and government agencies are requested under the Open Records Act (ORA).

In one known event, an ORA request was filed to obtain the directory information at a Texas university. This information included the email addresses of more than 50,000 current and former students, faculty, staff, and researchers. Within three days of compliance with the request, university staff members identified the list being offered for sale through a popular online auction site. Although the specific auction was removed by the site's host, the volume of spam being received by the university's servers increased significantly thereafter.

Address Mining

Downloaded utilities, animated cursors, network-distributed games, and other software, including spyware, might be performing their proper task while also mining a client's computer for email addresses stored in files or email client address books. These addresses are then relayed back to the agent's originator, who can use the new listing for added spam targeting.

Upcoming Legislation
With the prevalence of these mining agents, the U.S. legislature is currently reviewing legislation titled The Securely Protect Yourself Against Cyber Trespass (SPY ACT) Act. The proposed bill would carry fines up to $3 million (U.S.) for software developers that create illicit mining and browser-hijacking agents.

Many tracking cookies (small text files used by Web sites to "remember" your personalized settings from one visit to the next) include email addresses associated with a user's account, which other agents then can mine as a client moves between Web sites. Combining this information allows spammers to target their spam based on a user's past browsing activity.

Business Impact

It is a known fact that spam causes lost productivity in business. Employees who are required to read email for business purposes must wade through spam to find the legitimate business email.

The exact cost of lost productivity varies among organizations, with estimates ranging from $86 to almost $2,000 per employee per year. A company can perform some simple calculations based on its own statistics and personnel count, although administrators often feel the impact rapidly when attempting to calculate server storage requirements for the ever-increasing volume of email.

An Example Cost
If an employee making $20 per hour receives 25 spam emails per day and takes only 5 seconds to deal with each item, the company pays approximately $159 per year for that employee to read spam, based on a 230-day work year. Some individuals have reported hundreds of spam emails per day, many of which appear at first to be legitimate and so take far longer to deal with, magnifying this cost significantly.

In addition, spam takes a toll on the corporate network. Excessive spam steals needed bandwidth, wasting server storage space and taking up IT staff time. Phishing and other forms of fraud generate additional requirements for corporate response, depending on the type of information that was revealed by unwary clients. Phishing schemes involving legitimate businesses have also caused difficulties for those corporate entities that were targeted by the scam. Web sites must dedicate advertising and content space to notify clients of the scam, and customer confidence is often weakened by making clients more wary of using the legitimate Web site services provided by the vendor.

In addition to a loss of consumer confidence, a loss of legitimate communications with clients because of the client's difficulty in separating the real from the bogus phishing mail can impact sales and customer management efforts. If clients are fearful that any message from the spoofed legitimate business might be a scam, they might discard targeted email items such as sale notifications, electronic billing notifications, and other customer relations–related email out of fear. This can have an even more severe impact if business partners, manufacturers, or suppliers cannot trust their communications with the spoofed legitimate entity.

Fighting Spam

Attempts to track down and identify spammers can be very costly and time-intensive because spammers often use disposable or spoofed source email addresses, false names, and phone numbers, or might simply operate their servers within countries that do not recognize the legal systems of victims' home countries. Because a spammer need not be physically near his spam-generating SMTP servers, spammers often hide their activities this way—particularly when sending items including illegal content such as graphic material or fraudulent scams. The U.S. CAN-SPAM Act contains an assessment of the impact of spam, including the following:

- Threats to the convenience and efficiency of electronic mail
- Costs incurred by the recipients and agencies responsible for storing the unsolicited mail
- An increased risk that legitimate mail might not be received or might be lost

- Potential exposure to illegal or vulgar materials (noted by analysts as an increasing threat as minor children are accessing the network in growing numbers)

Legal Controls

Many countries have implemented legislation aimed at slowing the flood of spam:

- The U.S. federal CAN-SPAM Act of 2003 is the most comprehensive act of antispam legislation within the United States at this time. Critics claim that the law is too easily circumvented and that it overrides more restrictive laws passed at the state and local levels.

- Statutes requiring easy opt-out mechanisms, legitimate reply addresses, and specific labels in the subject field are common; they were passed in some form in almost all states within the United States. Many of these state laws are being contested by spammers, such as in a recent Wisconsin case in which the judge determined that the state law was not allowed to regulate interstate and international commerce; this was ascribed as the purview of the federal government alone.

- The European Union has passed extensive legislation regulating the use and distribution of personal information, and identifying specific penalties for identified spammers.

- Other countries have passed their own forms of similar acts of legislation. Among these are Austria, Argentina, Australia, Belgium, Brazil, Canada, Denmark, Finland, France, Germany, Greece, India, Ireland, Italy, Japan, Norway, Russia, Spain, Sweden, and the United Kingdom.

Shortcomings

Unfortunately, because of the lack of a single system of government, clients faced with spammers located in other countries find themselves stymied in their attempts to bring the spammers to justice. Spammers make use of this protection by locating their SMTP servers either in countries without such laws or in countries that do not recognize the laws of other countries.

Even when victims attempt to prosecute spammers operating within their own country, they often find the way fraught with political controversy. Because users are drawn to the open society of the Internet, the concept of freedom from governmental control remains a strong opposition to organized attempts to control what may be sent over the Internet, including spam. Civil-rights groups such as the Electronic Frontier Foundation and the ACLU frequently champion the cause of individuals charged with allegations of spamming, often claiming that unsolicited email is the only way small companies can possibly compete with the marketing giants.

This brings to bear many other entangling acts of legislation aimed at ensuring protections for competition in the marketplace, and even concerns over the constitutionality of any act abrogating freedom of speech. Other issues can also play a part in such efforts to limit spam traffic, such as the tradition of academic freedom enjoyed by most institutions of higher education. These traditional expectations were developed in a time well before a million-plus unsolicited email messages could be targeted at a single victim in a very short time—and yet, they continue to influence the pressure that can be brought when those victims attempt to redress their grievances.

The laws are not totally without success, however, as shown when email giant AOL was recently able to sue one of the highest-volume spammers in the world. Additional cases are pending all around the world, and additional legislation is presently being drafted in an attempt to provide protection for the clients and email-hosting agencies under attack by spammers. In the short term, however, companies must act to protect themselves from spam more directly.

Spam Protection

ISPs and corporate entities can make use of spam-blocking or spam-filtering technologies to screen email based on a number of criteria configured by the network administrator.

Server- and client-level defenses can be applied to provide a layered anti-spam defense around a client's inbox, as shown in Figure 9-3. Client-level

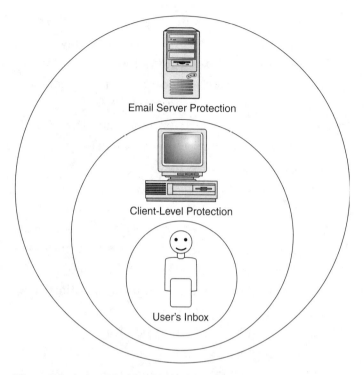

Figure 9-3 A simplified layered-defense strategy for antispam protection.

protections, such as Norton Antispam, can be used in a standalone fashion when no server-level email filtering is possible or desired or can be used in conjunction with server technology to provide a stronger defense-in-depth strategy for clients. This flexibility makes such protections exceptionally useful to a client beset by the ever-swelling tides of spam, whether the client's network is using a stand-alone solution or is protected by a layered-defense solution within the larger organizational setting.

Allow/Block List

One method of spam blocking involves using established listings of always-allowed (Allowed List) and always-denied (Blocked List) source addresses. This type of antispam defense relies on populating the permit and denial listings based on client preferences, corporate policies, or other similar measures. Because these listings are further refined by adding newly received email source addresses to a list, this type of protection will improve over time. Commercial Blocked List/Allowed List vendors are available for automated management of enterprise-level antispam defenses, while client-level filtering solutions allow clients to specify their own Blocked List/Allowed List options by selecting the appropriate action to be taken for a specific email address or range of addresses within an integrated email client such as Microsoft Outlook®.

Content-Based Filtering

Email can also be filtered for spam by an agent that scans each new item looking for known spam content, such as graphic content, malformed URLs, scripts, or words matching specified criteria, such as profanity, sexually explicit terms, or common names for pharmaceutical products. As with Blocked and Allowed Lists, this type of filtering can be implemented to provide general protection against emails that match a list of disallowed terms or phrases configured at the server level. Further refinement is also possible at the client level by configuring filters for phrases, terms, or sensitive information within the antispam agent running on the client's PC.

Heuristic Filtering

Heuristic algorithms make use of procedures that identify content, phrases, terminology, and other forms of potential-spam identification. For each successful match, weighting can be assigned to the suspect email. Based on this weighting, the spam email can simply be moved automatically to a spam folder or can be deleted outright depending on the policies in place for spam management.

Best Practices of Users

Individuals can also do many things to limit the amount of spam they receive, and some of the responsibility for limiting spam lies with them. Several groups, including The Center for Democracy & Technology, have identified a number of steps that people can take to protect themselves.

The most obvious action is to avoid giving out an email address at all. This is not feasible for companies whose employees use email for professional communications because their addresses are often published in some type of directory and can be transferred in the From field of each email that they transmit. Other strategies are detailed next.

Opt Out When Filling Out Forms

When filling out forms on the Web, clients should read carefully whenever a site or form requires their email address. When possible, they should opt out of offered email notifications, particularly those that offer to provide information or sales materials from partner organizations. Often these opt-out options are made grammatically difficult or vague to catch the reader unaware, with preselected check boxes and complex wording to make the proper response more difficult to discern.

Do Not Respond to Spam

Although at first this suggestion appears counterintuitive, unscrupulous spammers often use opt-out requests made by besieged clients to validate targeted email addresses. Users should take time to report spam to the proper agency, or to the spammer's ISP, if that information is readily identifiable. However, replying to a spammer's email directly might simply make the problem worse rather than better.

By responding to the original email, the user might see his address removed from that particular target listing for product A, but at the same time the now-validated address might be added to spam listings for the other few thousand clients paying the spammer to send their advertisements. In the worst case, the user might have just magnified their spam problems significantly, while not being removed from the original list as requested.

Do Not View Mail Using Active Content

Most modern email clients, such as Microsoft Outlook 2003, enable clients to view an email without including active content such as URLs and linked

280

graphics. Spammers often use active content elements, such as graphic images and Web bugs, to identify valid email addresses. By uniquely encoding the URL for loading a particular graphic image within an HTML-formatted email, the spammer can register which email was used to load that graphic image.

Web Bugs

The term *Web bug* commonly refers to small 1 pixel–by–1 pixel transparent graphic images that can be embedded in HTML-formatted email, Web pages, and other network-accessible documents. When the email client loads these images, they are not obvious in any way, yet they can be used to uniquely identify the client and to register information such as the targeted email address as a valid destination.

Other active content, such as executable files, script attachments, embedded JavaScript applets, and locked archive files, can carry additional threats. Clients should upgrade to an email client that supports reading only the text of an email before loading active content, to better protect themselves against these types of threat.

Future Forms of Protection

Many other forms of antispam protection are under investigation or development today. Two of these are challenge-response systems and SMTP server notification. Challenge-response systems are designed to allow email from humans and to block spam sent from automated senders. Most challenge-response systems work by requiring email senders to complete a simple task before accepting their email. These tasks are easy for people to carry out but impossible for machines to do so. Other solutions leverage the capability of SMTP servers to notify the originating SMTP server to wait before delivery. These systems eliminate mail that has a spoofed source email address and deliver other mail after a short delay.

Conclusion

As technologies evolve to slow the flood of spam, spammers continue to innovate as well, offering a steady and increasing flow of unwanted email. This flood is consuming increasing amounts of network bandwidth and email storage, without signs of a reduction in the flow impacting the costs and productivity of businesses. Companies of all sizes must take every precaution in protecting their systems against spam email, layering defenses where possible. The Norton Antispam solution provides automatic identification of spam and makes it easy to filter messages you don't want, without interfering with your legitimate email.

Chapter Review Questions

Question 9-1

The earliest email messages were used by _____. Select the best answer from those provided.

   ○ A. ARPANET administrators   ○ C. BITNET administrators

   ○ B. Mainframe administrators   ○ D. Internet clients

Question 9-2

Which two of the following options best describes spam?

   ❑ A. Unwanted email   ❑ D. Snail mail

   ❑ B. Unsolicited email   ❑ E. Email viruses

   ❑ C. Bulk email   ❑ F. All of the above

Question 9-3

What are some of the dangers of spam? Select all that apply.

   ❑ A. Scams   ❑ D. Lost time

   ❑ B. Phishing   ❑ E. Overloaded storage

   ❑ C. Viruses   ❑ F. All of the above

Question 9-4

Phishing describes _____. Select the best answer from those provided.

- ○ A. The advance-fee type of fraudulent scam
- ○ B. The Ponzi type of fraudulent scam
- ○ C. Email messages pretending to be from a known source asking for bank account or credit information
- ○ D. Email messages carrying viruses

Question 9-5

Scanning newsgroups, Web sites, and other network-accessible documents for email addresses describes which method of address list acquisition used by spammers? Select the best answer from those provided.

- ○ A. Brute-force spam
- ○ B. Business asset acquisition
- ○ C. Business partnerships transfer
- ○ D. Address harvesting
- ○ E. Address mining

Question 9-6

Spam is a problem at which levels? Select all that apply.

- ❑ A. Individual/personal
- ❑ B. Corporate
- ❑ C. Govermental bodies
- ❑ D. Global

Question 9-7

What are some of the methods used to block and filter spam email messages? Select all that apply.

- ❑ A. Using a Blocked List/Allowed List
- ❑ B. Content-based filtering

❏ C. Heuristic filtering

❏ D. Challenge-response filtering

❏ E. Using manual evaluation

Chapter Review Answers

Answer 9-1

Answer **B** is correct. The earliest email messages were used by mainframe system administrators to leave messages for one another on the same multi-user computer. Later development of batch-transfer and automatic-routing network email solutions were used by ARPANET and BITNET administrators, and are used by Internet clients today.

Answer 9-2

Answers **B** and **C** are the best answers here. Spam is unsolicited email sent in bulk. Although many additional email messages might be unwanted, spam generally refers to unsolicited bulk emails, often used for commercial advertising. *Snail mail* is a term used to refer to physical mail. Although spam can be used as a transport medium for viruses and other security risks, and although some viruses are used to send spam messages, the term *spam* is not identified specifically with viruses.

Answer 9-3

Answer **F** is correct. The dangers of spam include scams, phishing efforts, viral threats, overloaded SMTP server storage, and lost time for clients overwhelmed by the flood of messages in their inboxes.

Answer 9-4

Answer **C** is correct. Phishing describes email messages pretending to be from a known source asking for bank account or credit information. These email messages often carry the correct branding and links from the supposed source. Advance-fee fraudulent scams such as the Nigerian scam, as well as

Ponzi-type pyramid schemes, are intended to gain monies from targeted clients. Although spam can be used as a transport medium for viruses and other security risks, and although some viruses are used to send spam messages, the term *spam* is not identified specifically with viruses.

Answer 9-5

Answer **D** is correct. Scanning newsgroups, Web sites, and other network-accessible documents for email addresses is called address harvesting. Spammers use automated scanning agents to obtain lists of email addresses for targeted email transmission by scanning openly accessible documents on the Net; this differs from address-mining agents, which run in the background and stealthily obtain addresses from files and client input on the client's computer itself. Brute-force spamming attacks involve the attempt to send a test email to every possible address combination at a particular site. Spammers also acquire lists of email addresses during business asset acquisition and through transfer from affiliated "business partnerships."

Answer 9-6

Answers **A**, **B**, **C**, and **D** are all correct. Spam is a problem at all levels, as a threat to individuals and corporations as well as governmental bodies. Because spammers can operate from anywhere in the world, making use of the differences between legal systems, the problem becomes one of global scope as well.

Answer 9-7

Answers **A**, **B**, **C**, and **D**. Spam-filtering solutions include the use of automatic accept/deny filtration based on established Blocked List/Allowed List source address listings. Content-based filtering can be used to exclude specific content, while heuristic filtering often combines other types of filtration to identify spam that meets certain threshold criteria. Challenge-response and other methods of filtration are also being developed in an effort to slow the spread of spam, although each new solution is met by increasing efforts on the part of the spammers. Because of the tremendous volume of spam that a client might encounter, manual evaluation of each email message is not a viable solution.

CHAPTER 10

Norton AntiSpam Installation

Terms and Techniques to Remember

- Allowed List/Blocked List
- Ad blocking
- Subscription
- Activation
- Registration
- LiveUpdate™
- Features available within Norton AntiSpam™
- Minimum system requirements for Norton AntiSpam
- Installing Norton AntiSpam
- Integrating Norton AntiSpam with common email client applications
- Removing Norton AntiSpam

Introduction

Productivity is greatly affected by the amount of spam sent in today's world. Norton AntiSpam will reduce the amount of spam cluttering the inboxes of a small business making online communications safer and more efficient. Relatively few steps are necessary to prepare for and then perform an installation of Norton AntiSpam for your clients. This chapter provides you with the steps to install, activate and configure Norton AntiSpam for use with common email applications within a small business environment.

What Is Norton AntiSpam?

Norton AntiSpam is an application that runs on a client's computer to evaluate incoming email messages and filter those that match established criteria set by the client, to reduce the amount of spam that a client must wade through to use email for normal purposes.

How Does Norton AntiSpam Work?

Norton AntiSpam does not delete incoming messages; it moves identified spam into a separate folder to keep only meaningful messages in the client's inbox. This has the advantage of allowing a client to review identified spam, looking for false-positive identifications (emails that are not spam but that the application identified as such).

Norton AntiSpam makes use of multiple types of configurable spam filtration, including Allowed and Blocked Lists, content filtration based on language, or content containing remote images, invisible text, HTML forms, scripts, ActiveX objects, Java applets, and disguised or obscured Web links. Clients can specify particular email source addresses as being automatically allowed (Allowed List) or automatically filtered (Blocked List). Other email messages are evaluated for violations of content rules by including linguistic elements that match user-specified language-filtration criteria. Norton AntiSpam keeps spam definitions and program files up-to-date through the LiveUpdate service.

As a client employs Norton AntiSpam operating within a supported email client, its operation will improve as the system learns what is considered legitimate email by analyzing outgoing messages and as individual email addresses or even entire domains are added to the Blocked List. Norton AntiSpam can automatically add outgoing destination email addresses to the Allowed List so that responses to a client's own email messages will avoid filtration upon return.

Tip
Never respond to spam emails: A direct response can add the spammer's address to a client's Allowed List of allowed addresses. Not only can the response validate the recipient's address, but it also enables new emails from the spammer to be placed in the client's inbox unless the client later removes the spammer's address from the Norton AntiSpam Allowed List.

Norton AntiSpam also blocks pop-up windows and provides ad-blocking protection by monitoring for these types of intrusive events and preventing them from occurring. Together these capabilities enable Norton AntiSpam to reduce the amount of spam a client must endure and provide an improved browsing experience by reducing screen clutter by eliminating pop-up, pop-under, and banner ads.

Ad Blocking and Pop-Up Blocking
Ad blocking prevents automatically loaded ads from appearing when the client is browsing Web sites. Many ad-supported Web sites require ad-blocking software to be turned off to access the site. Pop-up blocking operates similarly, blocking the automatic opening of additional Web sites when a client navigates to a new Web page. Management of these options is discussed later in this section.

Norton AntiSpam makes use of Symantec's LiveUpdate service (shown in Figure 10-1) to maintain the most recent versions of spam definitions and program updates. The LiveUpdate service can be configured for automated execution on a regular interval or can be run manually, as desired.

As Figure 10-1 shows, the LiveUpdate utility provides updates to a number of different elements of Norton AntiSpam at one time. LiveUpdate also can operate in concert with other Symantec products, such as Symantec AntiVirus.

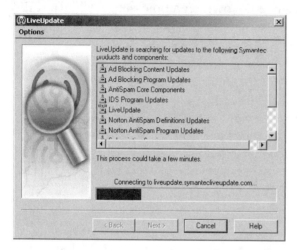

Figure 10-1 An example of Symantec LiveUpdate for Norton AntiSpam.

Requirements

Before installing Norton AntiSpam, you should make sure that the operating system and any installed applications have been fully patched with all appropriate service packs, patches, and hot fixes. Norton AntiSpam can be used with several versions of the Microsoft® Windows® operating system and can be integrated with many commonly used email client applications.

Operating Systems

To use Norton AntiSpam, you must be using one of the following versions of Microsoft's Windows operating system:

- Windows® Me/98/98SE

- Windows® 2000 Professional

- Windows® XP Home/XP Professional/XP Tablet PC/XP Media Center

Norton AntiSpam is not supported on Windows® 95/NT 4.x, Macintosh, Linux, or server versions of Windows 2000/XP computers.

Minimum System Requirements

The host computer must also fulfill the minimum system requirements identified in Tables 10-1–10-3, depending on the client's operating system version.

Table 10-1

Minimum System Requirements for Norton AntiSpam Installation on Windows 98/98SE/Me	
Component	**Minimum Required**
CPU	155 MHz or higher
RAM	32 MB or higher
HDD space	80 MB of available space
Medium	CD-ROM or DVD-ROM
Browser	Internet Explorer 5.5 or higher

Table 10-2

Minimum System Requirements for Norton AntiSpam Installation on Windows 2000 Pro	
Component	**Minimum Required**
CPU	155 MHz or higher
RAM	64 MB or higher
HDD space	80 MB of available space
Medium	CD-ROM or DVD-ROM
Browser	Internet Explorer 5.5 or higher

Table 10-3

Minimum System Requirements for Norton AntiSpam Installation on Windows XP	
Component	**Minimum Required**
CPU	300 MHz or higher
RAM	128 MB or higher
HDD Space	80 MB of available space
Medium	CD-ROM or DVD-ROM
Browser	Internet Explorer 5.5 or higher

This listing is correct as of this printing.

Deployment Scenario

Imagine that your client has 50 Windows 2000 systems with 64 MB of RAM and 10 GB of HDD space, and 50 Windows XP systems with the same configuration. What is necessary to install Norton AntiSpam on all of the client's systems (assuming that all other factors are sufficient)? When you review the list, you should note that the minimum RAM for a Windows XP system is higher than that for a Windows 2000 system (128 MB instead of 64 MB). The client will need to upgrade the RAM in the XP boxes to at least 128 MB before Norton AntiSpam can be installed on all systems.

Email Clients

Norton AntiSpam can be fully integrated with the following common email client applications, providing a custom email spam toolbar:

- Microsoft Outlook® 2000
- Microsoft Outlook® XP
- Microsoft Outlook® 2003
- Microsoft Outlook® Express (version 5.5 and later)
- Eudora™ (version 5.0 and later)

Norton AntiSpam can also be used with most POP3-compliant email programs, including these:

- Netscape® Messenger (version 4.x and later)
- Netscape Mail® 6.0/P
- Yahoo!® Mail
- Yahoo!® Mail Plus

Note

Support for Microsoft Hotmail® is provided only when accessed using Microsoft Outlook.

Norton AntiSpam does not support scanning email for the following email clients and protocols:

- Lotus Notes®
- America Online® (AOL®)
- IMAP
- POP3 clients that utilize Secure Sockets Layer (SSL) security, which can include ISP- and corporate-provided secure Web email access

> **Tip**
> Web-based email clients using SSL security can be identified by the locking symbol displayed by their browser client, as shown in Figure 10-2.

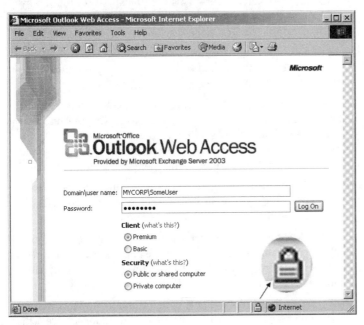

Figure 10-2 Secure Sockets Layer protection icon in Internet Explorer.

The Norton AntiSpam Package

Norton AntiSpam is licensed as a stand-alone package, as well as a component in the Norton Internet Security™ suite. Licenses can be individually purchased or obtained in 5-pack and 10-pack license bundles.

Features

Norton AntiSpam includes a number of features, allowing the client to configure spam filtration based on individual preferences. These features are listed in Table 10-4.

Table 10-4

Features Available in Norton AntiSpam 2005

Feature	Function
Integration with common email client applications	Norton AntiSpam can add spam-filtration controls to the email client's toolbar. This enables clients to access AntiSpam features within their usual email client, without requiring additional steps to open a separate console.
Allowed and Blocked Lists	User-defined address lists are used to automatically filter messages from allowed and blocked senders. This option can be configured by address or by email domain, enabling clients to easily allow all emails from a particular domain, such as *mycorp.com*.
Automatic address list import	Norton AntiSpam can automatically populate a client's list of allowed senders using the email client's Address List, avoiding the need for each client to manually configure a sender's list item by item.
Self-training	Norton AntiSpam can automatically add outgoing email addresses to the list of allowed senders, to avoid blocking responses. Norton AntiSpam can also automatically filter self-sent items to prevent spammers from sending messages with the same To and From addresses, which would otherwise appear as if they came from the client and would be allowed.
Custom rules	These enable the client to configure which spam-filtering and content rules will be applied to new email so that each client can configure antispam protection to suit individual needs and requirements.
Language filtering	The client can block all email written in specified languages, automatically blocking spam that is not written in the client's preferred language(s). This helps protect the user from spam messages composed in foreign languages to slip by less capable defenses.
Automatic updates	With their yearly subscription, clients gain automatic updates to their spam-definitions files through the Symantec LiveUpdate service. This process ensures that the client's inbox will continue to be protected against newly emerging mechanisms employed by spammers.
Yahoo! Mail and Yahoo! Mail Plus filtering	This enables spam filtering within the Yahoo! Mail and Yahoo! Mail Plus Web-based email system.

This is not intended to be a complete listing of all options provided by Norton AntiSpam. This listing is meant only to detail some of the more useful aggregate features available.

Subscription

Norton AntiSpam will function for up to 15 days before it must be activated using the unique product key provided with its source media. When activated, the Norton AntiSpam license extends for 12 months. During this time, the Symantec LiveUpdate service can be used to update the spam definitions and application components to meet emerging security and functionality goals. As the product's subscription expiration date nears, the client is visually prompted to renew the subscription for the following year.

Support

Norton AntiSpam has very detailed step-by-step instructions to guide you during the installation of this product, and a detailed set of help files is available after installation. In addition, the Norton AntiSpam User's Guide is available in PDF format (NAS.PDF), in the MANUAL folder of the installation CD.

Additional support is available on the Symantec Web site, accessible through the Norton AntiSpam Help menu or by browsing to www.symantec.com.

Preinstallation

Before installing Norton AntiSpam, it is important to perform a few simple preinstallation steps that are appropriate to most application installations:

1. Log in as a user with the appropriate privileges (any user in Windows 98/98SE/Me).

2. Close all open applications.

3. Ensure that mobile devices are plugged in, to prevent installation failure because of exhausted batteries.

4. Make sure that scheduled processes such as full-system virus scans or system automatic updates will not occur during the installation.

Installing Norton AntiSpam

Norton AntiSpam can be installed as a stand-alone application or as an element of the Norton Internet Security suite. Here we review the installation of the stand-alone client, which is identical to the component installed within the integrated suite. In preparation for taking the exam, you should be familiar with the stand-alone version of the product, although you can also use this text and the integrated version to practice its use.

Getting Started

 To install Norton AntiSpam, insert the installation medium into the CD-ROM drive. If auto-play is enabled, the welcome screen (shown in Figure 10-3) appears; otherwise, navigate to the proper drive and select **CDSTART** from the root folder.

Figure 10-3 The Norton AntiSpam 2005 welcome screen.

From this location, you can choose to install Norton AntiSpam, to browse the installation medium contents, or exit and abort the installation. You can open the Norton AntiSpam User's Guide in Adobe Portable Document Format (.pdf), by following these steps:

1. Select the option to browse the installation medium.

2. Select the MANUAL folder.

3. Select the NAS.PDF document to open the User's Manual.

The Adobe® Reader®
To read Adobe Portable Document Format (.pdf) files, the free Adobe® Reader® must be installed on your computer. The installation medium contains an installation package for the Adobe client, although you might want to check Adobe's site (www.adobe.com) for the latest version of Adobe Reader.

Installation

To install Norton AntiSpam follow these steps:

1. Select the option **Install Norton AntiSpam**, to begin the installation process. You will see the setup welcome screen, shown in Figure 10-4.

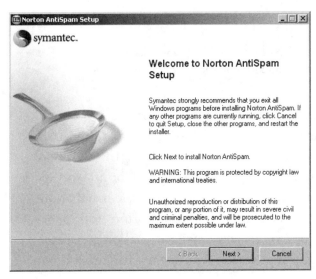

Figure 10-4 The Norton AntiSpam 2005 setup welcome screen.

2. Click the **Next** button to advance to the licensing screen, where you must choose to accept the license agreement and enter the unique product key, provided along with the installation medium, in the space provided (see Figure 10-5).

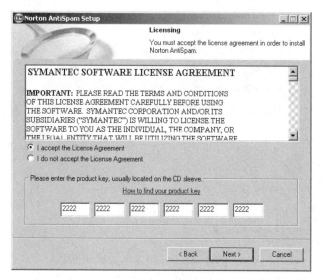

Figure 10-5 The Norton AntiSpam 2005 licensing screen.

Note
The key illustrated in Figure 10-5 is not a valid product key; you must use the product key that was included with the installation medium.

3. After accepting the licensing agreement and entering the product key, click the **Next** button again to select the destination folder for the application's files, as shown in Figure 10-6. Selecting the check box presented in the upper portion of this page allows Norton AntiSpam to be configured to filter Yahoo! Mail at the end of the installation. This configuration can also be started from the Norton AntiSpam interface after installation. We discuss email integration at greater length later in the "Integrating Norton AntiSpam with Email Client" section.

4. After making any changes to the destination folder, select **Next** to begin the installation process. As components are installed, the user interface (shown in Figure 10-7) displays the progress of the complete installation process.

5. When the installation process has concluded, you might be prompted to restart the system, (based on operating system and service pack

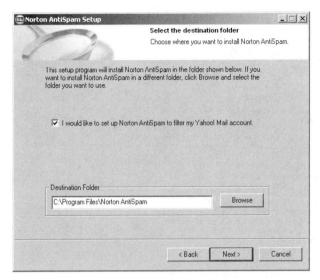

Figure 10-6 Selecting the installation destination folder.

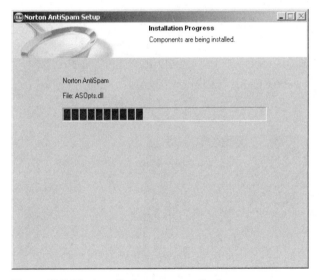

Figure 10-7 The installation progress display.

level) to complete the installation (see Figure 10-8). Selecting **Finish** here closes the installation wizard. You can elect to delay rebooting the system until later; however, if you are requested to do so, the Norton AntiSpam installation will not be complete until the next system reboot has occurred.

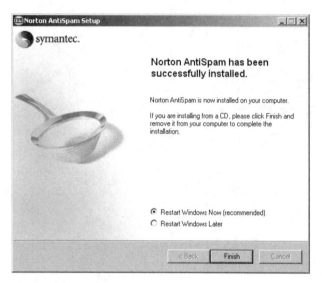

Figure 10-8 Completing the Norton AntiSpam 2005 Installation Wizard.

Before Using Norton AntiSpam

Following a reboot of the system (if needed), the newly installed Norton AntiSpam 2005 prompts you to perform an initial configuration, as shown in Figure 10-9.

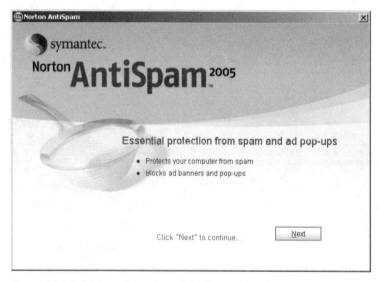

Figure 10-9 Initial configuration of the Norton AntiSpam 2005 application.

Activation and Registration

The initial configuration process consists of a series of steps in which you activate and register the software, as well as set up ad blocking and then run LiveUpdate.

1. Click the **Next** button to start the initial configuration of Norton AntiSpam, beginning with the product activation screen shown in Figure 10-10.

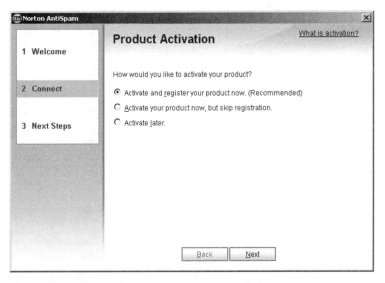

Figure 10-10 The product activation screen, with the option to activate and register selected.

Note

Activation requires connection with the Symantec server. If the computer has no current dial-up, broadband, wireless, or other form of connectivity to the Internet, you can skip activation now and activate later when connected to the Internet.

2. Select **Next** to proceed to the registration screen, unless you selected to skip activation at this time. If you selected to activate and register,

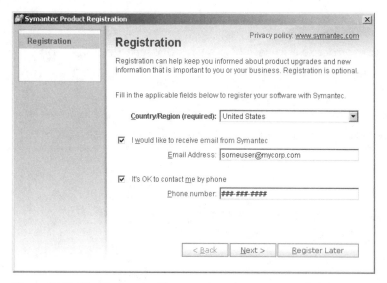

Figure 10-11 The Norton AntiSpam registration screen, with contact information provided.

the registration screen is presented next, as shown in Figure 10-11. Here you are prompted to select the client's country/region and to enter contact information.

> **Note**
> Registration is optional but is strongly recommended. Registering the product and providing email, phone or postal contact details will enable Symantec to keep you informed of product updates and other related information that will be useful to your business.

3. Select **Next** to proceed to the next portion of the registration wizard, where you can enter the client's postal mail contact information (see Figure 10-12).

4. Select **Next** again to initiate the activation process. During this procedure, Norton AntiSpam communicates with the Symantec server to validate the client's subscription and generate a unique key, which is displayed when the activation process is completed (see Figure 10-13).

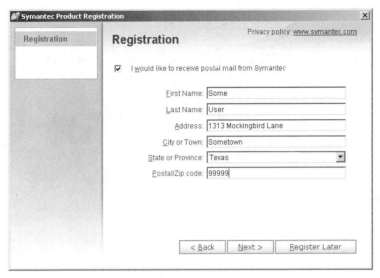

Figure 10-12 The Norton AntiSpam registration screen, with postal mail contact information.

Figure 10-13 The completed activation wizard displaying a simulated key value.

5. Clicking the **Print Key** button displays the text file generated by the activation wizard, containing the client's key, as here:

Example activation key text file (AntiSpam_Key.txt) generated by the wizard

```
Please print this page and keep it in a safe place.
You will need this key in the event that you need to
reinstall Norton AntiSpam.


BBBBBBBBBBBBBBBBBBBBBBBBBB


To print this page, press Ctrl-P.


For future reference, you can find this product key in
C:\Documents and Settings\someuser\My Documents\
Symantec\Norton AntiSpam_Key.txt
```

6. Select **Next** again to display the term of the client's subscription, as shown in Figure 10-14.

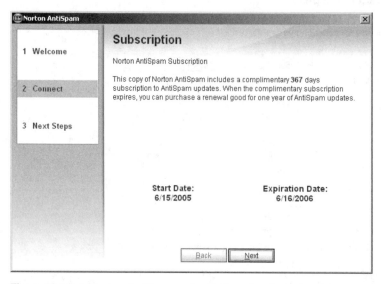

Figure 10-14 A Norton AntiSpam subscription showing term dates.

Yahoo! Mail Users
If you selected to configure Norton AntiSpam so that it will filter Yahoo! Mail access, the configuration wizard will prompt you to enter the client's Yahoo! Mail account information now. This process is covered later in this chapter, along with other forms of email client integration, as it can be run as part of the installation or manually from the management console.

Ad Blocking

1. Select **Next** again to configure ad blocking by default (see Figure 10-15). This setting can be changed later at any time.

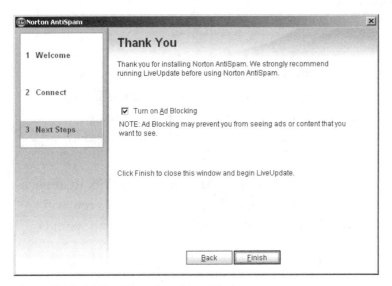

Figure 10-15 Ad blocking selected by default.

LiveUpdate

1. Select **Finish** to conclude the initial configuration steps for Norton AntiSpam. The Symantec LiveUpdate service prompts you to obtain any new updates available for Norton AntiSpam components (see Figure 10-16). Select **Next** here to begin the update process.

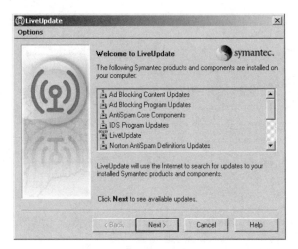

Figure 10-16 Symantec LiveUpdate showing multiple components used by Norton AntiSpam.

2. You might be prompted to select **Next** several times, depending on whether the client already has other Symantec products installed and updated. When LiveUpdate completes, you are prompted to finish and might have to reboot the system to apply the downloaded updates.

3. After the system reboots, you can open the Norton AntiSpam application for use. You will see the status OK and the product's renewal date in the main interface (see Figure 10-17) if Norton AntiSpam is activated.

Activating After Installation

After you have activated the product, the initial configuration process continues. If the product is removed and later reinstalled, the 15-day counter is not reset from the original 15-day period.

If during the activation process you opted to activate later or were unable to activate due to lack of an Internet connection, you would have seen an activation reminder, like that shown in Figure 10-18. The client is given 15 days in which to activate the product before it will stop functioning.

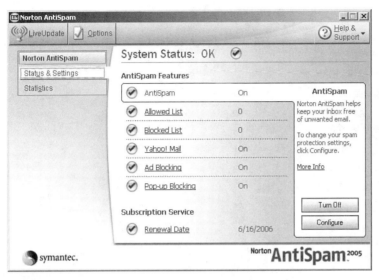

Figure 10-17 Norton AntiSpam 2005 showing status OK and subscription renewal date.

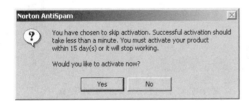

Figure 10-18 The Norton AntiSpam activation reminder showing 15 days remaining.

During the 15 days grace activation period Norton AntiSpam will function correctly but will remind you when you login each day that activation is still required. You will also be reminded when using the management console. As you can see in Figure 10-19, the System Status indicates that attention is needed, and the date by which activation is required is shown.

Launching Norton AntiSpam

Once the installation and initial configuration are complete, you can access Norton AntiSpam by selecting the desktop icon (see Figure 10-20) or by

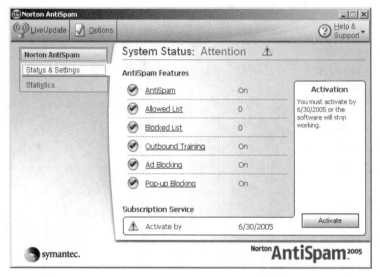

Figure 10-19 The Norton AntiSpam product showing an Attention status notifying you that activation is still required.

Norton
AntiSpam

Figure 10-20 Desktop icon for Norton AntiSpam 2005.

selecting options along the path **Start**, **All Programs**, **Norton AntiSpam**, **Norton AntiSpam**.

Integrating Norton AntiSpam with Email Clients

After Norton AntiSpam has been installed and updated, it can be integrated with many popular email client applications, including these:

- Microsoft Outlook 2000
- Microsoft Outlook XP
- Microsoft Outlook 2003
- Microsoft Outlook Express (version 5.5 and later)
- Eudora (version 5.0 and later)

It is also compatible with most POP3-compatible email programs, including these:

- Netscape Messenger (version 4.x and later)
- Netscape Mail 6.0/P
- Yahoo! Mail
- Yahoo! Mail Plus

The rest of this section discusses the steps necessary to configure Norton AntiSpam for use with Microsoft Outlook and Yahoo! Mail.

Microsoft Outlook

When Norton AntiSpam is integrated with the client's email client application, several spam-related controls are added to the client's toolbars to make spam processing easier. In the Microsoft Outlook client, Norton AntiSpam prompts you to specify whether you want Norton AntiSpam to be integrated into the client's client application (see Figure 10-21). This occurs the first time the client opens Outlook following the installation of Norton AntiSpam.

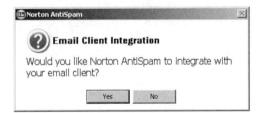

Figure 10-21 Norton AntiSpam integration prompt for Microsoft Outlook.

After configuration, the Norton AntiSpam controls appear in the Outlook toolbar and the new Norton AntiSpam folder is present in the client's list of mail folders, as shown in Figure 10-22. Email identified as spam is moved to this custom folder, where it can be later reviewed for deletion or, as in the example here, specified as not being spam so that the selected item's source address will be added to the client's Allowed List address listing.

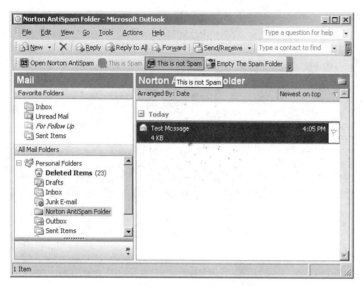

Figure 10-22 Outlook with Norton AntiSpam, illustrating the specification of a nonspam item in the new Norton AntiSpam folder.

Note

The This is not Spam option is displayed only while the client is reviewing items in the Norton AntiSpam folder; in all other folders, the This is Spam option is displayed instead. The options Open Norton AntiSpam and Empty the Spam Folder remain always visible within this interface.

Yahoo! Mail

Norton AntiSpam can also be used with other email clients. If your customer is a Yahoo! Mail client and you selected to configure Norton AntiSpam to filter that customer's Yahoo! Mail account during installation, three more steps would have been added following the activation process (following step 1 earlier in this chapter):

1. You would be prompted to select to add the client's Yahoo! Mail account information, as shown in Figure 10-23.

2. You would have been prompted to provide the client's Yahoo! Mail logon account information (see Figure 10-24).

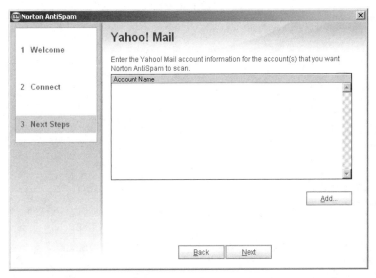

Figure 10-23 Norton AntiSpam Configuration Wizard with Yahoo! Mail integration selected.

Figure 10-24 The Yahoo! Mail account information dialog box.

3. After selecting **Test** to verify the account configuration (see Figure 10-25), you would have had to select **OK** and proceed to step 2 of the normal configuration process, detailed previously in this chapter.

When Norton AntiSpam has been fully configured and updated, its functionality is displayed when the customer accesses Yahoo! Mail, as seen

Figure 10-25 The confirmation message box
displayed after a successful test.

in Figure 10-26. In this example, you can see that the Norton AntiSpam folder
has been added to the list of available folders.

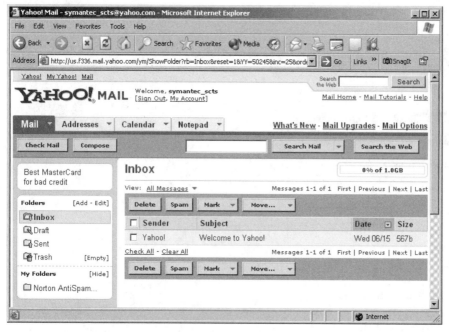

Figure 10-26 Yahoo! Mail with Norton AntiSpam integrated functionality.

Removing Norton AntiSpam

If your customer decides to uninstall Norton AntiSpam, you can do so by
using the Microsoft Windows Add/Remove Programs utility, located within
the system Control Panel, or by reinserting the original Norton AntiSpam
medium and selecting the option to install the application again. Both

solutions initialize the Norton AntiSpam Setup Wizard in its removal configuration, as shown in Figure 10-27.

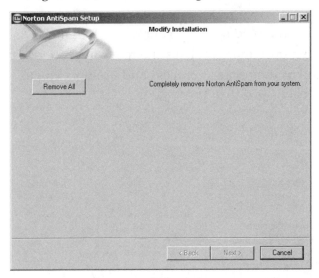

Figure 10-27 The Norton AntiSpam Setup Wizard displaying the Remove All option.

After clicking the **Remove All** button within the setup wizard, you are prompted to select whether to save the client's settings for a later reload of the Norton AntiSpam application (see Figure 10-28). This allows the client to

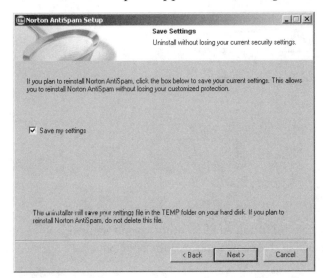

Figure 10-28 The Norton AntiSpam removal prompt to save settings.

keep all Allowed List/Blocked List address listings, along with the configured filtration rules. If you later reinstall the Norton AntiSpam client application, these settings will be maintained.

After selecting **Next**, you are prompted to verify your desire to remove Norton AntiSpam. Selecting **Next** once more initiates the removal process. The wizard confirms completion of the removal process and prompts you to reboot to finalize the changes (see Figure 10-29).

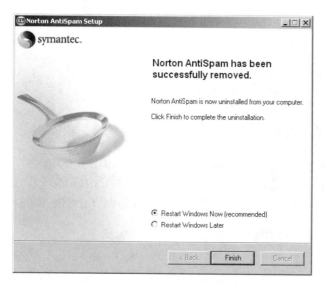

Figure 10-29 The Norton AntiSpam Setup Wizard confirming removal.

Note
When this process is completed, Norton AntiSpam has been removed and will no longer be protecting the client's inbox against incoming spam.

Conclusion

In this chapter, you learned how to install, activate and configure Norton Antispam for use with common email applications. Norton AntiSpam provides comprehensive filtering of spam and reduces time wasted responding to ad and pop-up blocking. By integrating a self-training email-filtering system with both rules-based and client-selection configuration options, Norton AntiSpam provides a versatile solution easily tailored to the requirements of a small business environment.

For additional details on the Norton AntiSpam product and the packaging options available for subscription services, check out the Symantec Web site at www.symantec.com/smallbiz/nas/.

Chapter Review Questions

Question 10-1

Upon receipt, blocked messages are _____, while allowed messages are _____. Select the best answer from those provided.

◯ A. Deleted, left alone

◯ B. Moved to another folder, left alone

◯ C. Left alone, deleted

◯ D. Left alone, moved to another folder

◯ E. Moved to another folder, deleted

Question 10-2

A false positive means that _____. Select the best answer from those provided.

◯ A. A wanted email has been identified as spam.

◯ B. A spam email has been left alone.

◯ C. An outgoing email's destination address has been added to the Allowed List.

○ D. An outgoing email's destination address has been added to the Blocked List.

○ E. A client's own email address has been added to the Blocked List.

Question 10-3

Which types of antispam filtering are available using Norton AntiSpam? Select all that apply.

❑ A. Content filtering

❑ B. Allowed Listing/Blocked Listing

❑ C. Heuristic filtering

❑ D. Ad blocking

❑ E. Pop-up blocking

Question 10-4

Why is it a bad idea to reply to spam email? Select all answers that apply.

❑ A. The client could increase the amount of spam received.

❑ B. The spammer's address could be added to the Blocked List of addresses.

❑ C. The client's address could be added to the Blocked List of addresses.

❑ D. The spammer's address could be added to the Allowed List of addresses.

❑ E. The client's address could be added to the Allowed List of addresses.

Question 10-5

Which of the following operating systems are supported by Norton AntiSpam? Select all that apply.

❑ A. Windows 95

❑ B. Windows 98

❑ C. Windows NT

❑ D. Windows 2000 Professional

❑ E. Windows XP

Question 10-6

Which of the following systems meet the minimum hardware requirements for Norton AntiSpam? Select all that apply.

❑ A. Windows XP, 155 MHz CPU, 128 MB of RAM, 100 MB of HDD space, CD-ROM

❑ B. Windows Me, 133 MHz CPU, 128 MB of RAM, 100 MB of HDD space, CD-ROM

❑ C. Windows 2000 Professional, 233 MHz CPU, 64 MB of HDD Space, 128 MB of RAM, DVD-ROM

❑ D. Windows 95, 350 MHz CPU, 256 MB of RAM, 100 MB of HDD space, CD-ROM

❑ E. Windows XP, 1.2 GHz CPU, 128 MB of RAM, 10 MB of HDD space, DVD-ROM

Question 10-7

Which of the following email clients can integrate or be filtered by Norton AntiSpam? Select all that apply.

❑ A. America Online (AOL)

❑ B. Netscape Messenger 5

❑ C. Microsoft Outlook XP

❑ D. Microsoft Outlook Express 5.5

❑ E. Eudora 6

❑ F. Lotus Notes

❑ G. Yahoo! Mail

Question 10-8

Norton AntiSpam 2005 can be installed without activation to evaluate the software for a short time. How long does the client have before it is necessary to activate the Norton AntiSpam installation? Select the best answer from those provided.

- ○ A. 7 days
- ○ B. 14 days
- ○ C. 15 days
- ○ D. 30 days
- ○ E. 45 days

Question 10-9

Which tasks should you perform before beginning your Norton AntiSpam installation? Select all that apply.

- ❑ A. Close all open applications
- ❑ B. Plug in mobile devices
- ❑ C. Check for conflicting prescheduled processes
- ❑ D. Make sure that you have your installation medium and product key

Question 10-10

Which steps are the minimum required to install Norton AntiSpam? Select all that apply.

- ❑ A. Accept the license agreement
- ❑ B. Activate Norton AntiSpam
- ❑ C. Enter the unique product key
- ❑ D. Register Norton AntiSpam

Question 10-11

After the initial configuration of Norton AntiSpam, which of the following methods will allow you to open the Norton AntiSpam application? Select all that apply.

- ❑ A. Selecting the desktop icon for Norton AntiSpam
- ❑ B. Opening CDSTART on the installation media

❑ C. Using the toolbar within an integrated Outlook instance

❑ D. Selecting the shortcut within All Programs, Norton AntiSpam

❑ E. Opening NAS.PDF on the installation medium

Question 10-12

Which of the following contact information elements are required to activate a licensed copy of Norton AntiSpam? Select all that apply.

❑ A. Email address

❑ B. Phone number

❑ C. Postal mail address

❑ D. All of the above

❑ E. None of the above

Question 10-13

Which of the following email client applications can integrate with or be filtered by Norton AntiSpam? Select all that apply.

❑ A. Microsoft Outlook 2000

❑ B. Microsoft Outlook Express 5.5

❑ C. Microsoft Hotmail (Web)

❑ D. Yahoo! Mail (Web)

❑ E. Eudora 5.0

Question 10-14

Your customer opens Microsoft Outlook, which you have integrated with Norton AntiSpam. Within the customer's inbox, which of the following options would be available within the toolbar? Select all that apply.

❑ A. Open Norton AntiSpam

❑ B. This Is Spam

❑ C. This Is Not Spam

❑ D. Empty the Spam Folder

Chapter Review Answers

Answer 10-1

Answer **B** is correct. Upon receipt, blocked messages are moved to the Spam folder but are not deleted; allowed messages are left alone.

Answer 10-2

Answer **A** is correct. A false positive means that a wanted email has been identified as spam.

Answer 10-3

Answers **A**, **B**, **D**, and **E** are correct. Norton AntiSpam provides language-based email content filtering, Blocked List/Allowed List email source address lists, and ad-blocking and pop-up blocking protections. Because of the processing requirements of heuristic spam analysis, this type of filtering requires a server-based antispam solution.

Answer 10-4

Answers **A** and **D** are correct. By responding to a spammer's email, the client validates the address for additional spam message listings. In addition, the outgoing target email address could be added to the Allowed List, allowing later spam from the same source to be left unfiltered.

Answer 10-5

Answers **B**, **D,** and **E** are correct. Norton AntiSpam is supported on Windows 98, 98SE, Me, 2000 Professional, and XP. Norton AntiSpam is not supported on Windows 95 or Windows NT.

Answer 10-6

Of the listed systems, only answer **D** is correct. Answer A is incorrect because Windows XP requires at least a 300 MHz CPU. Answer E is incorrect because the minimum installation on a Windows XP system requires 80 MB of HDD space. Answer B is incorrect because Windows Me installations require at least a 155 MHz CPU, and answer C is incorrect because Windows 2000 Professional installations require at least 80 MB of available HDD space.

Answer 10-7

Answers **B**, **C**, **D**, **E**, and **G** are correct. Norton AntiSpam can integrate with or filter several email clients, allowing the use of custom antispam controls added to the client toolbars. These clients include Netscape Messenger, Microsoft Outlook and Outlook Express, Eudora, and Yahoo! Mail and Yahoo! Mail Plus. Norton AntiSpam does not support America Online (AOL) or Lotus Notes from those provided.

Answer 10-8

Answer **C** is correct. Norton AntiSpam 2005 can be installed without activation to evaluate the software for up to 15 days. After this time, the client must activate the product for continued use.

Answer 10-9

Answers **A**, **B**, **C**, and **D** are all correct. Before beginning your Norton AntiSpam installation, you should close all open applications, plug in any battery-powered devices, check for conflicting scheduling applications such as virus scans or automatic updates, and make sure that you have your installation medium and unique product key.

Answer 10-10

Answers **A** and **C** are correct. The minimum steps required to install Norton AntiSpam are to accept the license agreement and provide the unique product key. Although activation is required to continue using Norton AntiSpam past 15 days, it is not required to evaluate the product. Registration is also optional and is not required in this case.

Answer 10-11

Answers **A**, **C**, and **D** are correct. After the initial configuration of Norton AntiSpam, you can access the application by selecting the Norton AntiSpam desktop icon or selecting its shortcut within All Programs, Norton AntiSpam. You can also select to open Norton AntiSpam from the toolbar within an integrated instance of Microsoft Outlook. Opening CDSTART on the installation medium opens the initial screen used to install or browse from the installation medium, and the NAS.PDF file is simply an electronic version of the User's Guide for Norton AntiSpam.

Answer 10-12

Answer **E** is correct. Registration is not required for activation; one of the three options for activation is to activate without registration of client contact information. Had the client desired to register as well, only the Region/Country selection would be required; all other contact information is voluntary and not required.

Answer 10-13

Answers **A**, **B**, **D**, and **E** are correct. Norton AntiSpam can be integrated into the functionality of Microsoft Outlook 2000, Outlook Express 5.5, and Eudora 5.0. Norton AntiSpam can also filter Yahoo! Mail and Yahoo! Mail Plus services through Web connectivity, but it cannot be configured to filter spam from a Microsoft Hotmail account unless it is accessed through Outlook or Outlook Express.

Answer 10-14

Answers **A**, **B**, and **D** are correct. With all folders of an Norton AntiSpam-integrated instance of Outlook, the options Open Norton AntiSpam and Empty the Spam Folder are always available. Only within the Norton AntiSpam folder is the option This Is Not Spam available. In all other folders, including the inbox, the option This Is Spam is available in its place.

CHAPTER 11

Norton AntiSpam Management

Terms and Techniques to Remember

- Management console
- Antispam level
- Language filter
- Configuring spam rules in the desired order of evaluation
- Establishing the desired AutoBlock settings

Introduction

This chapter provides a comprehensive review of the configuration options available within Norton AntiSpam to assist a small business in providing maximum spam protection. The capabilities within the management console include setting the spam level threshold, importing address book contacts, creating Allowed and Blocked lists and creating custom rules. While being a low maintenance solution, Norton Antispam has the flexibility to be configured to meet the needs of a small business environment to ensure security at the desktop.

The Management Console

After Norton AntiSpam has been installed, you can open the management console (see Figure 11-1) by selecting the **Norton AntiSpam** icon on your desktop; by selecting its shortcut within the **Start**, **All Programs**, **Norton AntiSpam** folder; or by selecting the **Open Norton AntiSpam** toolbar button within Outlook or other email client integrated with Norton AntiSpam functionality.

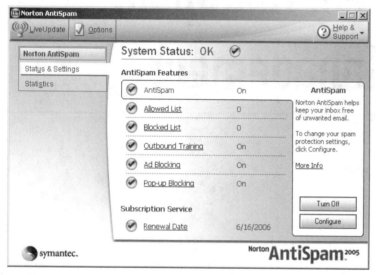

Figure 11-1 The Norton AntiSpam 2005 management console.

The Norton AntiSpam management console opens within the **Status & Settings** interface. This example portrays a system with a current status of OK and a subscription service renewal date of June 16, 2006. The status of OK indicates that Norton AntiSpam is turned on and currently within its subscription period.

> **Note**
> If you are unclear on the subscription and status details, review the previous chapter on installing Norton AntiSpam.

Status & Settings

The primary category of client configuration options can be found by selecting the **Status & Settings** tab. Within the Status & Settings interface, a number of common features are listed. These are selectable and display any available options when focus is directed to each, as in Figure 11-1. In that figure, the **AntiSpam** feature carries the current focus, displaying two option buttons, to **Turn Off** the AntiSpam filter or to **Configure** the general settings that apply to this option.

Selecting feature option buttons changes focus to the appropriate options page within the interface, as in the case of selecting the **Configure** button within the AntiSpam feature. When this control is selected, focus is redirected to the **General** AntiSpam options page, shown in Figure 11-2. Table 11-1 details the client options available within Norton AntiSpam.

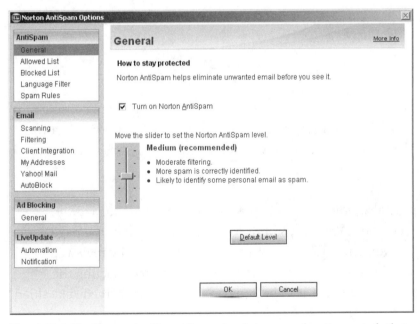

Figure 11-2 The Norton AntiSpam General options page, showing controls that toggle Norton AntiSpam on and off, as well as to select the level of filtering desired.

Table 11-1

Norton AntiSpam Options	
Category	**Options**
AntiSpam	General
	Allowed List
	Blocked List
	Language Filter
	Spam Rules
Email	Scanning
	Filtering
	Client Integration
	My Addresses
	Yahoo!™ Mail
	AutoBlock
Ad Blocking	General
LiveUpdate™	Automation
	Notification

Details of each option listed here are provided later in this chapter.

Statistics

In addition to the Status & Settings general page, the management console provides access to historical statistics, which detail activity since the product was installed or the last time the statistics were manually reset (see Figure 11-3).

Email Filtering Log

The **Statistics** page also offers access to the Norton AntiSpam log viewer, accessed by selecting the **View Logs** button at the lower right of the page. Within the log viewer, email filtering events can be individually reviewed (see Figure 11-4), allowing you to train the spam-filtering by selecting the **Retrain as Spam** or **Retrain as Clean** buttons on messages incorrectly classified.

Content Blocking Log

In addition to the Email Filtering log, Norton AntiSpam tracks all actions taken by its content-blocking function for the ad-blocking function, which

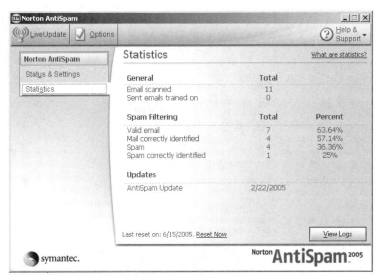

Figure 11-3 The Norton AntiSpam Statistics page.

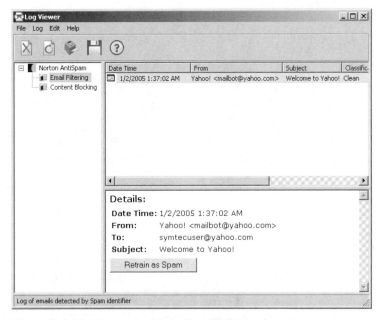

Figure 11-4 The Norton AntiSpam Email Filtering log view.

can be enabled or disabled according to client preference. Figure 11-5 illustrates this logging capability; here an advertisement has been blocked on the `http://mail.yahoo.com/` Web site.

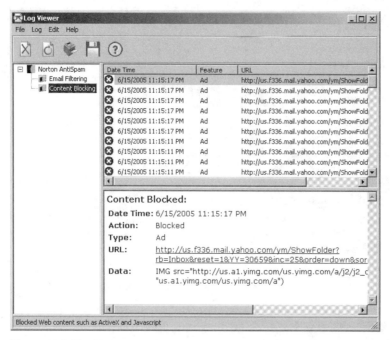

Figure 11-5 The Norton AntiSpam Content Blocking log view.

Other Functionality

In addition to the Status & Statistics page, the management console includes a number of functions available, including access to **LiveUpdate** (see Figure 11-6). LiveUpdate will download updates from Symantec to ensure that program components, antispam definition files and other functional elements are kept up to date.

Help and Support

The Norton AntiSpam management console also provides you with a number of **Help & Support** options, as detailed in Figure 11-7. Here Norton AntiSpam

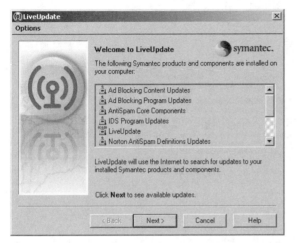

Figure 11-6 The Norton AntiSpam LiveUpdate service, detailing all of the elements that will be checked for update.

Figure 11-7 Norton AntiSpam Help & Support options.

can be activated after the initial installation by selecting the Norton AntiSpam Activation option to open the activation wizard.

Norton AntiSpam provides access to rich user-support options, including both Web-based solutions provided through the Symantec Security Response option and detailed Symantec Help Center help files in a standard Windows® help file format (see Figure 11-8).

Options

The Status & Settings page provides access to many common configuration options within each of the provided AntiSpam features. These options are also accessible by selecting the **Options** button at the top of the management console (shown previously in Figure 11-1).

AntiSpam

The AntiSpam section of the options includes five pages: **General**, **Allowed List**, **Blocked List**, **Language Filter**, and **Spam Rules**. Details of each page follow.

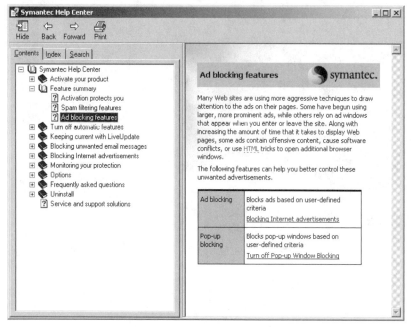

Figure 11-8 The Symantec Help Center interface.

General

Selecting the **Options** button brings up the **General** page for the Norton AntiSpam solution shown previously in Figure 11-2. Here you can toggle the antispam protections on or off. Additionally, the General options page allows adjustment of the current level of protection used. Table 11-2 details the settings provided at each level. The **Default Level** button can be selected to return to the Medium level, recommended by Symantec.

Scenario

If you want to ensure the highest possible level of security that rarely identifies personal email as spam, you would select Low to minimize the personal email falsely identified as spam. If you want the highest level of protection, regardless of what might be incorrectly identified as spam, you would specify the High setting.

Table 11-2

Norton AntiSpam Levels

Level	Settings
High	Maximum filtering Most spam correctly identified More likely to identify personal email as spam
Medium-High	Moderate filtering Almost all spam correctly identified More likely to identify some personal email as spam
Medium (Recommended)	Moderate filtering More spam correctly identified Likely to identify some personal email as spam
Medium-Low	Moderate filtering More spam correctly identified Less likely to identify personal email as spam
Low	Light filtering Some spam correctly identified Rarely identifies personal email as spam

These are general levels of antispam filtering. Obviously, individual settings and training of the Blocked List/Allowed List address listings will improve spam identification as the client continues to use the product.

Allowed List

The second options page within the AntiSpam section is the **Allowed List** page (see Figure 11-9). Norton AntiSpam does not filter email coming from addresses in this listing.

One highly useful feature of this interface is the **Import Address Book** feature. By clicking this button, you can automatically populate the Allowed List with the email addresses of your email contacts, as illustrated in Figure 11-10. As with entries in the Blocked List, individual email addresses or entire email domains can be specified. Your corporate email domain should be added to this list, to ensure that internal email is not accidentally identified as spam.

Blocked List

As a counter to the Allowed List, the **Blocked List** (see Figure 11-11) details addresses identified as spam sources. Messages received from addresses in this list are automatically filtered and moved into the Spam folder as they are received.

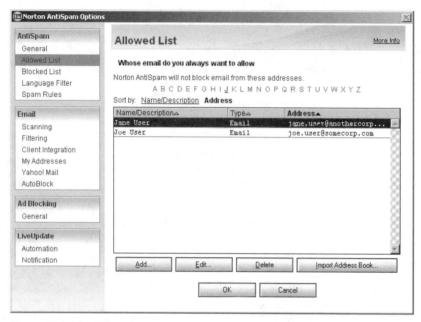

Figure 11-9 The Allowed List populated by importing the client's address book contacts.

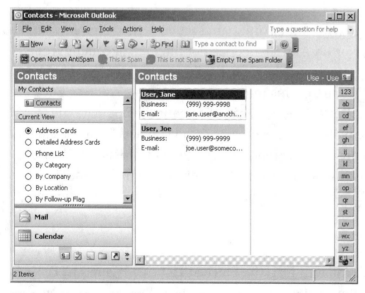

Figure 11-10 Microsoft Office contacts used to populate the Allowed List.

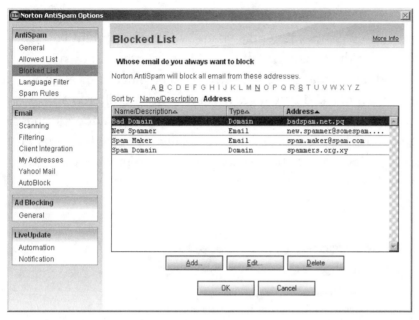

Figure 11-11 The Blocked List populated by individual email and domain addresses.

Addresses can be entered into this list using the controls within the email application, or can be directly added, edited, or deleted within this interface. Figure 11-12 shows the options available for a new Blocked List entry: allowing blocking by an individual email address or by the entire email domain of the identified address. By selecting to block all email from any address within a domain, Norton AntiSpam can protect against spammers that incrementally change the *<name>* portion of *<name>@somecorp.com* type of email addresses each time they send a new message.

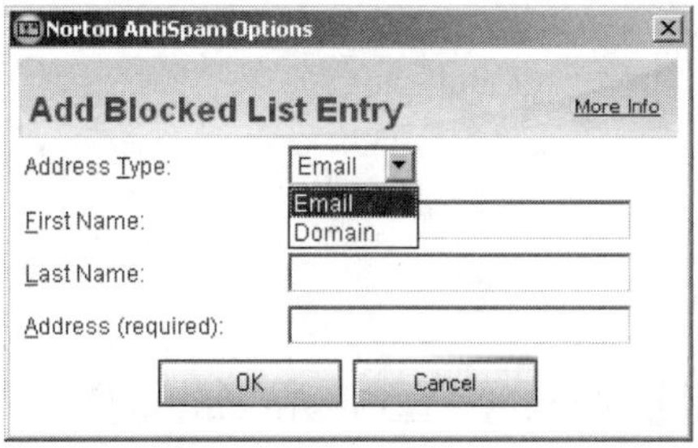

Figure 11-12 Individual email and domain options for a new Blocked List entry.

Language Filter

Norton AntiSpam also identifies potential spam by filtering content based on your preferences. In the **Language Filter** selection interface, shown in Figure 11-13, individual languages can be selected to be blocked or allowed. Email messages sent in blocked languages automatically are filtered and sent to the Spam folder if their senders have not already been added to the Allowed List. You should configure the Language Filter to only allow email in languages that they might reasonably expect to receive, to provide the best possible antispam defense.

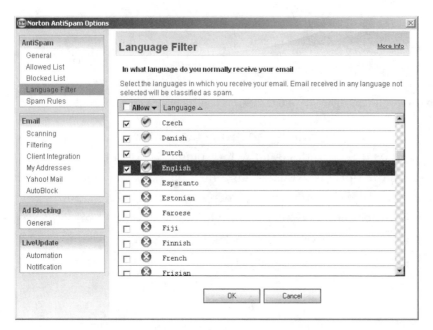

Figure 11-13 The Language Filter interface, showing the selection of multiple allowed languages.

Spam Rules

In addition to language-based content filtering, Norton AntiSpam can filter email messages based on specified **Spam Rules**, as shown in Figure 11-14.

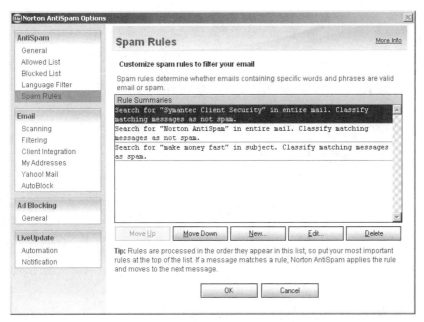

Figure 11-14 The Spam Rules management interface showing several client-defined rules, which are evaluated in order from the top of the list down. The first matching rule is implemented.

Tip
Rule order is important. The first rule that matches an incoming email message, evaluated top down in the list, is applied to that message. The Move Up and Move Down buttons enables you to reorganize the listing of spam rules as desired.

Creating a new spam rule allows you to first specify a target word or phrase to be used as the search term for the new rule, as shown in Figure 11-15. Messages containing the target word or phrase, including versions of the search term with alternate capitalization and punctuation markers, will be processed as spam or not spam, depending on the configuration assigned.

After selecting **Next**, you are prompted to specify which part of each incoming message will be evaluated (see Figure 11-16), to determine if a match has been made with the new custom spam rule.

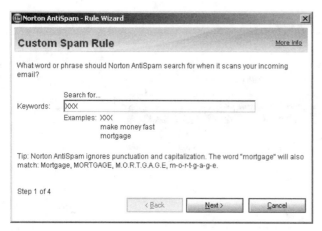

Figure 11-15 Defining the search word *XXX* as a new custom spam rule to block explicit advertisements employing the triple-*X* keyword.

Figure 11-16 Defining the search scope to search only in the message's subject line.

After selecting **Next** again, you are prompted to specify whether a match to this rule is to be filtered as spam or allowed as not spam (see Figure 11-17).

When the rule has been defined, you are select **Next** and then **Finish** to create the new rule. The rule can then be moved up or down in the listing of custom spam rules as desired to provide the best filtering of spam email messages.

Figure 11-17 Defining the custom spam rule to send matching items to the Spam folder.

Email

The **Email** section of options provided within Norton AntiSpam allows the configuration of email-related configuration settings. The Email section of options includes six pages: **Scanning**, **Filtering**, **Client Integration**, **My Addresses**, **Yahoo! Mail**, and **AutoBlock**. Details of each page follow.

Scanning

The **Scanning** option page is used to configure the host system's scanning response when a new email message arrives. Figure 11-18 illustrates this page, which includes options to configure how Norton AntiSpam will handle timeouts during scanning of large email messages. This page also provides user interface customization of whether Norton AntiSpam will be displayed as an icon in the system tray, and whether you want to see a display of progress during spam filtering.

Filtering

Figure 11-19 illustrates the **Filtering** options page, which includes options to configure how Norton AntiSpam will handle automatic training of Allowed List/Blocked List addresses based on normal email use. You can specify whether Norton AntiSpam should prompt before adding source addresses to either the allowed or filtered listings, or whether Norton AntiSpam should

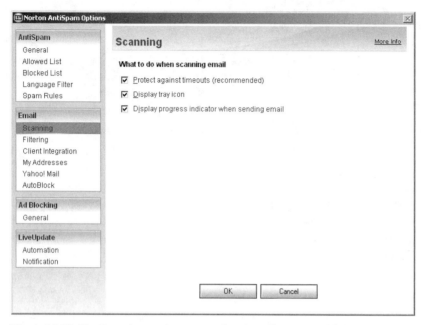

Figure 11-18 The Scanning options page, showing all items enabled.

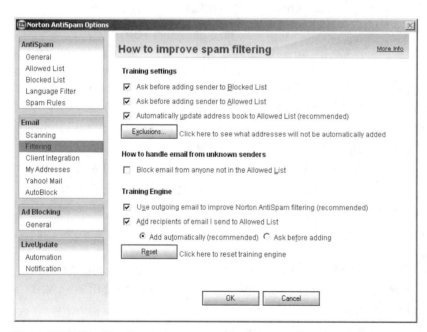

Figure 11-19 The Filtering options page, with all items selected except the option to block all email messages from anyone not on the Allowed List.

maintain automatic synchronization with the email client address book. The **Filtering** options page also allows you to configure addresses that will never be automatically added to the Allowed List.

> **Note**
> Although the option is provided to block all email that does not come from a source on the Allowed List, this setting is likely to cause many false-positive filtering actions, classifying nonspam email messages that come from addresses that have not yet been added to the list. This will keep the inbox empty of all items that do not come from preapproved senders, but it could create an added burden for regular review of items in the Spam folder, to avoid missing valid email messages sent from unexpected source addresses.

The **Filtering** options page also enables you to control whether Norton AntiSpam will use the destination addresses of outgoing email messages to improve its filtering of returning potential spam messages. The feature includes the capability to automatically assign all target email addresses to the Allowed List so that responses will not be filtered.

Client Integration

Norton AntiSpam allows you to manage integration with many common email client packages, as discussed earlier in this chapter. The **Client Integration** options page, shown in Figure 11-20, allows you to select which available email clients will be configured for Norton AntiSpam–integrated functionality. You can also select address book listings from these clients that will be used to automatically populate the client's allowed senders listing.

> **Note**
> This options page allows configuration of client integration for installed client applications only. Filtering for Yahoo! Mail is managed using the Yahoo! Mail options page detailed later in this chapter.

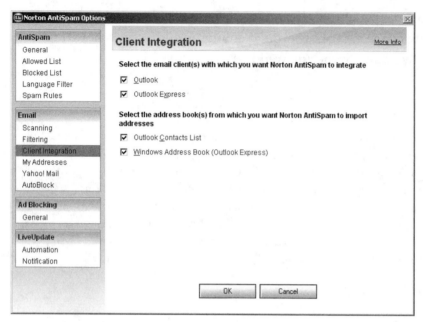

Figure 11-20 The Client Integration options page, showing options available for Outlook and Outlook Express, which are installed on the Norton AntiSpam host system.

My Addresses

Norton AntiSpam supports the capability for you to specify which addresses should not be automatically added to the allowed senders listing, in case you maintain multiple email accounts and occasionally sends messages to the alternate addresses. By adding your own email addresses to the **My Addresses** listing (see Figure 11-21), Norton AntiSpam prevents spam from bypassing the protective filtering by pretending to originate from your own address.

> **Note**
> Users who regularly carbon-copy their outbound email messages to themselves might not want to configure this option, to avoid having their correctly sent duplicates from being identified as spam.

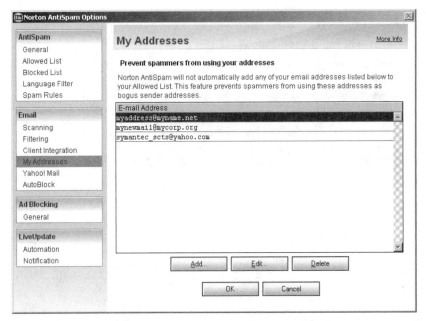

Figure 11-21 The My Addresses options page, showing several addresses the client has blocked from automatic addition to the allowed senders listing.

Yahoo! Mail

Norton AntiSpam supports automatic spam filtering of Yahoo! Mail and Yahoo! Mail Plus accounts. The **Yahoo! Mail** options page (see Figure 11-22) allows you to add, edit, or remove Yahoo! Mail accounts that Norton AntiSpam will automatically filter. This page also allows you to configure how often you want Norton AntiSpam to scan the Yahoo! Mail message store for new messages.

AutoBlock

The final email configurations option page allows you to configure Norton AntiSpam to automatically block email messages containing content of a variety of types. Figure 11-23 shows the **AutoBlock** page, which allows you to filter email containing remote or local images, invisible or hidden text, and obscured or disguised Web links, a mechanism commonly used in phishing scams.

Here, you can also elect to block emails containing potentially dangerous active content, including scripts, ActiveX controls and Java applets, objects that could perform unwanted actions.

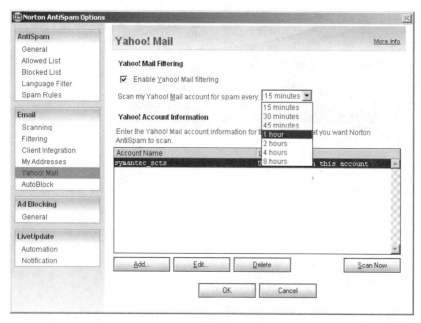

Figure 11-22 The Yahoo! Mail options page, illustrating selection of the scanning interval.

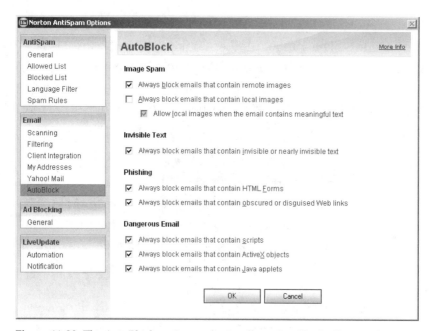

Figure 11-23 The AutoBlock options page, configured to block all active content except for local embedded images.

Ad Blocking

In addition to email filtering, Norton AntiSpam includes functionality designed to improve the Web-browsing experience by reducing the number of Web-based ads and pop-ups. By blocking advertisements and pop-up Web elements that automatically load additional unsolicited pages when a client browses to a target site, Norton AntiSpam can extend its umbrella of protection to include more of a user's online efforts.

Figure 11-24 provides an example of the **Ad Blocking** options page, currently configured to block both advertisements and pop-up windows during Web browsing. Because some sites require these protections to be turned off, if you want to visit such a site, you can toggle Norton AntiSpam protection on and off here. By selecting the **Advanced** button, you can configure ad blocking for individual sites according to individual preference (see Figure 11-25). This listing is regularly updated during LiveUpdate (discussed next), providing the best possible protection.

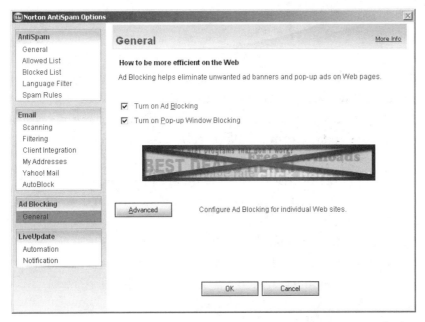

Figure 11-24 The Ad Blocking options page, illustrating protection against both advertisements and pop-up windows.

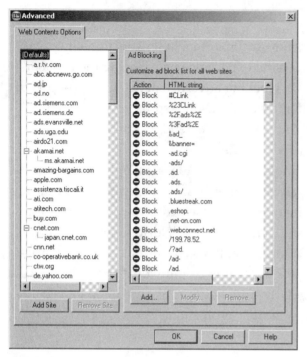

Figure 11-25 The advanced interface for by-site ad blocking and pop-up windows blocking.

LiveUpdate

We previously discussed the use of the Symantec LiveUpdate service to allow Norton AntiSpam and spam signatures files to be updated during the term of the subscription. You can configure Norton AntiSpam to automatically perform a regular LiveUpdate from the **Automation** option page, as shown in Figure 11-26. This recommended option is enabled by default to ensure that the most recent elements of Norton AntiSpam are provided. You should not disable this setting, or you risk missing critical updates to their AntiSpam protection.

You can further refine the automatic LiveUpdate process from the **Notification** option page by configuring Norton AntiSpam to create a notification when updates are available or when they have been applied, or to allow Norton AntiSpam to update itself whenever new updates are made available (see Figure 11-27).

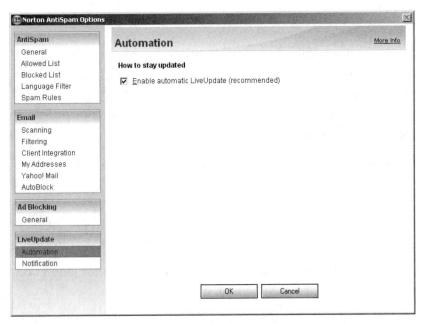

Figure 11-26 Automated LiveUpdate enabled.

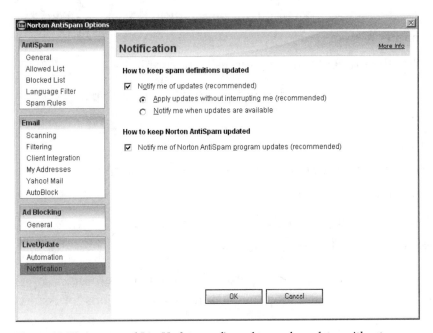

Figure 11-27 Automated LiveUpdate configured to apply updates without notification.

Troubleshooting

During installation and operation of Norton AntiSpam, errors might occur that require your assistance to correct. Common error messages and their corrective actions can be found at the Symantec Web site, www.symantec.com/smallbiz/nas/. Following are a few of the more common errors you might encounter:

- You get this error message: "The setup has detected that a previous install or uninstall has completed but requires a restart."

  1. Restart the computer and determine whether this corrects the problem.

  2. If not, delete all leftover installation files and reinstall the application.

- Norton AntiSpam 2005 installation appears complete, and although you do not see an error message, you cannot start the program.

  1. Ensure that the system is virus free.

  2. Delete any conflicting Registry keys.

  3. If this does not correct the problem, run SymKBFix3.exe (available at the Symantec support site).

  4. Verify that the proper Symantec services are running.

- Email is not properly identified as spam with Norton AntiSpam or Norton Internet Security.

  1. Verify that the computer is virus free.

  2. Make sure that previously installed adware is not conflicting.

  3. Delete third-party email client add-ins.

  4. Update other protections, such as Zone Alarm Pro.

  5. Remove and reinstall Norton AntiSpam.

Many other error corrections can be performed simply by running LiveUpdate. Updates to Norton AntiSpam 2005 include corrections for issues such as these error messages:

- "Norton AntiSpam has finished configuring Outlook . . ." when changing users in Outlook or Outlook Express

- "Managed MAPI Service Catastrophic Failure," with Norton AntiSpam and Microsoft Outlook 2003
- "Runtime Error Visual C++: \Outlook.exe, Abnormal program termination," after installing Norton AntiSpam

Conclusion

In this chapter you have learned to use the management console capabilities to configure Norton AntiSpam to provide protection to meet the custom needs of the small business environment. The functionality provides granular yet simple features to control the handling of the ever increasing amount of spam users must wade through to get to their real business email, decreasing the productivity losses that spam causes, and protecting companies from some of the risks associated with spam carrying viruses and phishing attacks.

> **Note**
> For additional details on the Norton AntiSpam product and the packaging options available for subscription services, check out Symantec's web site at http://www.symantec.com/smallbiz/nas/.
>
> Additional detail regarding the installation, configuration and registration of Norton AntiSpam can also be found on the installation media, as well as within the Norton AntiSpam client itself.

Chapter Review Questions

Question 11-1

If you want to activate an already-installed copy of Norton AntiSpam, where would you find the activation wizard? Select the best answer from those provided.

- ○ A. Status & Settings
- ○ B. Statistics
- ○ C. LiveUpdate
- ○ D. Options
- ○ E. Help & Support

Question 11-2

If you want to configure Norton AntiSpam to provide moderate filtering in which almost all spam is correctly identified, at which level should configure Norton AntiSpam? Select the best answer from those provided.

    ○ A. High

    ○ B. Medium-High

    ○ C. Medium

    ○ D. Medium-Low

    ○ E. Low

Question 11-3

You need to make sure that email messages from important business contacts are not accidentally filtered as spam. What is the most efficient way to obtain this result? Select the best answer from those provided.

    ○ A. Turn off AntiSpam filtering using the General AntiSpam page

    ○ B. Select messages within an integrated email client and select This Is Not Spam for each

    ○ C. Configure automatic addition of outgoing email addresses using the Email Filtering page

    ○ D. Import the address book using the Allowed List page

    ○ E. Enter the important contacts' email domains (rather than their individual addresses) using the Allowed List page

Question 11-4

What methods of antispam filtering are available in Norton AntiSpam? Select all that apply.

    ❏ A. Block/Allow (Allowed List/Blocked List)

    ❏ B. Language filtering

    ❏ C. Content filtering

    ❏ D. Custom spam rules

    ❏ E. File attachment filtering

Question 11-5

You have created several custom spam rules, arranged in the following order:

- Search for "make money fast" in subject. Classify matching messages as spam.
- Search for "money fast" in entire mail. Classify matching messages as not spam.
- Search for "fast" in entire mail. Classify matching messages as spam.
- Search for "money" in subject. Classify matching messages as not spam.

You receive a mail message from an unknown source address with the subject line of "~gE.t–Mo,ne.y__FaSt!" and a body message of "Want to make money fast? Contact <url> today!" Based on the custom rules, will this message be handled as spam or not spam? Select the best answer from those provided.

- ○ A. Spam
- ○ B. Not spam
- ○ C. Unable to tell from the information provided

Question 11-6

When creating custom spam rules, which of the following parts of the email can be searched? Select all that apply.

- ❑ A. From
- ❑ B. Recipient
- ❑ C. Subject
- ❑ D. Body
- ❑ E. Entire mail

Question 11-7

If the option Block Email from Anyone Not in the Allowed List is in its default state, what condition is most likely with regard to spam from a new source, provided that no other rules apply? Select the best answer from those provided.

- ○ A. You could experience false-positive spam filtering.
- ○ B. The email message will be placed in the inbox.

○ C. The email message will be placed within the Norton AntiSpam folder.

○ D. The sender's email address will be added to the Allowed List.

○ E. The sender's email address will be added to the filtered list.

Question 11-8

You configure all email AutoBlock options to block incoming spam, what types of spam will be filtered by this action? Select the best answer from those provided.

○ A. Image spam

○ B. Invisible text

○ C. Phishing Web links

○ D. Attached ActiveX controls

○ E. Attached Java applets

Chapter Review Answers

Answer 11-1

Answer **E** is correct. If you want to activate an already-installed copy of Norton AntiSpam, you can do so by selecting the Norton AntiSpam Activation option within the Help & Support drop-down listing. This is necessary only if you did not activate the Norton AntiSpam subscription service during the initial application installation.

Answer 11-2

Answer **B** is correct. If you want to configure Norton AntiSpam to provide moderate filtering in which almost all spam is correctly identified, you must select the Medium-High level within the General AntiSpam options page.

Answer 11-3

Answer **D** is correct. When you need to make sure that email messages from important business contacts are not accidentally filtered as spam, the most efficient way to obtain this result is to import the email address book from the email client. Although all solutions listed can be used, this populates the listing in a single step.

Answer 11-4

Answers **A**, **B**, **C**, **D**, and **E** are all correct. Norton AntiSpam supports spam filtering based on Allowed List/Blocked List address lists, as well as content filtering based on custom spam rules, file attachment rules, and language rules specified by the client.

Answer 11-5

Answer **B** is correct. The first rule does not match because the phrase "make money fast" appears in the body of the text, not the subject line. The second rule will test successfully because Norton AntiSpam has been configured to search for the phrase "money fast" anywhere in the email. Norton AntiSpam ignores punctuation marks and case when performing content matching, allowing the garbled phrase to be successfully identified as not spam. The third and fourth rules are not evaluated because the first successful match is used to determine the email's destination if no other rules apply. As a new source address, the sender's address will not be in either the Allow or Filtered listings.

Answer 11-6

Answers **A**, **B**, **C**, **D**, and **E** are all correct. When creating custom spam rules, various parts of the email can be searched. These include the entire email, the From and Recipient address lines, and the message subject and body text.

Answer 11-7

Answer **B** is correct. If the option Block Email from Anyone Not in the Allowed List is in its default state, it is not enabled. Without other rules to the contrary, an email from a new source address will be left in the inbox.

Answer 11-8

Answers **A**, **B**, **C**, **D**, and **E** are all correct. If you configure all email AutoBlock options to block incoming spam, invisible text and image spam will be filtered in addition to spam containing hidden Web links commonly used for phishing scams and file attachments such as scripts, ActiveX controls, and Java applets.

Index

browser-hijacking adware programs, 29
brute-force spam, 271-272
business, impact of spam, 274-275
business issues, 49-51

C

capacity, impact of security risks and
    threats, 47
Center for Democracy & Technology, 279
Central Quarantine
    server requirements, 175
    Symantec AntiVirus, 75
Central Quarantine polling, 171
CertTracker, 12
.cfp (Client Firewall policy) files, 228
.cfu (Client Firewall update) files, 228
challenge-response systems, 281
changing
    client management state, 135
        Symantec Client Security, 217
    server groups, Symantec System
        Center, 121
child domains, installation
    environments, 71
Children's Online Privacy Protection Acts
    (COPPA), 48
choosing management hierarchies, 146
    client groups, 149
    server groups, 146-147, 149
Client Firewall, 166
Client Firewall policy (.cfp) files, 228
    creating, 232-234
Client Firewall update (.cfu) files, 228
    creating, 232, 234
client groups
    choosing management
        hierarchies, 149
    managing, 131, 133-134
    Symantec Client Security, 208-209,
        215-216
    Symantec System Center, 116-117
Client Integration options page, 339-340
client management, Symantec Client
    Security, 215
    changing client-management
        state, 217
    client groups, 215-216
    client migration, 216
    client scans, 217

client-management state, changing, 135
    Symantec Client Security, 217
client-management strategies, 150-151
client migration, Symantec Client Security, 216
client migration paths, 105-106
client requirements
    Symantec AntiVirus, 74
    Symantec Client Security, 174
client scans, 135-137
    Symantec Client Security, 217
Client Settings tab, 251
client software, migrating, 107
ClientRemote Install tool, 67
clients
    client scans, 135, 137
    client software, migrating, 107
    client-management strategies, 150-151
    integrating Norton AntiSpam, 339
    logon script Symanted Client Security
        client installation, 196
    managed clients, 64-65
    managing, 131
        client groups, 131, 133-134
    migrating, 134
    mixing with parent servers, 117
    remote network clients, deploying, 193-194
    Symantec Client Security, deploying,
        188-190
    unmanaged clients, 64-65
command-line installation, Symantec AntiVirus
    (examples), 103
command-line options, Windows Installer, 197
components
    of antivirus risk management, 144
    Symantec Client Security, 168-170
computer security, impact of security risks and
    threats, 49
configuration priorities, Symantec System
    Center, 117
configuration tasks, Symantec Client
    Security, 215
configuring
    Installer options, 101-102
    Windows Installer options, 196-197
Connection Management tab, 237
Connection property, 244
Connections, Symantec Client Firewall policies,
    239-240